the complete guide to

SAGE

STERLING +2

FOR WINDOWS

ADELE WARD

COMPUTER
STEP

First published in 1994

Computer Step   Tel. +44 (0)926 817999
Unit 5c, Southfield Road   Fax. +44 (0)926 817005
Southam, Leamington Spa
Warwickshire CV33 OJH
United Kingdom

Notice of Liability
Every effort has been made to ensure that this book contains accurate and current information. However, Computer Step and the author shall not be liable for any loss or damage suffered by readers as a result of any information contained herein.

Trademarks
Microsoft® and Windows™ are registered trademarks of Microsoft Corporation. Sage Sterling +2, Sage Financial Controller, Sage Accountant Plus, Sage Accountant and Sage Bookeeper are all registered trademarks of The Sage Group Plc. All other trademarks are acknowledged as belonging to their respective companies.

Acknowledgements
Computer Step and the author would like to thank the staff at The Sage Group Plc for their help in the preparation of this book. We are particularly grateful to Graham Wylie, the managing director, for providing information on the main questions asked by users and how the technical support team answers them. Also Henry Wallace, the technical director for making time to answer queries on getting the best possible performance out of the software. Without this level of direct assistance this book would not have been this complete and helpful to the readers.

British Library Cataloguing in Publication Data
A catalogue record for this book is available from the British Library.

Printed in England

ISBN 1 874029 17 2

A Note from Sage ....

The Sage Sterling +2 range of Windows accounting software is renowned for its revolutionary design and ease of use, with real life forms such as cheques, invoices and VAT returns simulated on screen so you intuitively know what to do. But while the same procedures and logic used in manual bookkeeping are followed, there are many aspects to business accounting and bookkeeping that benefit from a more detailed understanding of what's going on "behind the scenes" in the software.

Many Sage users seek help on practical bookkeeping matters and can benefit from having guidance on how the software deals with particular accounting activities, such as what to do when an invoice is refunded, how to handle asset sales, how to make adjustments for profit and loss accounting and how to get the most from the reporting features. All these subjects are covered in this book plus guidance on opening balances, VAT procedures, correcting errors and much more.

Although Sage recommends that users get professional advice from their accountants, you'll find plenty of information in this book to help you understand the bookkeeping procedures and get the most out of Sage Sterling +2.

This book compliments the user documentation by providing the guidance and practical advice on accounting with Sage Sterling +2 that you'll want to keep by your computer for day-to-day reference.

Graham Wylie
Managing Director
SageSoft Limited

About the Author

Adele Ward was the technology writer for Accountancy, the journal of the Institute of Chartered Accountants in England and Wales, for five years before going freelance six years ago. She specialises in accounting software, technology and general management. Her work appears regularly in the financial and technological press both in the UK and internationally.

Dedication

For my family

Foreword

Financial software is no longer purely the tool of the qualified accountant but has also found its way into businesses of all sizes. At the Institute we run a scheme to evaluate and recommend functionally sound products to our members. Sage Sterling +2 has been evaluated and included in our list of recommended products and is widely used both by accountants and by small to medium sized businesses. Our Recommendation Scheme aims to put good software and members in touch with each other, and this applies to accountants both in practice and in industry.

As part of our testing we stipulate that the software must be easy to operate as well as demonstrating accuracy and integrity of accounting functions. Although Sterling +2 is designed for ease of use, businesses will still need to understand the principles of accounting to make the most of its facilities. In this book the author seeks to explain basic accounting skills so that you will gain the confidence needed to tackle this work.

Another key requirement in the Institute's testing is that the software supplier must be financially sound and able to provide adequate support. The technical team at Sage have worked together with the author to provide troubleshooting advice and to give many useful tips on how to exploit the software to best advantage. Like many books this one gives step-by-step guidance on how to use the software, but it also goes beyond the manual in answering the type of questions users are most likely to ask.

Apart from explaining accounting principles the author ventures into the area of general management. Business guides at the end of relevant chapters describe ways to improve profitability, including effective credit control, debt collection and reclaiming VAT. Businesses need to gain as much information as possible on their rights to VAT refunds and how to make successful claims.

The case studies at the end of this book show how both a qualified accountant and a non-accountant are using Sterling +2 and their experiences in implementing the system provide helpful advice to newcomers. Professional accountants are well aware of the benefits of acounting software so the following chapters will be useful mainly for the technical advice given. For non-accountants the advice on accounting principles and general management will be equally valuable and should help in producing an accurate set of final accounts at year end.

Trevor D'Cruz FCA
Managing Director - Accountancy Business Group
The Institute of Chartered Accountants in England and Wales

Table of Contents

CHAPTER 1

An overview of Accounting with Sterling +2

Sterling +2 was the first Windows based accounting software to be evaluated and approved by the Institute of Chartered Accountants in England and Wales for inclusion on its Recommended Products Scheme. The Institute's recommendation assures users that the software is functionally sound, but many who tried the first version wanted more Windows functionality. The new release (Version 2) is no disappointment, providing a major upgrade which looks completely different and takes full advantage of the Windows environment.

For accountants and non-accountants alike a computerised method of keeping the books is the best way to simplify the day to day recording of business transactions. Companies are required by law to maintain accurate accounting information in order to prepare a set of final accounts each year for inspection by the Inland Revenue and also to complete a VAT return for submission to HM Customs and Excise. The computer won't lead to a paperless office for the accountant, as each transaction needs to be accompanied by the right documentation which can be used as evidence in cases of legal dispute.

Software solutions are of tremendous benefit to businesses which don't have a qualified accountant on board as they can perform all the intricate calculations necessary in double entry bookkeeping (see the next section). Sterling +2 comes with standard settings to let you start keeping your company's accounts without any great understanding of how this all works. However, you still need to find out about the basic accounting principles so that you can exploit the system to the full. There are also opportunities to amend the settings to suit your needs more exactly, but you need to be confident that you know exactly what you're doing.

At times you will have to adjust the figures, for example when you detect errors. As this requires some bookkeeping knowledge it's worth reading as much as you can about basic accountancy practices. Once you gain some understanding of accounting and learn how to get the most out of your software it will be possible to keep your own accounts. You will only need to pay for professional help in the early stages when you need to enter opening balances and make initial business decisions. Limited companies will also need an auditor at the end of the year when preparing the final accounts. At these times an accountant can suggest ways of setting up the business, deciding on the financial year start date and making sure all the allowable expenses will be deducted from your profits before tax. All of this can save you money, especially as many small business owners don't realise just how many items they can claim as allowable expenses - the benefits can be greater than the accountant's bill. Some businesses have quite simple accounts to keep and many of them can follow the methods set up by the accountant to do even more by themselves in future years.

Sage helps users to learn about accounting in detail if they subscribe to SageCover. This entitles members to unlimited help from the telephone support staff as well as software maintenance revisions which update the programs each time there are changes in legislation.

Double entry bookkeeping

All bookkeeping systems use the double entry method and even the most basic software package will have a sales ledger, a purchase ledger and a nominal ledger. This entry level package is provided by Sage in the Sterling +2 Bookkeeper product. The double entry method is so called because for every transaction two entries are recorded, a debit and a credit. For example, in the sales ledger when your company sells a product to a customer the price of the goods will be listed as a credit to you and a debit to the customer. In this case you are the creditor (you are owed money) and the customer is a debtor (they owe money). This example is the most obvious one and it illustrates a simple rule of accounting: always credit the giver and debit the receiver. When customers return goods to you they become the giver and you are the receiver. In this case the customer will be credited with the amount and you will be debited.

Unless you are an accountant you may feel that debits are always bad for your company and credits are always good. This is not the case as the purchase ledger shows that the reverse can also be true. When you buy goods or services from a supplier this will be recorded in your purchase ledger as a credit to the supplier and a debit to your company. The supplier is the giver and you are the receiver - a fact which may sound obvious but can cause confusion when you're keeping the books. In Sterling +2 an invoice in the sales ledger will be a credit to your company, whereas an invoice in the purchase ledger will be a debit.

The two sides of all transactions, the credits and debits, are always equal and this is why each time you run your trial balance the figures should be the same or you can be sure you're not getting your double entry bookkeeping right. The sales and purchase transactions balance in an obvious way, but the same is true for all transactions recorded in Sterling +2. Apart from sales and purchases, the company's net assets will also be equal to the amount of finance the owners have invested in the business. If this sounds complicated be thankful that the software will do much of the work for you, as long as the figures are entered correctly.

The finance invested is called the owner's funds and is made up of the capital the proprietors have put into the business, the amount shareholders (if there are any) have contributed, bank loans or other borrowings and the retained profits. The term retained profits is used to describe all money generated by the business which the owners have not taken out in drawings or dividends. This amount is balanced by the net assets which are worked out by taking the total assets and subtracting the total liabilities. The assets include fixed assets (plant, equipment, property and vehicles), stock, debtors, cash and money in the bank. The liabilities are amounts owing to creditors and the bank overdraft.

Debits and credits are quite obvious terms to use in certain transactions, such as in the sales and purchase ledger, but in other parts of the system they are less clear. For example, debit is the term used to describe an item of expenditure or a decrease in owners funds. This is simple to understand for non-accountants, as is the fact that credits represent an item of income or an increase in the owner's funds. However, credits and debits are also used to represent changes in the values of assets and liabilities and here the situation is different. A debit represents an increase in the value of an asset or a decrease in the amount of liability, whereas a credit represents a decrease in the value of an asset or an increase in the amount of liability.

Imagine entering details on wages paid to your staff and deciding where to put the debit and credit for this transaction. You would have to debit the wages account and credit the cash account, which may seem suprising. The wages account should be debited as this is an item of expenditure. The cash account should be credited because this transaction represents the decrease in the value of an asset. This type of transaction occurs when moving amounts between accounts in the nominal ledger and sometimes you can apply the simple rule of credit the giver and debit the receiver. Here you must credit the giver, which is the cash account and debit the receiver - the wages account. Similarly if you take money out of the bank for the petty cash float you would credit your bank account and debit the petty cash account.

Debit	Credit
An increase in the value of an asset	A decrease in the value of an asset
A decrease in the amount of a liability	An increase in the amount of a liability
An item of expenditure	An item of income
A decrease in owner's funds	An increase in owner's funds

Ledger accounting

Sterling +2 uses the ledger method of accounting with the sales, purchase and nominal ledgers fully integrated, so that transactions entered in one place can update the entire system. When you update the sales and purchase ledgers the transactions will be posted to the nominal ledger, meaning that the information is entered in the correct nominal accounts.

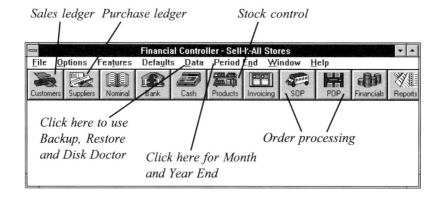

Nominal ledger

The nominal ledger is sometimes also referred to as the general ledger as it is at the heart of the bookkeeping system, taking figures from all other ledgers. All the debits and credits recorded for each transaction arrive here and are sorted into accounts - for example all money owed to you is in the debtors control account, while all money you owe is in the creditors control account. The total figure for each set of transactions is stored and easily viewed here, such as the overall balance for the wages account. The nominal ledger tidies up the figures and stores the results which can then be used to produce financial reports. To analyse each account in detail, you will need to produce one of the many reports available as standard from Sage.

Apart from the derived total balances resulting from sales and purchase transactions the nominal ledger includes balances for every type of income and expenditure, assets, liabilities and owner's fund figures. When you choose Nominal from the main Sterling +2 menu you can see a list of all the nominal account codes and names to get an idea of how all of these types of transaction are listed in the default chart of accounts. Should you list the balances of all nominal ledger accounts the total credits should equal the total debits.

The nominal ledger, therefore, takes data from throughout the system - the sales and purchase ledgers as well as transactions entered via the Bank and Cash options. You will need to use the nominal ledger to record recurring payments such as monthly rent, prepayments which include money paid in advance for items such as insurance, and accruals which are payments made in arrears such as telephone bills. These types of payment are entered directly into the nominal ledger, as are details on the depreciating value of assets such as office equipment.

The nominal ledger also lets you set budgets for each nominal account and compare these with the actual figures. For example, you could enter a budget setting the amount you want to spend on casual workers (7005 on the default chart of accounts) and keep a close eye on the actual figure to make sure you don't overspend. Figures for budget, actual and prior year appear on the nominal record for each account so it's also quick and easy to compare this year's performance with that achieved last year. This would be useful when checking the sales accounts to see if you are meeting your targets as set in the budget. It also highlights whether the business is performing better or worse than at the same time last year. For presentations, Sterling+2 also provides graphs to highlight the significance of these comparisons. All of the versions except Bookkeeper have budgetary control and management reports features.

Tip

You can also set budgets in other parts of the system including the sales and purchase ledgers.

Sales ledger

Sage has called the sales ledger Customers, so this is the choice you should make on the main menu. Here you record all transactions with your customers and all sales will result in a credit to your company and a debit to the customer. For this reason whenever you update the records, the transactions will be posted to the debtors control account and the sales account in the nominal ledger which will show the totals from all transactions. In this way the nominal ledger can be kept as small and tidy as possible as it doesn't need to have an account for every single customer. Similarly, the VAT liability from each sale will be posted to the nominal ledger VAT account, so that your VAT return can be calculated automatically.

The Sterling +2 sales ledger keeps detailed records on all of your customers and includes automated telephone dialling and preparation of fax files for quick and easy communication. For the credit controller there are ways to set credit limits and produce the standard reports to highlight customers who are exceeding the amount of credit they are entitled to or time they have been allowed for payment. There are standard letter and fax designs but you can also produce your own using Windows Write. Standard invoice, credit note and statement designs are provided or you can create your own to fit into your stationery layouts rather than the range of documents available from Sage.

Tip

Although you can design your own, check the prices for personalised stationery available from Sage. This is one supplier with a policy of undercutting the competitors including high street printers.

For each sales transaction there is a documentary record. The Sage sales ledger reflects this by dividing transactions into Invoice and Credit Note facilities. Receipts are recorded separately using the Bank or Cash option from the main menu. To enter details on a sale you will fill in an invoice and the software will credit you and debit the customer. When customers return goods you will fill in a credit note and in this case the software will debit you and credit the customer.

If you have one of the two entry level systems, Bookkeeper or Accountant, you will enter your invoices in the sales ledger by choosing Customers from the main menu. If you have Accountant Plus or Financial Controller it's best to enter the invoices to customers using Invoicing or the sales order processing option, SOP, on the main menu. This can seem slightly confusing at first as the addition of extra invoicing and order processing functions means there are two places where you can enter invoices. It's important to choose one method and not enter the invoices both in the sales ledger and through Invoicing or SOP as this will post the transaction to the nominal ledger twice and duplicate your figures. If you're using Sterling +2 for stock control use the sales order processing option to generate invoices, then continue to work on them using the Invoicing option from the main menu. This way the details you enter can be used to allocate stock and update your stock levels as well as to produce an invoice and post the transaction to the nominal ledger.

The balance in the nominal ledger debtors control account is the total you expect to receive from sales and it will be given as a debit amount. This is because amounts owed to you by customers are an asset and are classed as a debit item according to the rules described earlier. When you receive payment this is recorded using the Bank or Cash option on the main menu. This will automatically allocate the payment to the correct invoice.

Purchase ledger

The Sterling +2 purchase ledger is called Suppliers and this is the option to choose from the main menu. Don't be confused by the similarity in appearance between this and the sales ledger. Here an invoice records goods the supplier has sold to your company so they are a credit to the supplier and a debit to you. If you need to return goods you will be issued with a credit note which is a credit to you and a debit to the supplier.

The purchase ledger keeps track of all the money you owe to suppliers and the total figure is stored in the nominal ledger in the creditors control account. Don't be surprised to see the total figure you owe to suppliers stored in the creditors control account as a credit balance. This is because the amount you owe to suppliers is a liability and is therefore classed as a credit item. The nominal ledger also stores total figures for purchases and VAT you have paid suppliers.

Remember to keep all the documents linked to each transaction, here these will be the invoice or credit note from the supplier. The software can be used to print out a remittance advice to give details on payments made towards outstanding supplier invoice amounts. You can redesign the layout of the remittance notes, as you can with all Sage documents.

Note
The purchase ledger is also used for goods or services bought on credit.

Bank payments, cash payments and receipts

The Bank and Cash options on the main menu are used to record all payments and receipts. For petty cash payments it's important to keep the till receipts as a record for possible inspection. You should also keep a copy of receipts issued to customers. For payments and receipts by cheque a record of the cheque details will serve as valid documentation.

The payment and receipt facilities in the banking function are separated into transactions made purely through the nominal ledger and transactions which link to customer or supplier accounts. You will use the supplier option on the Bank menu to enter details on payments you make to suppliers only if you have recorded the invoice in the purchase ledger. The customer option on the Bank menu is to record payments made to you by customers in response to invoices in the sales ledger. When you pay a supplier or receive a payment from a customer you can allocate this payment to the relevant invoice or credit note. The nominal method of banking payments and receipts is for all transactions which have nothing to do with outstanding supplier and customer invoices and credit notes.

Sterling +2 provides a particularly useful method of checking your bank statement against your own record of transactions. This reconciliation process helps you to ensure the bank statement is correct and that you're not paying more than necessary for bank charges and interest. A 1993 survey by the Daily Mail showed that less than 5% of business bank accounts had been charged the right amount of interest. Even though the bank may later correct any mistakes you have the right to reclaim any losses due to the error. The software can help you to negotiate the exact figure taking each transaction into consideration.

Financials and Reports

Standard reports are available from different options on the main menu. It's important to familiarise yourself with the different techniques in order to take advantage of the wide range you can produce using information from throughout the system. In each of the ledgers there are simple reports which can, for example, list all the records or give a balance of accounts. Even these basic listings can be sorted and selected using criteria to give useful analyses of each ledger.

The Financials option from the main menu gives the ever-important trial balance as well as offering reports on profit and loss and balance sheet. The balance sheet report shows the balances for all of your assets and liabilities. The profit and loss report shows the figures for sales, purchases, direct expenses and overheads. These are used to calculate your gross and net profit or loss. The trial balance report lets you check all of the transactions entered to see that the credits equal the debits - this means the books balance and you are doing the accounting correctly!

Financials is also the place to find the budget report, comparisons with the prior year and asset valuation which will show how much assets are worth, taking into account the monthly depreciation.

When the time comes to fill in your VAT return the Financials menu offers this choice. Here you will find the standard HM Customs and Excise form with nine boxes to be filled in. The software prompts you to fill in the details and automates the process, then it provides reports to help you check the figures and reconcile your VAT. Most of the figures will be entered in the boxes automatically by Sterling +2 so long as you are careful from the outset and fill in the correct VAT tax code for every transaction.

The third option for reporting is more aptly called Reports on the main menu. This provides a report generator as well as standard reports. This is the option to choose if you want to see and print out the audit trail, and there is also a full selection of fixed transaction reports. The fixed transaction reports are for each type of transaction, from customer invoices through to tax analysis. The report generator lets you design and produce your own reports which will select and lay out data according to your specifications using figures from the audit trail.

Stock control

Basic stock control is handled by choosing Products from the main menu, which will let you record details on all your products. The order processing options then let you record all the transactions associated with goods you buy from suppliers and the resale of these items to your customers. The sales and purchase order processing facilities (SOP and POP) on the main menu automatically allocate stock to customer orders and keep a record of stock levels. You can keep a close watch on your stock to see when you need to re-order, and can also monitor the progress of sales and purchases of goods from the moment of order right through to delivery.

If you have Financial Controller and are using sales order processing make sure you generate the invoices here and then use the Invoicing option to complete this task. Don't duplicate the invoices by entering them in the sales ledger as you only need to type in an invoice once to update the whole system. If you have Accountant Plus, use invoicing to raise invoices from stock. Unfortunately invoices entered through the Customers option won't update your stock records so you need to use SOP for a fully integrated approach. The Customers option has also been designed for buyers who don't have the full stock and order processing functionality and need to enter their invoices this way.

Month and year end

Every month you will need to run the month end routine which is on the pull-down Period End menu on the menu bar. This will tidy up your records, automatically posting all the transactions which have been set as monthly payments and receipts. For example, all the recurring payments such as monthly rent, all the prepayments and accruals, and the depreciation percentage for your assets, will be posted and recorded for use in reports and analysis. The Year End choice is also available by selecting Period End and this will make all the postings necessary to get your books ready for the new financial year. The third choice on the pull-down menu under Period End is called Consolidation and is used at the end of the financial year by groups of companies to consolidate the data from subsidiaries in the parent company's nominal ledger (this option is for Financial Controller users only).

Data security and utilities

It's vital to make regular backups, especially when you start using Sterling +2 and will be entering a massive number of records which you will not want to lose. Sage makes this easy by asking if you want to make a backup each time you try to exit and you should certainly do so whenever you have spent a few hours entering records or transactions. Once the system has been completely set up, you may be able to make backups just once a day. Even so you should do so more often on days when the workload is heavy, for example when you have just typed in a large number of invoices. Backup and Restore routines can also be run by choosing Data from the menu bar on the main menu screen.

Many of the utilities are discreetly incorporated in the software and will be offered as options while you work - this is the main way you are prompted to make backups for instance. Other utilities include changing the document designs and again this can be handled by a simple switch to Windows Write while running the Customers letter writing facilities. Sage has provided many system set up details as defaults which you can choose during configuration or at a later date. These include the chart of accounts for the nominal ledger, the control accounts, company preferences and VAT rates and codes. You will find out how to amend the default specifications in the configuration section of

Chapter 3. If you're unsure about changing these settings then refer to your accountant and you will be able to run the software without major amendments using the defaults to get you started. The most important detail to alter is the start date for the financial year which you should agree with your accountant as this can't be changed once you start to post transactions and a bad choice can be detrimental.

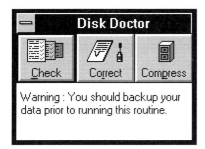

Disk Doctor (all versions except Bookkeeper) offers impressive error correction facilities for a small to medium-sized business package. It is selected from the pull-down menu under Data on the menu bar. It offers methods of checking your data for errors and can also put these problems right, if possible, so that you can avoid using a backup version of your accounts. If you keep regular backups it might prove better just to restore data from the last copy and re-enter work done since that time, especially if there are major errors or corruption. Disk Doctor will prove particularly useful for removing all the records you have deleted, such as fully paid transactions, to free extra disk space using the file compression function. Many users don't take advantage of this feature, which is a pity, as it can help to keep the software running quickly. The error correction routine on Disk Doctor is also a handy way of cancelling unwanted transactions such as invoices and credit notes.

Q&A

Which version of Sterling +2 do I need?

The following chapters cover all functions available in Financial Controller, the top level version of Sterling +2. If you have one of the other versions you won't be able to use all the features described. Check the list below and the table on the next page to see what is available on each version of Sterling +2. The following list shows which facilities are *not* available on one or more versions.

Bookkeeper users will not have the following functions:

Monthly budget, sales/purchase analyses, department analysis, direct mail letters, balance sheet, assets valuation, data file input routine, Disk Doctor, credit control letters, budget v actual report, prior year comparison report, recurring journal entries, prepayments and accruals, report generator, contra entry processing, bad debt write-off, auto processing of refunds, recurring bank payments, full and partial refunds.

Bookkeeper and Accountant users will not have the following functions:

Skeleton invoices, stock control, stock explosion, re-order level report, free text invoicing, invoicing from stock, invoice generation, stock recording, graphical stock analysis, auto invoice numbering, credit note generation, price list generation, stock valuation, item VAT amount/discount, print index/enquiries, interactive stock level index.

Bookkeeper, Accountant and Accountant Plus users will not have the following functions:

Sales order processing/purchase order processing, stock allocation, multicompany use.

Note

Credit control includes standard overdue letters. Invoicing lets you raise invoices from stock - this is only relevant on Accountant Plus and Financial Controller which have stock control facilities. With Invoicing you can also print out invoices on plain or pre-printed stationery. The invoices on the Customers and Suppliers menus are only for entering details on sales and purchase ledger transactions - they don't handle printing.

	Bookkeeper	Accountant	Accountant Plus	Financial Controller
Sales Ledger (Customers)	*	*	*	*
Purchase Ledger (Suppliers)	*	*	*	*
Nominal Ledger	*	*	*	*
VAT Management	*	*	*	*
Credit Control		*	*	*
Management Reports		*	*	*
Stock Control (Products)			*	*
Invoicing			*	*
Order Processing				*
Multicompany				*

CHAPTER 2

Windows and Sterling +2 - First simple steps

If you already have other Windows applications you will find it particularly easy to run Sterling +2 as it uses standard Windows techniques. In many places you switch to Windows to do basic tasks such as writing text, copying files, changing the screen colours and setting up your printer. For those who have never worked in the Windows environment here are some of the main methods of menu selection, opening and closing options and also taking advantage of the special facilities that make this approach more interesting and functional than DOS.

In the next chapter you will be shown how to install and configure Sterling +2 for your particular company needs. Once the software is up and running you will select it by first loading Windows (type WIN at the C> prompt) and then use the mouse to move the pointer on the screen to the Sage icon in the Program manager window. Click the mouse button twice to load Sterling +2, using the left hand button. If you have trouble getting Sterling +2 to load you're probably not doing the double-click quickly enough but the right technique soon comes with practice. Next you will see the Sage group window. Here you double-click on the Sterling icon. Beside it is an icon labelled Read Me. You should read and print this file as it gives guidance on all the changes made to the software since the manual was written.

The Sterling +2 main menu then appears and, as all the choices are displayed as buttons with a picture and a label, it's especially attractive and self-explanatory. Make choices from the main menu by using the mouse to position the arrow over the desired option and click once with the left mouse button.

At the top of the display is a title bar and under it a menu bar for more general functions. If you click on any of the options on the menu bar you will be shown a pull-down menu.

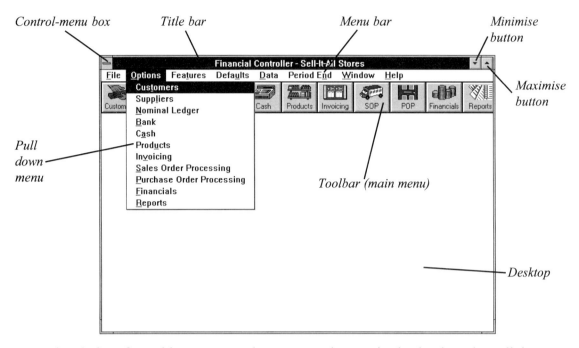

Control-menu box   *Title bar*   *Menu bar*   *Minimise button*

Maximise button

Pull down menu

Toolbar (main menu)

Desktop

To make choices from this you move the arrow to the required selection, then click to highlight and load it at the same time. For example, on the main menu you can click on Options on the menu bar to be presented with a complete list of main menu choices. From this you can choose Customers, Suppliers or any of the options which are also offered as buttons on the Toolbar. Choose Data and you will be offered Backup, Restore, Import (to transfer data from other applications such as spreadsheets) and Disk Doctor. Try each of the menu bar choices to see what the pull-down menus have to offer.

Working with windows

The main screen has several other standard Windows features which will be available on most displays throughout Sterling +2. You may want to move this window to a different position on the screen so that you can look at the windows underneath (at this point these will just be the Program Manager and Sage group window). To do this, position the arrow on the title bar (this has the name of your version, such as Financial Controller), press the left mouse button and keep it held down, then move the mouse to drag the window to the new position. Release the mouse button and your Toolbar and Desktop window will stay where you have placed it. This technique is called 'dragging' and can be used throughout the system and when using other Windows applications.

Just because you're running Sterling +2 doesn't mean you can't load another application and work on both simultaneously. On the right of the title bar is a small down arrow (the minimise button). If you click on this Sterling +2 will be minimised. This makes the window disappear and the Sage icon will appear at the bottom of the screen. Next, double-click on any of the other applications you have installed under Windows to load them and then click on the Sage icon to maximise it. The Sterling +2 window you were working on will appear on top of the window of the application you have just loaded. You can carry on with the accounting work you were doing, or switch to the second application by positioning the arrow anywhere on it's display and clicking. Work on the second application then return to Sage by clicking the arrow on the Sterling +2 window. You can minimise applications at any point in your work as you will be returned to the same position when you maximise again. This is also true when you switch between two application windows. This means you could be working on your accounts using Sterling +2 and writing a word processor document or analysing figures on a spreadsheet at the same time.

Windows applications also have a small up arrow on the title bar (the maximise button) which is used to make the window larger - in fact, it will take up the whole screen. This can be useful if you intend to work for a long period on an application such as a word processor and want to take advantage of the whole screen for the document display. If you do this you won't be able to see the other windows hidden underneath so it's not a good idea if you want to switch between two active applications by clicking alternately on the overlapped windows. However, you can still look at the windows underneath by clicking on the minimise button to minimise the full-screen display to an icon if you want to occasionally refer to other Windows software.

The main menu has been called the Toolbar by Sage. It runs along the top of the screen when you load Sterling +2 and also when you are working on the ledgers or any other part of the system. This lets you work on different options simultaneously, so you could be working on both sales and purchase ledgers by clicking on Customers and then Suppliers on the Toolbar. The Customers and Suppliers windows will overlap under the Toolbar - you simply work on the top window then click on the bottom window when you want to make it active. Sterling +2 lets you decide how you want the windows to appear on the screen. You can change the layout by pressing Window on the menu bar. The pull-down menu offers Tile or Cascade as the first two choices. Cascade creates the standard display with windows overlapping from the top of the screen to the bottom, Tile offers an alternative arrangement with windows overlapping side-by-side and top to bottom so that more of each window is visible.

Tip

If you need more space on the screen you can remove the Toolbar temporarily. To do this choose Defaults from the menu bar and click on Toolbar - the screen will be clear with only the title and menu bars remaining. When you need the main menu again press Defaults and click on Toolbar again to activate it - it will be automatically marked with a tick on the pull-down menu.

All of the windows throughout Sterling +2 can be resized. This is often useful if you are working on one window but want to see more of the information on the window underneath. To do this, place the arrow pointer on the window border and the arrow will change to a double-sided pointer. Press the mouse button and hold it down while you move the pointer to the place where you want the window boundary to be repositioned. This technique is also useful for some of the windows in Sterling +2 which hold too much information to be visible on the standard sized display. Once you load an option, such as Customers, you may find that the command buttons have disappeared off the bottom of the window - simply resize the bottom boundary of the window in order to see them.

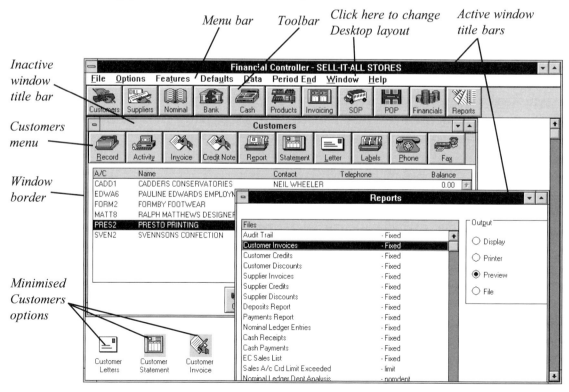

The title bar on all of the options has its own maximise and minimise buttons in the right hand corner. In some parts of Sterling +2 you will want to click on the maximise button to make the screen display bigger, particularly for options which have too much information to appear easily on a smaller window. The minimise button should be chosen when you want to reduce any of the options to an icon. For example, you could reduce the sales ledger to an icon at the bottom of the screen while you work on a separate application. Then click on the Customers icon to return to sales ledger work exactly where you left off. When you load Sterling +2 the window with the Toolbar and Desktop takes up the whole screen display as it has already been maximised, so if you want to see the windows underneath you must click on the restore button. You will find the restore button on the right of the title bar on a maximised window - it's the one with both up and down arrows. Any time that you maximise a screen but then want to revert to standard window size this is the button to press. Unless you are going to be working on another application, such as a word processor, keep Sterling +2 on maximum so that you can use the whole screen space to see all the detail on each of the options available from the main menu.

If you minimise parts of Sterling +2 but can't see the icons clearly you can drag them to a different part of the screen where they can be maximised more easily. To do this use the mouse to position the pointer over the icon, hold the left button down and move the mouse to pull the icon to a better position. Should you later decide to tidy all the icons back to the bottom of the screen this can be done by selecting Window from the Sterling +2 main menu bar and clicking on Arrange Icons. To maximise an icon (i.e. to reload the application) you need to double-click on it; if you click just once a menu of choices appears which includes Close and Maximise.

Sometimes you will find that you have minimised a variety of different options and don't want to waste time closing all the icons. You can save time by choosing Window from the menu bar then Close All from the pull-down menu. This is also the best method if you have opened too many windows and want to close them all at the press of a single button! To see how many windows you have opened at any one time choose Window from the menu bar and all the open windows, such as Customers or Suppliers, will be included in the list with a tick by the active window. The top window is always the active one, and you can only work on one window at a time. When you read how to change the screen designs in Chapter 3, you may want to use the Windows control panel to set a different colour for active windows so that it is always obvious which one you are currently able to work on.

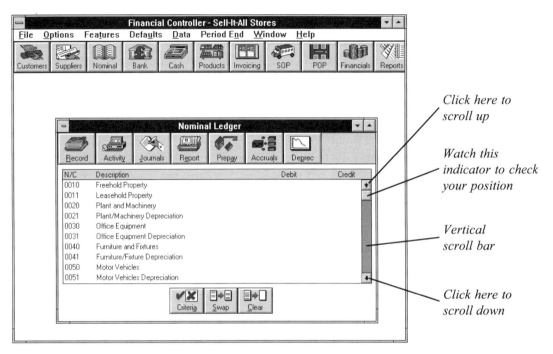

At times you will be working on a part of Sterling +2 where the software holds more information than the screen can display. In this case you will be presented with scroll bars running from the top to the bottom or from left to right across the bottom so that you can see if there is extra information beyond the limits of the window. When you load the nominal ledger, for example, you will be immediately presented with the default chart of accounts which is far too long a list for you to view all at once. You will know there is more to see because to the right of the list is a scroll bar with scroll arrows at the top and bottom for you to scroll up and down through the list. Move up or down by clicking on the correct scroll arrow. As you move through the list a box on the scroll bar moves to show your exact position so that you will know if you have reached the end. Try this technique by choosing Nominal from the main menu and scrolling through the list; then try a different method. Click on the Nominal title bar, hold the mouse button down and drag the Nominal window to the top of the desktop. Next position the arrow on the bottom boundary of the Nominal window so that it becomes a double pointer, hold the mouse button down and resize the window by dragging the boundary down to the bottom of the Desktop. This instantly makes the Nominal window longer and you can see more of the nominal account list. On some displays this method would let you see the whole list without having to use the scroll bar.

The scroll bar from left to right along the bottom (a horizontal scroll bar) works in exactly the same way as a vertical scroll bar. Horizontal scroll bars are most common in reports as these may well have too many columns to fit onto the computer screen. When you see the scroll bar on the bottom of a display click on the left and right scroll arrows to make sure you have seen all the available information. If you have word processing and spreadsheet software which runs under Windows horizontal scroll bars are present and work in the same way. Sage has also included scroll bars so that you can move around any windows which are not entirely visible, for example to find the command buttons at the bottom of a screen. This technique saves you resizing or maximising a window.

Exiting Sterling +2

The quickest way to exit from a window and return to the main menu or close down an application completely is to double-click on the control-menu box to the left of the title bar. In Sterling +2 there is also an exit option available by selecting the first choice on the menu bar (File) and then choosing Exit from the pull-down menu, but this is only to be used for closing down completely. Only exit in this way if you have first saved your work, whether transactions or new records. Don't make the mistake of pressing the Close button or the control-menu box without saving your last record or transaction as this will exit without saving. The best way to close any of the options is to save your work then double-click on the control-menu box. It's important to choose the correct control-menu box as it's easy to close Sterling +2 completely if there are a few windows open and you press the top left-hand corner by mistake. As the main menu is now constantly available, a major difference from the first version of Sterling +2, the whole system will also be closed down if you use the menu bar to select Exit from the pull-down menu. Don't do this accidentally when you only want to close one option.

Warning

If you minimise different options, such as Customers and Suppliers, Sterling+2 will let you close down these icons even if you haven't saved transactions. It's best to check if you were in the middle of a transaction before closing icons.

These are just basic steps in working with Windows and Sterling +2. As you progress through the chapters you will find out more about how to make the most of your operating environment and your accounting software. Different aspects of Windows will be explained at the times when you actually need to use them, so that you will become more familiar with Windows as you learn to handle the accounts using the Sage approach.

Tip

For more detailed information on working with Windows you can refer to the popular graphical guide, Windows in Easy Steps, also published by Computer Step.

As you install, configure and begin to use Sterling +2 for your daily work you will also have some business questions to ask. To help answer these questions there are business guides throughout the book with practical advice on areas such as banking, ledger processing, VAT and preparing your final accounts. These are at the end of chapters so that readers with accounting expertise can concentrate on the sections dealing with Sterling +2 functionality.

Tip

Set up sample data to practice working on Sterling +2. This way you can try out all the functions without risking damage to your actual accounting files. Even when you are experienced and know how to use the software, demonstration data can be helpful when you want to try out a particularly complicated procedure. If you have Financial Controller it's best to set up a demonstration company which can be used to try out functions and also to train your staff on Sterling +2 - find out how in Chapter 11. If you have a version which doesn't include multicompany facilities you will have to set up demonstration data on a floppy disk.

The multicompany approach is the easiest way to work on demonstration data, but with care you can also use a floppy disk to practice complex functions. First you need to clearly label a disk DEMO DATA and run the backup routine to copy your accounting data onto it. Whenever you want to use the demo data to try out Sterling +2 functions you must start by backing up your actual data onto another clearly labelled disk. Next run the restore routine to copy the demo data onto Sterling +2 and use it for training. When you are confident simply restore your actual accounting data onto Sterling +2 and use your newly acquired expertise to work on the company accounts. Backup and Restore are both described in Chapter 11. It's vital that you remember to back up your accounting data each time and to restore it before you start doing actual work. It's easy to forget which set of data you're working on, especially if you get called away from the computer while working on the demo files - you could damage your actual records if you leave the demo data on the system by mistake.

CHAPTER 3

Getting started

The latest version of Sterling +2 is only available to run under the Windows environment, unlike its predecessor which also offered a DOS option. As more than 90% of the users wanted to work with Windows the company decided to free itself of the limitations caused by trying to develop identical products for two such different operating environments. There is still a DOS product, Sterling V6, which offers similar functionality. Anyone upgrading from the previous version will find that the interface has been improved as a graphic designer has sharpened up the appearance of the already attractive icons. The main menu is now in a band across the top of the screen, giving a tidier appearance and making the options easier to find.

What type of equipment do I need?

To get the best out of Sterling +2 you will need an IBM AT or compatible PC with a 386 or 486 processor and a mouse, although it is possible to use a keyboard. Minimum requirements are MS-DOS version 3.1, Windows version 3.1, an EGA resolution monitor and a printer (both supported by Windows), 2MB of memory with all memory over 640KB configured as extended memory, and a hard disk with at least 3MB of free disk space left over after installing Windows. Sterling +2 offers communications facilities for the telephone and fax, and if you want to use these options choose a Hayes compatible modem and a Windows compatible fax card. So far, few users have opted to use the automatic fax facilities as it can be cheaper simply to print out documents to send via the standard office fax machine rather than paying for a fax card. Small businesses which haven't bought a fax machine yet could save by installing a fax card for their general office faxes and to use this extra Sage feature.

Installation

Sterling +2 is installed from a single master disk. It's best to start by making a copy and storing the original away so that you always have a backup. Although there is only one disk this doesn't mean that the software is in any way limited - Sage has compressed the files so that they can be contained on one disk. To make a copy insert the master disk in the A drive, load Windows and choose Main then File Manager. On the File Manager window click on the A drive icon, then choose Disk on the menu bar and Copy Disk on the pull-down menu. Confirm that you want to continue and you will be prompted to insert the source disk (the Sterling +2 master disk) and then the second disk for your copy.

Insert the copy of your Sterling +2 master disk into drive A, then load Windows and point and click on the File option on the Program Manager main menu. From the pull-down menu select Run and a dialog box will be displayed prompting you to fill in the Command Line.

Type A:\SETUP then point and click on OK. The Install Program is now loaded and will automatically lead you, step by step, through the whole process.

The first screen gives four choices including Exit which lets you cancel installation and return to the Program Manager if in any doubt. The main choices are Install for the First Time and Install Program Files Only. Both total newcomers to Sterling +2 and those upgrading from Version 1 should choose Install for the First Time. This is because the software is stored on a completely different subdirectory. You will need a completely new installation because this version is so different from its predecessor.

Warning

Don't be tempted to try Install Program Files Only if you are upgrading from Version 1 to Version 2. This routine has been designed for future upgrades when you move from Version 2 to Version 2.1 and beyond. Using this option now may copy incorrect settings from Version 1 to your new software.

First time users

Once you have selected Install for the First Time you will be prompted to fill in your company name and address in a box titled Company Details. The Name box expects a company name of at least 6 characters, and the address fields will accept up to 30 characters each. To move between fields use either the TAB key or point and click the mouse at the place where you want to enter information - this is the standard Windows method used to move between fields throughout Sterling +2.

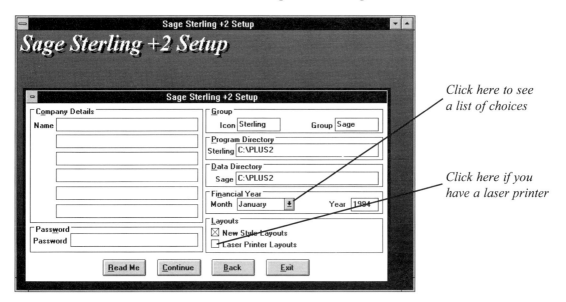

On the same screen it is possible to enter a password. If this is left blank anybody will be able to access the information held on Sterling +2 simply by switching on the computer and loading the software. If you want to wait until later a password can be added at any time. Remember to keep a record if you do specify a password as it will be impossible to load the software without it next time you start working on Sage.

To the right of the screen the Financial Year box contains a default setting and this may have to be changed. Think carefully about the start date for the company's financial year, because this can't be altered once accounting figures have been processed by the software - for example once you post your first invoice. There will be another opportunity to change this date later as you progress step-by-step through the initial configuration settings. Don't start working on Sterling +2 without checking that the financial year specification is correct. To change to a different month type the first letter and the whole word will be displayed (keep typing the letter if there is more than one month with the same initial); or click on the arrow at the end of the field to see a list of months in a pull-down box, then scroll through them using the scroll arrows and point and click on the correct one. Remove the pull-down menu by clicking on the arrow a second time. Change the year simply by moving to the Year field using the mouse or TAB key and typing.

There are set rules about which dates you can choose - your accounts will always cover a 12 month period starting from that time. If you are not registered for VAT you can choose any date, but if you are registered for VAT it's best to select a date which falls at the end of the month. This is because VAT accounts are calculated at month end and it's best if you can finish your year end accounts for VAT and all other records at the same time. Even if you are not registered for VAT now you may well have to register in future and once you set a financial year start date you will probably not want to change it.

You may choose the actual day you start trading but this is unlikely to be the first of the month. Alternatively you could choose the end of your first month - then your first year will be slightly longer than 12 months. Financial years can also be set according to the calendar year or the tax year. The calendar year runs from 31st December for 12 months, while the tax year starts on 5th April.

Many businesses choose 31st March as this is a handy end-of-month date and falls close to the tax year start date. If you choose the calendar year but start trading well afterwards and not on January 1st your first year is likely to be up to a month short. If you pay VAT quarterly you will want a date which ties in with the month when your VAT is due. This is not a great problem as you can ask the VAT office to alter your dates.

It's best to ask an accountant to advise you about the appropriate financial year start date. Tax is assessed based on profits from previous years - a short year can reduce your profits and prove advantageous. The Inland Revenue has special ways of working out the way you are taxed in the early years of trading which can reduce your tax bill. It's well worth consulting an accountant who will tell you how to make the most of this legislation.

In the bottom box on the same screen are options for the stationery layouts: New Style Layouts and Laser Printer Layouts. Click on the check boxes beside the required layouts to activate your choices, and remember that if you have a laser printer you will need to put an X in both boxes. The X activates an option, while a second click removes the X and deselects it. Sterling +2 includes both the old and new designs for stationery layouts so there is a choice, while the laser printer layouts are vital if you are not using continuous stationery. You will also be able to switch over to a different type of printer with continuous stationery, but the laser printer settings will be the default choice.

Tip

Click on the down arrow at the end of fields to see a list of choices.

The remaining boxes on this screen have default settings which can be changed, but it's safest to leave them as they are. They specify the drive and directory where the programs and data will be stored on the hard disk as well as the icon label and group window which you will choose from the Windows Program Manager each time you want to load Sterling +2. Once all the information is correct, point and click on Continue or select Read Me for extra guidance. If in any doubt choose Exit to close without completing installation. Once Continue is selected all the program files will be copied to the hard disk. A final message will appear to say the installation has gone successfully and there's a reminder to fill in the registration card and return it to Sage. It's a good idea to do this straight away as it entitles you to free support for 90 days, giving unlimited access to the telephone hotline. Point and click on OK to start working with Sterling +2.

Tip

Select Read Me before pressing Continue on the installation screen, then click on File on the menu bar and choose Print from the pull-down menu. This will print out a supplement to your manual with guidance on all changes to the software since the documentation was written and includes important variations to menu commands and screen designs.

Installation is now complete and next time you load Windows the Program Manager will have a Sage icon which you need to choose to see the Sage group window. On the Sage group window there will be an icon labelled Sterling which should be chosen when you want to work on the accounts software. There is also an icon labelled Read Me which you should use to print out extra software instructions before continuing, unless you did so using the command on the installation screen.

Upgrading from the first version of Sterling +2

The initial release of Sterling +2 Version 2 has no upgrade option on the menu for users moving up from Version 1. You will need to press Install for the first Time and use the same steps described for first time users. Make sure you also refer to any upgrade notes provided with your software, and if in any doubt choose Exit to cancel the installation without altering your files.

The first time installation routine is the only way to load the software onto the correct subdirectory C:\PLUS2. The previous version used the subdirectory C:\SAGE2 so you need to choose Install for the First Time to put the program files in the right place. Watch out for early versions of the manual which still mistakenly call the new subdirectory C:\SAGE2.

If you have been using the first version of Sterling +2 you will already have accounting data which needs to be transferred to the upgraded software (the new installation on the subdirectory C:\PLUS2). To do this it's necessary to convert the data using a routine which will either be offered on the installation display (not on the early releases) or provided on a separate disk. If you have a disk with the data conversion software take the following steps.

Load Windows then click on Main in the Program Manager window followed by the MS-DOS prompt icon. When the DOS prompt appears type CD \PLUS2 to change over to the directory where your Sterling +2 version 2 program has been installed. Place the disk labelled Convert2 into your floppy disk drive (the A drive if you have two). At the MS-DOS prompt type COPY A:\CONVERT2.EXE C: and press Enter. A message will appear to tell you one file has been copied. Type EXIT and you will return to Windows.

The data conversion program has been copied but you still need to create an icon. From the Windows Program Manager window choose the Sage icon. Next select File from the menu bar and New from the pull-down menu. A dialog box titled New Program Object appears and you should click on the Program Item option button. Press OK and the Program Item Properties dialog box will be displayed. In the Description box you should type CONVERT +2. In the Command Line box type C:\PLUS2\CONVERT2.EXE. Type C:\PLUS2 in the Working Directory box. Finish by clicking on OK.

An icon labelled Convert +2 has been added to the Sage Group window - just select it when you want to convert your data. When you double-click on the Convert +2 icon a window appears headed Sage Sterling +2 Convert. In the options box you should only click on the Convert Data check box to insert an X. The other check box (Convert Layouts) is for future releases so there should be no X inserted here. The software will automatically insert the path in the final box - this is C:\PLUS2. Only change this path if you have specified a different subdirectory for your Sterling +2 program. The Browse button lets you search for the files if you can't remember where you have stored them. Press Exit if you are unsure about the data conversion routine, or choose Continue if you want to convert your data.

If you press Continue a window headed Convert Data appears. This has just one field with the path leading to the location of your old data files. If you use the Sage default settings this will be C:\SAGE2\ACCDATA. If you chose a different subdirectory for your previous version of Sterling you should specify the correct path before pressing Continue. Again there is a Browse button to help you search for the files in the right subdirectory, or Cancel to exit without converting data. When you are happy with the settings press Continue and your data will be converted and transferred to your new software.

If you didn't buy one of the early releases of the software the conversion routines will be integral to Sterling+2 and are provided as an extra option on the installation display. Respond to the prompt to indicate you have data to convert and you will be presented with the same windows described earlier. The method is the same as it is for those who have an early version of the software and run the conversion routine off a separate disk.

Tip

You will be able to run the conversion program at the installation stage or you can wait and do this task later by clicking on the Convert +2 icon. Remember that the first version of Sterling +2 used the subdirectory SAGE2 but the latest release uses the subdirectory PLUS2.

Warning

Before converting your data, make sure you have an up-to-date backup in case anything goes wrong. See the Backup and Restore section in Chapter 11 for full details on how to do this.

First Steps

You are now ready to start working with Sterling +2. Each time the computer is switched on you will have to load Windows, select the Sage icon from the Program Manager window and then the Sterling icon from the Sage group window. At this point the software will prompt for a password before you can continue unless you have chosen not to set one. Although it's necessary to configure the system for each company's specific requirements it is possible to work on Sterling +2 straight away, so have a look through the software before continuing. Don't start any serious work until the software has been completely set up for your company - the first major task will be entering information on all the customers, suppliers and products. This is a good time to do some housekeeping and tidying to get your files in order and up-to-date!

The Sterling +2 main menu (Toolbar) has been set out along the top of the screen and presents a particularly attractive and intuitive interface to the user. Try selecting some of the options to see how the graphic designer has added a touch of animation for a little bit of fun. The sales ledger is called Customers - selecting this option makes the cheque change hands. The Suppliers option opens the purchase ledger with the cheque quickly being signed. Use the standard Windows techniques described in Chapter 2 to close each option and clear the display. The quickest way is to double-click quickly on the control-menu box at the top of each window, or choose Window from the menu bar and Close All from the pull-down menu.

Help! Useful function keys

From this point onwards, if you get stuck it's possible to find some instructions on how to use the software by reading the online manual although this is not a complete guide. This is a standard Windows facility and Sage has put step-by-step instructions on how to use Sterling +2 features listed under main contents headings. Try it out now to see how to enter customer records. Don't start entering any customer records yet as there are still some important settings to enter or amend. You will find that some functions are not covered by the online help or are not detailed, in which case refer to the relevant chapter for more instructions.

Call up the help screens by pressing F1 or by selecting Help from the menu bar and again from the pull-down menu. A list of main contents appears under headings, typed in black. It's possible to point and click on any of the sub-headings typed in green. Choose Customers from the first display, then Records from the second and, finally, Creating New Customer/Supplier Records from the third list. Finally a display appears which asks if you want information on how to fill in the fields or how to use the buttons when entering records in your customer database. There is also general information giving guidance on creating a customer database. With Windows it's possible to be working on the Sterling +2 software in one window, whilst looking at the help screen for guidance in a second window - just point and click on the windows to move between them and the window you click on will become active.

A second Windows facility, the calculator, can be called up by pressing F2. The pop-up

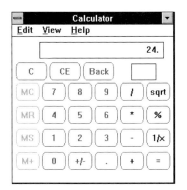

calculator appears to help with your maths and results can be pasted into Sterling +2 fields by selecting Edit from the Calculator menu and then Copy. Place the cursor in the Sterling +2 field where you want to Paste the figure then press Shift and Insert. The calculator can be moved to a more convenient position using the mouse to drag it by the title bar as described in Chapter 2. Switch between two versions of the calculator, standard or scientific, by choosing View from the Calculator menu and highlighting your choice.

Sage has set more function keys to give quick access to parts of the system you need to use regularly. Apart from F1 for help and F2 for the calculator you can press F11 to use the Windows Control Panel without exiting from Sterling +2. The Control Panel is particularly important for setting screen colours and printer defaults. The F12 key calls up Windows Write for creating and editing documents. This gives access to an extra feature - the ability to add variables which can be used to redesign all your stationery (see Chapter 5). The other function keys are for working on particular parts of Sterling +2 . F7 creates adjustments when you are reconciling your bank account, F6 will delete a complete line from a record you are editing and F5 will paste the system date into a date field. The handy F4 key will show a list of available choices or records for the field you are working on. For example, if you press it when entering a customer account number, it will show you a complete list of customer accounts. Try out these function keys to get a clear idea of how helpful they can be.

Tip

Some function keys, such as F1 and F2, are useful throughout Sterling +2. Others, such as F7 and F6 are used in specific places and you will be reminded about them throughout the book as you learn to handle the relevant functions.

Set up and defaults

The software is fully functional from the time of installation as Sage has set defaults which fit in with standard business practices. You will, however, have to check certain details such as the financial year start date and the method of VAT accounting.

Before entering records on customers, suppliers and products it's possible to make optional changes to the default settings so that the software fits your company's business methods exactly. Don't try to tackle any detailed tailoring unless you are an expert both at handling software and accounting. Even then make changes only after careful consideration of your company's particular needs.

Even when the software is set up to your satisfaction it's important to keep running the existing accounting system as a safeguard until any initial problems have shown up and been overcome. It's vital to keep regular backups of data held on a new accounting system. Sage offers this option each time you try to exit - make full use of it. Hard disks don't last for ever, and with an expected life of about five years, failure is certain just when you have grown complacent about taking backups. Some cheaper computers have hard disks which fail even sooner. Get in the habit straight away of copying all data onto separate disks as information lost on a failed hard disk is gone forever.

Replacing the hard disk is not expensive, but the data you lose could be invaluable. Don't be tempted to buy a do-it-yourself manual and tackle your own repairs as you could do irreparable damage. You may only need a new battery, or perhaps a board has slipped out of place and needs to be pushed firmly back. At worst you will have to buy a new hard disk, but in all cases use a qualified maintenance engineer.

Before starting work you need to set the VAT accounting method, currencies, departments, products and the printer installation. It's also a good idea to ensure the financial year start date is correct, to add a password if this has not already been done and to decide whether or not you want to change the colours on the screen display. These choices used to be available from the Configure option which has now been removed from the menu bar, and the instructions in your manual may have been superseded by changes to the software so take the following steps instead:

Configuration

From the main menu select Defaults to see a pull-down menu. Start by clicking on Company Preferences to check your current choices for the company name, address and password. These fields can be changed at any time. To do so move between fields using

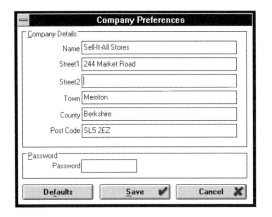

the TAB key, then move within fields using the directional arrow keys and type the amendment. To keep any amendments remember to point and click on Save, or choose Cancel if you change your mind and want to retain the original settings.

To do more detailed tailoring select Defaults from the Company Preferences display. This will let you change the screen display colours and specify the correct VAT method.

Most of the settings on the Company Preferences Defaults screen can be left as they are, but you will have to check the ones in the boxes labelled System Defaults and also Communications. The box headed Editor shows the link to Windows facilities for wordprocessing as the software will then switch easily to the Windows Notepad. Sage has set the function keys F11 and F12 to call up specific programs and you can change these keys by specifying the programs you want them to initiate in the box headed Function Keys. Leave the F12 key as it is because the program specified here lets you switch easily to Windows Write each time you want to work on the document editing facilities. F11 switches you easily to the Windows Control Panel, so only change this if you need to access a different application more urgently. The Text Labels box is to set out the prompts which will appear beside the address fields for customers and suppliers. All of this has been carefully designed by Sage so you can leave the defaults as they are unless you have specific company requirements to meet.

Screen display

Under System Defaults, you can test out the method for changing the screen display. Point and click on the check box beside Use Default Windows Colours to insert an X. Once the X has been inserted this option becomes active and the screen display will change appearance immediately. Point and click again on the check box to remove the X and the colours revert. If you put an X, the display will use the colours you specify for all your Windows software - if you haven't changed the screen designs this will be the default Windows colour scheme. You have two choices: either insert an X to use the same colour scheme for all your Windows applications, or remove the X to set an individual colour scheme for Sterling +2.

Screen colours

If you want to change the screen colour for Sterling +2 alone without affecting all of your other Windows applications use the following technique. Make sure first of all that the Company Preferences Defaults screen does not have an X in the Use Windows Default Colours check box. If you're using Windows default colours no changes can be made via the Sage menus.

Next click on the Set Colour button on the Company Preferences Defaults display. This switches over to the Windows Color dialog box which you can also run from the Windows Control Panel. The simplest method is to click on one of the basic colours, then point and click on the small arrow to the right of the screen and drag it up and down the luminosity bar to make the shade lighter or darker. Click on OK and return to Sterling +2 to see how your choice appears. Alternatively point and click on the rainbow-coloured palette and drag the marker around to locate the exact shade you want, then point and click on the Add to Custom Colors box and your creation will be included on the palette to give an extra choice. Point and click on the custom colour and on the OK box to view Sterling +2 with your favourite shade as background.

Changing the screen colours can be fun and it is appealing to see attractive shades, but remember that softer hues are easier on the eyes. Don't be tempted to make the display too garish. The gentle greys and light blues of the default Windows colours have been chosen because these soothe the eyes, allowing operators to work for longer periods without discomfort. The end result is fewer mistakes caused by eye-strain. Those working on accounts software need to be accurate when inputting numbers, so keep the colours relaxing in order to avoid errors.

If you want to set a colour scheme for all of your Windows applications including menus, choose Defaults from the main menu, then Company Preferences then press Sterling +2, it's possible to make more changes using the Windows Control Panel. To do this you need to put an X in the Use Windows Default Colours check box and the colour design you specify on the Control Panel will appear on all of your system software.

Next press F11 to load the Control Panel from within Sterling +2 and choose the icon of three crayons labelled Color. If you are not running Sterling +2 load Windows then choose Main from the Windows Program Manager. From the Main group select Control Panel and then choose the icon labelled Color. This loads the colour schemes display and if you click on Color Palette it will also load the colour palette described above. Press Define Custom colors if you want more choice. At the top of the colour palette is a box labelled Screen Element and if you click on the arrow at the end of the field you will see a list of all the parts of the screen design which you can change. Scroll through the list, click on the elements you want to change including background and text, and choose the colours from the palette or by creating a custom colour. The Desktop is the whole area of the window below the title bar, menu bar and main menu Toolbar.

There are already a few screen designs set up by Microsoft and to try them out press the arrow at the end of the field labelled Color Schemes on the Windows Color panel. Just point and click on each of the colour schemes to see how they appear. If you like the design choose OK at the bottom of the screen to use it. If you are creating your own colour scheme take full advantage of the Screen Element box which lets you set the colour for every part of the display, including highlighted text as well as menu bars and buttons - the background and text are just the basics! Once you have chosen colours for all parts of the display press the Save Scheme button and give it a name to add it to the list. It will then be in use when you return to the Program Manager and throughout your Windows applications. In future you can return to the Windows Colour panel and select a different colour scheme including the Windows default colours. If you want to use this colour scheme just for Sterling +2 you could call it Sage so that you can easily identify and select it. If there are a few operators in your company they could each give their name to their favourite colour scheme and select it when they start work.

Tip
Choose a different colour for the title bar on your active window so that you can easily identify it when you have a number of open windows.

Warning
If you're experimenting with different background and text colours be careful not to switch to a background colour you are already using for text or vice versa. All of the text will disappear on the Windows Control Panel and throughout the system so choose your shades carefully!

VAT

The second setting on the Company Preferences Defaults display is the method of VAT accounting. There are two options: standard VAT accounting and VAT cash accounting, with the default being set as the former. Standard VAT accounting bases the values of input and output VAT on the VAT elements of *all* invoices and credit notes, plus taxable cash and bank transactions. VAT Cash Accounting bases the value of input and output VAT only on invoices and credit notes *which have been paid* plus bank or cash transactions. Output VAT is the tax you must add to the price of goods before selling them to customers, whereas input VAT is the tax you pay to your suppliers.

If your company uses VAT Cash Accounting put an X in the check box. In this case the VAT control account will not agree with the results of the VAT return analysis. This is because the VAT control account adds together amounts for all taxable transactions regardless of whether or not they have been paid. See Chapter 9 for more detailed guidance on VAT.

Communications

The communications box on the Company Preferences Defaults display contains important information for anybody using the communications and fax facilities. The first box labelled Port shows COM1 as the place where the communications equipment is attached - change this if you are using a different serial port. The second box is for the name of the modem to be used - make sure this is a Windows-supported Hayes compatible device. The delay box shows the time in seconds which you want the equipment to pause when processing a telephone number. This will work when you use the automatic dialling button to phone a customer or supplier by disconnecting the line after the specified delay.

Once all of the defaults have been set to suit your exact company needs, point and click on OK to return to the Company Preferences window which needs to be closed to return to the main menu. Remember to press Save or your specifications will be lost.

Tip

Choose Defaults from the Help menu then Company Preferences and scroll through the list of definitions to see exactly what each option means. Don't be surprised to find some slight variations from your software as the manual and online help have fallen behind rapid improvements to Sterling +2.

VAT Rates

Sage has set up standard VAT rates as defaults but it is possible to change or add to these. Select Defaults from the menu bar, then Tax Codes from the pull-down menu. A maximum of 100 VAT rates can be set and these are numbered from T0 to T99. The default setting includes T1 with the current standard percentage rate. Look at the VAT Code Setup box which shows the current settings with the code number, percentage rate and Y/N (for yes or no) to show if the code is in use and if it is for European Union transactions. The default settings can be used for the following standard codes:

T0   Zero-rated

T1   Standard rate

T2   Exempt

T4   Sales to EU customers (not UK)

T7   Zero-rated purchases from EU suppliers (not UK)

T8   Standard rated purchases from EU suppliers (not UK)

T9   Transactions not involving VAT

To amend or add to the table, point and click on the line you want to change to highlight it and then select Edit. This displays a Tax Code Setup box which gives the code number and prompts for the rate: enter the percentage required in the Rate field then point and click on the check boxes to make the code active and to indicate whether or not this is for EU transactions. An X in the check box makes the choice active and will appear as a Y for yes in the main VAT Code Setup display.

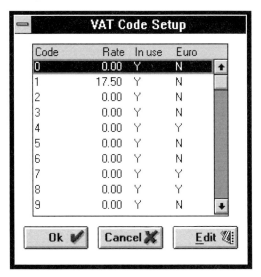

Try out the tax code setup by using the scroll bar to move down to the code T10 - you can see that this is the first free code because there is an N in the column headed In use. Be careful not to use a code which has a figure of zero in the Rate column as this may just be a tax exempt setting. Click on T10 to highlight the line and press Edit then put 3 in Rate field and point and click on the first check box to make the code active. Finish by pressing OK to see the code added to the VAT settings. Now you can use the code T10 when recording insurance transactions as insurance companies charge 3% and pay the same amount to HM Customs and Excise.

Tip

Keep a close watch on changes to rates of VAT as they can vary with every Budget and you will need to amend your tax table accordingly.

Currencies

Sterling +2 is not a multicurrency product as it doesn't handle the *processing* of different currencies, but foreign currencies can be specified for overseas customers and suppliers. This feature is only used for reporting or purely for notes and memorandum purposes. Sage has already set a wide range of currencies which can be viewed or amended by selecting Defaults from the menu bar then Currency from the pull-down menu. Check the list of currencies already set to see if your company needs any additional countries to be included. The currencies are listed by number, name of the currency, name of the country and a two-letter abbreviation for EU members.

Note
The software was written before the Maastricht Treaty and uses the old term EC instead of EU.

When you create a database of customers and suppliers in the next chapter you will be able to give each of the overseas businesses its correct currency and country code. Although the software can't perform any currency conversion calculations this will be useful for your own reference and for reports. You may want to create a report sorting out customers or suppliers by country and currency, in order to check your VAT liability figures for EU trade. Alternatively you may want to reclaim VAT, which has to be done by contacting the tax authority in the relevant country. This could all be done using the report generator method described in Chapter 10 to help you find the relevant customer and supplier accounts.

Tip

See the Business Guide in Chapter 9 to find out how to reclaim VAT from EU member countries.

The currency settings are also useful for reference when you have to make manual conversions as this is not always straightforward. Although you will have to convert the amounts yourself when trading with overseas customers and suppliers it will be necessary to watch these figures carefully. The conversion rates are likely to change before invoices are settled and you will have to make manual adjustments to allow for the difference between what was charged on the invoice and what is actually paid. Find out how to do this in the overseas customers and suppliers section of Chapter 6.

To add to or alter the currency settings select Edit to see the Currencies setup box. Simply type in the name of the currency in the Currency field (e.g. Pound Sterling, French Franc, Swiss Franc), then in the field labelled Country enter the name of the relevant country. Finally enter a two-letter abbreviation in the EU member box if the country is a member of the European Union and click on OK to amend the currency list.

Departments

The software lets you set up to 99 departments, although small businesses will have far fewer! Make a list of departments such as accounts, sales, marketing, purchasing and training. Each of these can then be recorded by name and code, and the code will appear on invoices, credit notes and bank and cash transactions. The code is also useful when producing reports analysing figures by department.

Choose Defaults from the menu bar then Departments from the pull-down menu. The display shows the Departments window with code number 1 highlighted, so click on edit to add the first department. The Departments box will then prompt for the name of the department to be typed in and accepted by clicking on OK. To add a second department point and click on number 2, then click on Edit and continue storing names in the same way.

Products

Again make a list - this time of all the company product categories. Up to 99 can be recorded by name and code number. These are used for reports on any one group of products.

Tip

Product categories are for groups of products of the same type, not individual products. For example, a product category of Clothing would be used later to store information on separate items such as trousers, dresses etc.

Select Defaults from the menu bar, then Product Categories from the pull-down menu. The Product Categories window appears with number 1 highlighted and to start listing products click on Edit. When the Product Categories box appears type in the name of the product group and click on OK. Click on number 2 and Edit to continue listing products. Any of these settings can be changed in future by highlighting the product category and editing using the same technique.

Control Accounts

It's best to leave the default settings for the control accounts, although these can be changed if you wish. Only attempt changes if you have the necessary expertise. Control accounts are used for automatic double entry postings and can be viewed or altered by selecting Defaults from the menu bar, then Control Accounts from the pull-down menu. Point and click on the account code you want to change. Then either enter a new code directly or click on the magnifying glass icon at the end of the field to see a list of nominal codes. Scroll through the list by pointing and clicking on the scroll arrows on the vertical scroll bar.

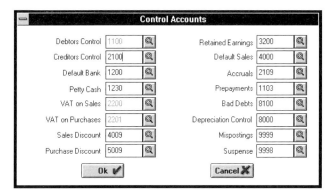

Even if you don't want to alter the default settings now, you may need to later as you start to do more advanced work on the software. These alterations will be described as you progress through later chapters and start to find out how to amend the chart of accounts. The default control accounts work with the Sage chart of accounts for the nominal ledger. This means that changes to the chart of accounts which affect any of the control accounts will also have to be amended on this (Control Accounts) screen. To do so you must first set up the account as a nominal ledger record (see Chapter 4) then specify the nominal code on the control accounts screen. For example, it would be important to change the control accounts for your main bank and petty cash accounts using this option should you create new records in the nominal ledger. If you didn't enter the new codes for bank and petty cash accounts both in the nominal ledger records and on the control accounts screen the software couldn't post bank and cash transactions correctly.

Thanks to the control accounts you can depend on the software to make most of your double entries accurately. The debtors control account records all customer invoices as debits, while purchase invoices cause credit postings to the creditors control account. These calculations may appear complicated for non-accountants, but the software automatically makes the correct credit and debit postings into all the control accounts, including VAT.

Warning

Don't change the Control Accounts if you are in any doubt. These have the nominal code specifications so that the software knows where to post accounting transactions. Mistakes on this screen will cause problems throughout Sterling +2. For this reason some Control Accounts will be 'greyed out' and can't be amended once in use for actual transactions.

Financial Year Start Date

This was already input during installation, but it's important to check and amend it before starting work on Sterling +2 because once amounts are posted to the nominal ledger it's impossible to change your mind. Refer to the advice given earlier (in the first time users section) and don't enter any invoices or other transactions until you're sure this specification is correct.

Choose Defaults from the menu bar, then Financial Year from the pull-down menu. Type in a new month, or point and click on the arrow to see a selection of months and click on the desired option, then type in the year and finish by clicking on OK. If you have already tried posting a few transactions your initial financial year setting will appear in lighter grey characters and can no longer be altered.

Installing and setting up the printer

If your main problem in getting started is caused by difficulties with the printer don't be embarrassed. This can be the most complicated part of setting up your system and the Sage hotline is buzzing with callers with printer problems. This procedure is easiest if you already have a printer installed and running under Windows for other applications.

For those who have set up one or more printers beforehand using the Windows Control Panel, the Sterling +2 menu gives access to setup commands for connecting and switching between printers. You may want to switch between a laser and a dot-matrix printer for different quality documentation, for example. To do so, choose File from the menu bar and then Printer Setup from the pull-down menu. This will display a list of printers you already have connected. To switch between printers simply highlight the desired option and press OK.

It's more complicated to get started if there are no printers installed. This will have to be done using the Windows Control Panel. If you are running Sterling +2 press F11 and choose the Printers icon on the Control Panel group window. Alternatively load Windows on the PC, then choose Main followed by Control Panel and the Printers icon. Scroll through the List of Printers to see if your equipment is included: if so highlight it and click on Install. The printer will automatically be installed and will be included on the Sterling +2 printer setup menu.

If your printer is not included, make sure that it is compatible with Windows then choose Install Unlisted or Updated Printer, from the List of Printers box. Click on the Install button and insert the disk supplied with your printer when the screen prompt appears. Select OK and your printer should be added to the list. When the procedure is complete click on the Close button. If there are still problems contact the printer supplier to check you have the correct disk with the printer driver file.

Windows is also used to specify which ports your printers are connected to and this needs to be done before printing out information from Sterling +2. The same technique can be used to change the port specification at a later date. Press F11 or load the Control Panel via Windows, highlight the printer you want to connect to a specific port and click on the Connect button. A dialog box displays a list of ports for you to highlight the required one and click on OK to complete the selection process. If you're not sure which port you require, check the port name on the computer - this is the place where you connect your printer. It will be something like COM1, COM2, LPT1 or LPT2.

Once the printer has been installed you're ready to start working on Sterling +2 and the next major job will be to input all of your records. The software is ready for daily accounts work straight away, but to start making full use of all its features try to organise and input the company's records as soon as possible. Follow the steps in the next chapter to build up your complete database of customers, suppliers and products. Make the most of this chance to tidy and update the records. Sort your invoices into date order for input and soon all the company accounts will be computerised.

Q&A

Every time I load Sterling +2 it fills the whole screen and I can't see the windows underneath. Do I have to minimise it to work on other applications?

Instead of minimising you can press the restore button in the top right of the display to make the window smaller but still active. This way you can switch between two applications, such as Sterling +2 and a word processor or database. Some parts of Sterling +2 have so much information on the screen that you will need to use the whole display. To do this click on the maximise button to enlarge the display. You can also press Defaults and click on Toolbar to remove the main menu from the top of the screen and free some extra space, then replace it by pressing Toolbar a second time.

I changed the background colours using the Set Colour button on the Company Preferences screen and now I want to switch back to the original Sage setting. How can I do this?

Use the Set Colour button again and choose the light green shade on the top row of the colour panel, then press OK. This will replace your settings with the original background so long as you do not have an X in the Use Default Windows Colours check box.

Will it be possible to change to a different method of VAT accounting if I choose the standard method on the Company Preferences screen? I intend to change over to VAT cash accounting.

You can change to VAT cash accounting at a later date. Remember that you can only use VAT cash accounting if your turnover is below a set limit (£350,000 in the 1993 Budget) and this can vary from year to year. See Chapter 9 for full details on VAT.

I haven't bought a printer yet and I've heard that some are not suitable for Windows or accounting software. What should I look for, apart from Windows compatibility, to make sure I select the right printer?

Accounting software produces lengthy reports, so if you are not using a printer with continuous stationery it will need a sheet feeder well stocked with paper. If some of your documents need to be copied using carbonised duplicate forms the printer will have to be dot-matrix or daisywheel in order to make the necessary impact (you can also have a laser printer as a second choice for documents where high quality is the important factor). As some of the reports are wide the printer must be able to handle more than 80 columns - check that 80 column printers can be switched to condensed mode to cope with this.

Laser printers may have to be set on landscape if the report will not fit on the standard portrait format.

Your printer may offer a variety of fonts which you can use on any of your documents. Before a major print run you should check to see that the size of the characters will fit easily onto the stationery. Some printers can produce graphics as well as offering a variety of fonts and Sterling +2 exploits these facilities. For example, you can create a bitmap image of your company logo and have it printed at the top of reports. The different fonts can be used to vary the appearance of text to distinguish headings from statistics and to highlight the column totals. However, be careful not to overdo it and create a messy appearance with too many different character styles. Find out more about reports in Chapter 10.

I have a copy of the Accountant version of Sterling +2 and I would like to consolidate the accounts for a small number of companies. Do I have to upgrade to Financial Controller or is there a cheaper option?

If you have Accountant and don't need stock control or sales order processing it would be cheaper to get a bureau licence from Sage. This will let you handle multicompany accounting and will give you the extra software together with advice and instructions on consolidating the accounts in your main company's nominal ledger. People with Accountant Plus would find the cost of upgrading to Financial Controller similar to the cost of a bureau licence, but whereas Financial Controller offers multicompany processing for up to 10 companies, the bureau licence option can deal with a greater number. The bureau licence is suitable for companies which want to handle multicompany processing, or for accountants in practice. It's also suitable for businesses which manage the accounts for other companies (such as payroll bureaux) where it's necessary to put the data for each client onto the system.

CHAPTER 4

Creating a Database

Once the software is installed you can start adding records. It's a good idea to get all details of customers, suppliers and products onto the database as soon as possible. The last chapter explained how to set the default codes which will help organise this database. Sage has already planned the most difficult set of codes as defaults for the nominal ledger.

Tip

You will be told how to change nominal account codes whenever this is necessary. The chart of accounts is described later in the chapter - you can also refer to Chapter 9 for more details on the nominal ledger. In Chapter 10 you will learn how to change the layout of the chart of accounts so that the correct data goes into the profit and loss or balance sheet sections.

Building up a complete database means painstakingly entering all the company records and will take a long time, so make sure whoever does this task remembers to make constant backups. The work may be rather monotonous, but it's even more soul-destroying to have to repeat the entire task due to system failure combined with the lack of backup data. You will be prompted to make backups each time you exit. Remember that it's vital to make copies onto floppy disks in case of hard disk failure. Backups can be made onto hard disk subdirectories, but these will be useless on the day the computer screen informs you that there is no access to drive C.

Backup is offered under Data on the main menu as well as from the prompt each time you attempt to close Sterling +2. Choose Data, then Backup. Put a formatted disk into the A drive, then click on the a: drive graphic in the drives box. Finally, click on the OK button. Label the disks and number them, as you may need more than one disk to back up the data. It's a good idea to keep more than one copy of each disk in case the data is mistakenly overwritten - this way at least there is a copy of the last complete backup. There is no longer any warning that the backup will overwrite all the data you have on disk.

Tip

See the Backup and Restore section of Chapter 11 for a detailed guide to backing up and restoring data.

Customers, Suppliers and Products

Sage provides easy to complete screens for your records, but before starting it's important to check the default settings to see if and where they need to be changed. You can set defaults for fields in your records where information which will be true for the majority of cases. These fields will then be automatically filled in, saving you time and effort as you create your database. Start with customers by choosing Defaults on the menu bar, then Customer Defaults from the pull-down menu. The Customer Defaults display shows the settings already selected. The tax code will be automatically set at the current percentage for VAT and the currency is set on your Number 1 choice. To change to one of the other currencies or VAT settings click on the arrow at the end of the field to see a complete list, click on the desired choice to highlight it and it will appear as the default. Whenever there is an arrow at the end of a field you can use this technique. When the pull-down list appears for selection, it will have scroll arrows to let you scroll through any choices which are out of view.

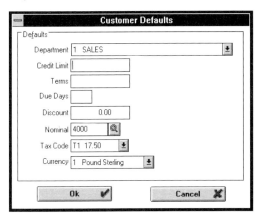

If you have set up a variety of departments click on the arrow at the end of the Department field to view them all and make a selection. The nominal code specified is for the standard type of sale. Click on the magnifying-glass icon to see the complete set of codes and use the scroll arrows to scroll through the whole list. It's possible to set other defaults at this stage, such as a standard credit limit for customers, discount, terms and due days for payment. Only put figures in these fields as defaults if they are likely to be true for the majority of your customers. They will appear on all your customer records and it might be easier to fill in blank fields. Even if you set defaults, these fields can be changed on the final customer record input screen.

Tip

If you get the default settings wrong they can be changed when you start adding records. Don't put up with incorrect default settings - change them as soon as you notice your error.

The supplier defaults can be viewed by choosing Defaults from the menu bar then Supplier Defaults on the pull-down menu. The display is similar to Customer Defaults and can be amended in the same way. Again you should only set defaults if they will apply to the majority of suppliers, such as in the Tax Code field. This will save you inputting the same information repeatedly - you will only need to change the fields with default settings in a small number of records.

The Product Defaults display is not so detailed and is accessed by choosing Defaults then Product Defaults. The extra fields (Stock Unit and Category) probably don't need to be changed. Typical stock units to show how products are bundled for sale would be box, dozen, single or six-pack and there is usually too much variety to allow a default. As most of your products will fit into a wide range of product categories it is also unlikely that a default setting would be helpful. However, you may be able to select a default nominal account to analyse sales of each product, as well as department and tax code.

Adding records

With all the defaults set, it's time to start entering customers, suppliers and products. Choose Customers from the Toolbar then click on the Record button. The Record option has a picture of a card index and using this computerised method really is as straightforward as the old manual method. In future, each time you choose Customers you will be shown a list of existing customer records before you can proceed. If any are highlighted it's important to click on Clear before selecting Record so as not to change existing data. If you have a few windows open you may not be able to see the whole display so click on the maximise button to enlarge the record card and to make sure it is completely visible. To shrink it again press the minimise button. You will know when parts of the display are not showing if you can't see the function buttons at the bottom of the window. You can also use the scroll arrows to the right and bottom of the screen to see the hidden information. Try out all the Windows methods described in Chapter 2 to make the displays more accessible. For example, drag windows to a different part of the desktop by clicking on the title bar and moving the mouse, then resize the boundaries to see extra information at the bottom or sides.

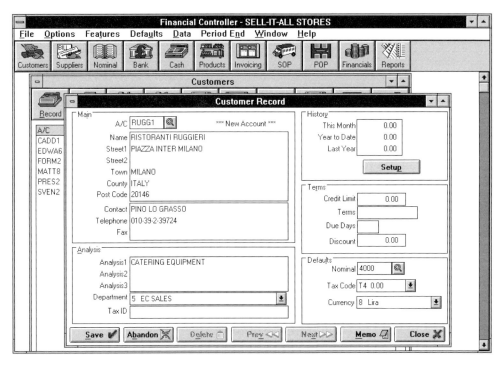

The first time you use the software there will be no existing data on store. The first Customers screen will be blank and you can select Record to start the database. The first field is for a code number or name (this can be numeric or alphabetic) and this field must be filled in. All of the other fields can be added later, but think carefully before selecting a code. For customer records it may be easiest to have an alphabetic code using the first four or five letters of the customer's name so that they can be easily located. The code can have up to six characters but the last character could be a number when customers have the same name and a distinction has to be made, i.e. FRED1, FRED2 etc. Alternatively the code can be completely numeric if this ties in with your existing system. To make sure that records are sorted in the correct order you must keep numeric codes the same length by adding zeros. This means that instead of using the simple numbers 1 to 10 you would have to type 0001, 0002 and so on up to 0010.

The customer record screen is as easy to fill in as a standard card index by typing in the name and address. Add the name of the person you usually deal with in the Contact field, then check if any of the defaults need to be changed in the Credit Terms box or in the box labelled Defaults. The Analysis fields are for identifying individual records for analysis reporting so the first three fields could contain information such as the salesman who deals with this customer, the type of business the customer runs and any other criteria to be used in reports. Look at the case study on Acoustic Records at the end of the book to see how the Analysis fields can be used to target potential customers. Fill in the department dealing with this customer and the customer's tax ID (both the VAT registration code and the country code) as these must be included on invoices and credit notes.

The Customer Record screen holds important information on the customer history for this month, the year to date and last year. These fields are only completely accurate when period end routines are run. For example, all figures entered during the current month will be included in the field for this month, even if the payment was for a previous month, until the month end procedure is completed. The history fields will become useful once the opening balances are entered (find out how later in this chapter).

The box labelled Terms is particularly useful for credit control, as customers who exceed their credit limits will be asterisked on reports and can be quickly identified. It's still possible to continue trading with the customer and sending out invoices, but you will know when payment is overdue. In fact the best time to ask for payment is when the customer is on the phone with a new order, so the software can help you call in your debts. The Terms field in this box is for any information you want to add about the customer terms (the maximum number of days allowed for payment) with up to 14 characters permitted. Follow up by filling in the Due Days box with the number of days within which the customer can pay and receive the discount entered in the next box. The Discount field allows any discounts to be entered as a percentage which can be offered for payment received within the number of days stated in the Due Days field.

How can I add extra information on individual customers?
Sterling +2 lets you add memos to each record, so this could be used to make a note of any special arrangements made with a particular customer. It could also include information such as names of extra contacts should problems arise with payments and best ways to ensure quick payment judging by past experience. All of this is of great help for the credit controller. Simply select Memo from the commands at the bottom of the Customer Record screen - if you can't see the Memo button, maximise the display.

When all the data has been filled in, plus any memos, click on the Save button to save or on Abandon to delete the entire entry. The software then presents a clear screen so that you can quickly fill in the next record. Carry on in the same way to build up the database. When you want to stop, click on the Close button or use the standard Windows method to close this function. To exit from the Customers option completely, double-click on the control-menu box or choose Window from the menu bar and Close All from the pull-down menu to clear the Desktop area completely.

Warning

Click on Save each time you complete a record or your work will be lost. If you click on Close the software only checks if you want to exit - later on you'll find you have no records despite all your typing!

Tip

Stop from time to time when entering records and look at the main Customers screen to see the list of customers growing. If there are no records listed you must be forgetting to click on Save for each one. If just some records are missing you may be pressing Close when you enter the last record in a batch - you must press Save after each record and only press Close when you have an empty record window.

Updating records

Next time you select Customers the first screen will show a list of existing records. Select the one you want to change by highlighting it and then click on Record. The selected customer record will be displayed for alterations. To work on a number of records, first press Customers and select them from the list of customers by highlighting all of your choices. Then press Record and after amending the first customer details, select Next to move to the second, third and so on. Remember to press Save after amending the final record in the batch to keep all of the changes (or Abandon to leave them as they were). The Next and Prev (for previous) buttons for moving backwards and forwards through the customers you selected for editing are at the bottom of the screen with the other commands. If they have disappeared from view try maximising the display or resizing the window.

Tip

The reference code can't be altered so think carefully about your method of allocating codes before starting. To change codes you would have to create a completely new record with a different code, re-enter all the details and then cancel the transactions stored under the old record - a sure recipe for confusion.

Records can only be deleted if they have a balance of zero and no outstanding transactions. Choose Customers, then highlight the record to be deleted and choose Record. Click on the Delete button and you will be prompted to confirm whether or not the record should be erased - choose Yes (No to leave the record as it is). If the Delete button is greyed out and won't function this means you have some outstanding transactions for the customer so the record can't be erased. Once you have finished working on your customer records close this option by double-clicking on the control-menu box in the corner. Alternatively, select Window from the menu bar and Close All from the pull-down menu.

Supplier records

Enter details on suppliers using exactly the same techniques you have learnt for creating a database of customers. The supplier record screen is just the same - the information provides a mirror image of the customer data. Here you are the customer, so you will be using the details on credit terms and the memo facility to keep a record of how you can delay payment while still getting the best out of possible discounts from the supplier.

Tip

You can record all suppliers here, although a traditional purchase ledger only includes details on suppliers whose goods you buy for resale to your customers or when goods or services are bought on credit. The Sterling +2 nominal ledger can also take supplier information from these records for other goods you need to purchase and pay for staightaway (including consumables such as stationery) and use it to process transactions.

Product records

The database of products is built up in a similar way to those for suppliers and customers.

Select Products from the main menu, then Record. Think carefully about the type of code you want to give each product as this will be used for sorting. The code can be alphabetic as well as numeric so it might be best to choose the first few letters of the product name, or its initials, followed by a number. For example a fashion company could give Wellington boots the code WB102, fill in Wellington boots in the Description field and footwear in the Category field. The company should have set footwear plus a code number when Product Categories were specified during configuration. It's possible to click on the arrow at the end of the Category field to see a selection of product groups.

The product Description field accepts up to 30 characters, but it will be possible later to add extra details on order, invoice and credit note records. The VAT code must be filled in. It appears initially with the standard percentage rate unless you entered a common code for most of your products on the Product Defaults screen. If you need to change the default VAT setting to a different code for this product press the arrow at the end of the VAT field to see the full selection. Choose T0 for zero rate, T1 for standard rate and so on (refer to the table in Chapter 3). If you haven't already set defaults it is possible to press Defaults on the menu bar and Product Defaults to set them as you are working - perhaps they now make more sense. Unless you change the settings, the Sage default is number 1 for each type of code, then you can click on the down arrow at the end of the field to see a complete list of choices.

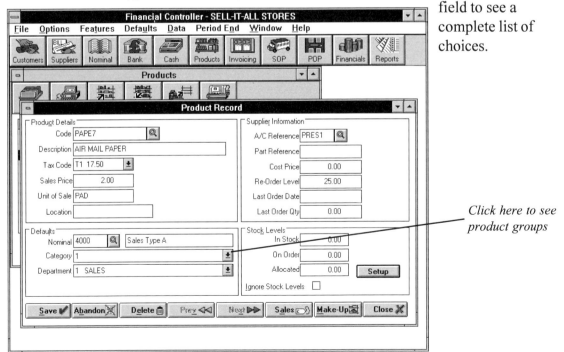

Click here to see product groups

The product record screen also has fields for the net sales price, the unit of sale (e.g. 6-pack, carton or each), and the location where the product is stored (warehouse, bin number etc.). The stock levels will only come into action and give meaningful figures when you enter opening figures together with opening balances for the ledgers a little later on. The fields in the Stock Levels box will then be updated automatically as the products are included in daily transactions throughout the software. This box gives useful information on how many products are in stock, how many are expected to arrive from suppliers due to outstanding orders and how many have already been allocated to customers.

The box on the top right of the Product Record display gives information on suppliers. This has already been set up in the supplier record database. The A/C Reference code field for suppliers has a magnifying-glass icon, so click on it to search through the complete list. The next field lets you enter a Part Reference - this is useful if the supplier uses a different code to the one set up by your company. The Cost Price field is updated during product and order processing, so this field can't be amended from here. Set a Re-Order Level giving the minimum quantity that should be left in stock before new products are ordered. Once this level is reached there will be a reminder on the re-order report. Once products are on order the Last Order Date field will present updated information, as will the Last Order Quantity field.

From the Product Record screen click on the Sales button to see the complete sales history for each product. This gives month-by-month figures for the year and at the bottom of the screen is the date of the last sale. The figures are by quantity and by sales value, each with three columns to compare actuals, budgets and previous year's results. The actual sales figures by quantity and value can then be compared to budgets the company is setting and constantly amending. To start off you will need to enter the previous year's figures, but in future this will be done automatically when year-end procedures are run. This information is particularly important in deciding which product lines are profitable and should therefore be continued and which should be discontinued. Click on the Graph button to see the data presented as a column or line graph. This is a handy option for reports and presentations.

Some companies stock a number of separate products which can also be grouped together and sold as a complete set - a typical example would be a toolset which comprises different items that customers may also want to buy separately. Sterling +2 provides a method of grouping these individual items together, to help keep track of the required stock levels for both types of sale. First you have to make sure all the separate products in the set have been recorded in the product database. Next give the set a name and code on the Product Record screen - in our example this would be a toolset. Then select the Make-Up button to fill in all the component products which together form a complete set - this would be the different types of screwdrivers, spanners etc. Give the code number under Stock Code, and the name of the set under Description, then fill in the names of the separate products which make up the set under Description and put their code numbers in the fields headed Code. The Code fields have the handy magnifying-glass icon to help you search for details on all available products. Put the quantity of each product required to make up the set in the fields headed Qty.

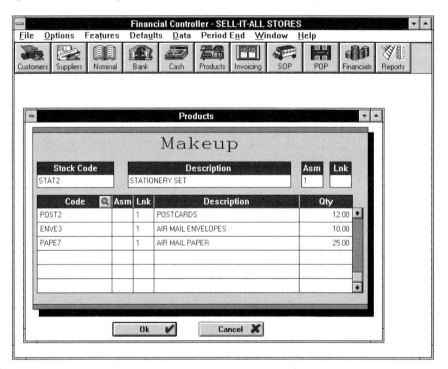

There are two more fields to fill in labelled ASM and LNK and these are slightly more complicated. If a number of tools which comprise a toolset are stored under the name Toolset you would need the number 1 in the ASM box. This shows that the set has only one level of assembly with the toolset at the top and the separate products underneath. However, if one of the products listed in the set also comprises a group of separate items there are then two levels of assembly (imagine a toolset which contains within it a separate set of screwdrivers). The toolset would then need a 2 in the ASM box to show that there are two levels of assembly (two separate sets of products) and it's at the top.

The LNK box is for sub-sets of products which form part of another complete set (e.g. a toolset which is sold in different do-it-yourself kits). If they are only used in one set of products the number entered should be 1. If they are used in a variety of product sets this number should increase accordingly. A toolset sold in three different do-it-yourself kits would have the number 3 in the LNK box.

Nominal account records

Sage has put together a complete chart of accounts and it's best not to alter this without professional advice, unless you have the necessary accounting skills. You may just want to change the names of some of the account descriptions so that they are more suitable for your company. For example Sage simply gives general names such as Sales Type A and Sales Type B for the sales accounts and you could make these more specific. Take a look at the complete list to see where the names could be altered to suit your company's working methods. To see the Sage chart just choose Nominal from the Toolbar and use the scroll arrows to the right of the window to scroll through the whole list. Resize the window to lengthen it and see more of the list at any one time by clicking the arrow on the bottom boundary and dragging it further down the Desktop. To print out the chart of accounts, select Nominal, then Report, highlight Nominal List, click on the Printer option button and press Run.

Change the sales type to suit your business

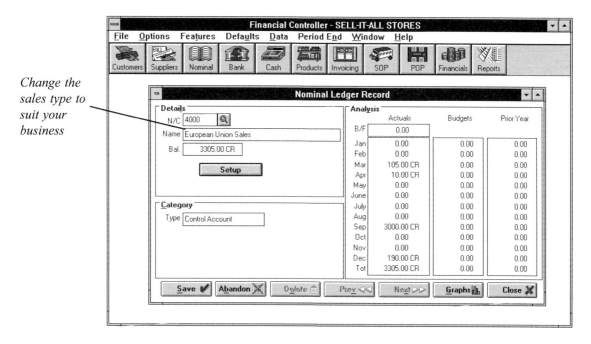

If you want to keep the Sage default chart of accounts and just add some of your own, then try to fit in with the way these accounts have been set up. Although the codes can have up to six digits you should only use four to match the existing records. Accounts have been put in groups with the same number sequence so that similar types will be presented together on the trial balance. The profit and loss and balance sheet reports allocate nominal ledger accounts to various categories. These are: sales, purchases, direct expenses and overheads (profit and loss reports); and assets, liabilities and financed by (balance sheet reports). When you add an account give it a code which will put it into the right category grouping - for example, look at the current settings and put any new sales accounts into the range 4000 to 4199. These codes have already been allocated by Sage to sales accounts. There are plenty of free numbers for your own additions.

Warning

Be careful not to use a number already allocated by Sage - this sounds obvious but is surprisingly easy to do!

What's the difference between profit and loss and balance sheet accounts, and which number should I allocate to a new account?

Look at the printout of the Sage default chart of accounts to see how all the accounts are separated into either profit and loss or balance sheet. Within these groupings they are then put into more specific categories. The balance sheet uses the numbers 0010-3299, and the profit and loss accounts run from 4000-8299. There is also a mispostings account (9999) and a suspense account (9998). The suspense account takes all figures which can't be accounted for in any other way, so keep an eye on this one to make sure you're posting the figures correctly. If you're completing transactions in the right way the suspense account should have a balance of zero. The mispostings account comes into use when you need to adjust the figures to alter posted transactions - for example when making refunds to customers (see Chapter 6 where this is covered in more detail).

Within the profit and loss set of accounts there are the following groups: Sales (4000-4999), Purchases (5000-5299), Direct Expenses (6000-6999) and Overheads (7000-8299). The numbers from 8000 to 9999 are miscellaneous expenses. If you need to create a new account in the profit and loss category and it doesn't fit in anywhere else you probably need to allocate a number in this section.

The balance sheet set of accounts consists of these groupings: Fixed Assets (0010-0059), Current Assets (1000-1209), Current Liabilities (2200-2209), and Financed By (3000-

3299). Even if you don't want to change the chart of accounts print it out and look at it to get an idea of how it has been put together. As you become more familiar with the system you will find it easier to set up nominal records and understand how they work. In later chapters you will have to create some nominal records, but will be given exact instructions on how to do this.

Tip

Print out the chart of accounts and mark the names of the different categories by the number ranges given above. Then read the Business Guide at the end of the chapter for more details on how the profit and loss and balance sheet sections are used in practice.

If you are already confident and want to amend the nominal account records, select Nominal from the Toolbar and click on Record. Choose an account code, then put the name in the Name field if you're creating a new account. Alternatively, use existing codes to make Sage's account descriptions more meaningful for your company. For example change the record name Sales Type A so that it refers to one of your sales categories. The Bal field is automatically updated by the software with the current balance. The Setup button can be left alone for the moment: it will be used later to enter opening balances. The Category Type field can't be altered as it is set automatically to show the nature of the account in one of three ways. The three options are: a bank account set up using Bank on the Toolbar; a control account specified on the Control Accounts screen; or a nominal account which covers all other types.

Tip

Ask your accountant to help you work on the nominal ledger accounts if you are in any doubt.

The month by month breakdown of figures gives Actuals, Budgets and Prior Year. The Actuals totals will be calculated automatically. For the Budgets column either enter an annual amount in the Totals field and this will be divided by 12, or set your own figures for each month. Even if you start with a total amount you can alter the figures in separate month fields. The figure for the Prior Year will be changed automatically in future when you run the year-end procedures, but is derived for the first year. To start off you will need to enter an amount for the previous year.

Bank and cash account records

Look through the nominal accounts by choosing Nominal from the Toolbar, then scrolling through the list. You will find a selection of bank accounts already set up. The bank current account code has been specified as the default by Sage for banking transactions (this is number 1200 and is grouped with the other types of bank account). You can add extra bank accounts as Sterling +2 allows more bank account records than you are ever likely to need. Only one cash account is allowed and Sage has set up a petty cash account in the nominal ledger. If you're designing a completely new chart of accounts remember to amend the cash account code using the Control Accounts option (choose Defaults from the menu bar then Control Accounts) and also by amending the nominal accounts record (choose Nominal, then Record). Cash transactions can only be posted if you have recorded the code in the nominal ledger and on the Control Accounts screen.

 If most of your transactions use the same bank account set it up as the default to save time. The default bank account set by Sage can be viewed by selecting Bank then Records. Fill in this screen with the details of your main bank account. If you want to change to a different default bank account in future do so by selecting Defaults from the menu bar, then Control Accounts. On the Control Accounts display change the nominal ledger code number to that of your chosen default bank account making sure that you have also specified it as a nominal ledger record.

To enter more bank account records select Bank from the Toolbar, then Records. The first record will be the default current account already set up by Sage with the correct code. To enter details on your deposit account and building society account, highlight them on the Bank window and press Records. Fill in the name and address of the bank and the type of account will be filled in automatically according to the nominal code. The Account Name field is for the bank account name, for example, your company name. Fill in the bank sort code and your account number which is printed on statements and cheque books. The Balance field can't be altered as it is updated automatically once you have taken the next step and entered the opening balances. Always finish by clicking on Save to make sure your records are stored and not erased. Only click on Close when you have saved all the records and want to go back to the main screen. To enter extra types of bank account, make sure none of the existing ones are highlighted on the main Bank display. Click on Records to see a blank Records screen. Choose a code which fits in with other bank accounts (four digits, starting with 12). Put the type of account, such as

VISA, in the Desc field. Finish by entering the account details as on the current account record.

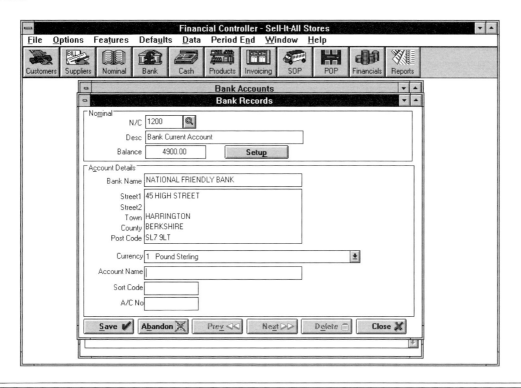

It also makes sense to print out all the records entered so far, both for reference and as an extra backup. Start with the customer records by selecting Customers from the Toolbar. Click on the Clear button to make sure none are highlighted and all will be included. Then choose Report and highlight the type of report you want from the box headed Files, press the Printer option button and click on Run to print it out. At this point print out a list of customers, suppliers, nominal accounts and products, plus any of the other reports you would like to keep on file.

Tip

Check the printout to see everything you input is included. If just some of the records are missing you're probably forgetting to click on Save for the last record in each batch.

Opening balances

Now that all the records have been entered it's time to set the opening balances and then Sterling +2 will be ready for your daily transactions. Unless you are just starting out in business there will be active balances on different accounts. The current status of products will also have to be recorded. Opening balances can be entered as a lump sum or as individual outstanding transactions and Sage allows you to use special setup procedures or you can post the transactions in the standard way.

Those using the VAT cash accounting scheme can't run the Setup options. They will have to enter opening balances by posting each transaction with the correct VAT rate code. To do this, select Customers and then click on Invoice or Credit Note to fill in the details on individual transactions (see Chapter 5). The Invoice and Credit Note displays appear just like the standard forms to fill in. This method has to be used in the VAT cash accounting scheme as only when payment has been made will the amount be calculated for VAT purposes.

For those using standard VAT accounting there are other considerations to ponder before entering the opening balances. How does your company want to allocate payments and receipts (allocating payment and receipts means matching them to the relevant invoice or credit note)? If you want to be able to match up invoices and credit notes with receipts and payments it's best to enter individual transactions. If you enter a lump sum receipts and payments will have to be part allocated at some stage. This is so that Sterling +2 can match them to invoices and credit notes at month or year end. The software can't clear debit and credit items until they are allocated.

How do you want to see the transactions aged on reports and statements? If you would like to see each transaction aged separately it's best to enter transactions individually so that the exact date can be filled in. Entering opening balances by filling in data on each transaction may be more time consuming than giving a lump sum, but in the end this method provides more useful information.

Tip

Entering opening balances as individual transactions takes longer, but provides greater benefit. This is true for those using cash accounting or standard VAT accounting.

Do you need to analyse the opening balance for VAT purposes? If you use the Setup button on the customers, suppliers and nominal record screens the opening balances can be set swiftly and without complications. However, this will not allow any analysis of VAT on opening balances and the balances can't be linked to separate nominal accounts. The Setup option means that entries will be given T9 as a VAT code and on the audit trail the figures will be marked with the words Opening Balance to separate them from other transactions.

Sales and purchase ledgers

To enter opening balances, select Customers or Suppliers from the Toolbar, highlight the customer or suppliers in the list, press Record, then click on the Setup button. The screen displays a window headed Opening Balance Setup. Under Ref type the reference number for the invoice or credit balance and this will be used in the nominal ledger audit trail. Under Date you can put the present date or the date of the transaction for more accurate ageing. Under Invoice or Credit you can either enter the amount of each separate invoice

Opening Balance Setup

Ref	Date	Invoice	Credit
102	01/03/94	200.00	0.00
99	02/01/94	0.00	100.00

Save ✔   Cancel ✗

or credit note, or if you are entering a lump sum just fill in the total figure. When you are happy with the information entered click on the Save button. Otherwise click on Cancel if you need to rethink the method you want to use for entering opening balances. It's a good idea to print out reports on the balances and account histories at this point, to double-check that the information has been input correctly. Select Customers or Suppliers, then Report and highlight Balances in the list of reports. Click on the Printer option button and press Run.

Nominal ledger, bank and cash accounts

Before setting the opening balance for the nominal ledger it's important to make sure all accounts are set to zero. This will not automatically be the case as you have been entering opening balances for customers and suppliers. These will have been transferred to the nominal ledger's control and suspense accounts. Those using VAT cash accounting will have recorded transactions by invoice and credit note which will have sent a balance to the nominal ledger VAT control account. All of these must be set to zero, otherwise when you start setting the nominal ledger opening balance these figures will be duplicated.

To set the amounts to zero you need to print out a trial balance in order to see the exact figures. Select Financials from the Toolbar, then Trial. Click on Print, press the Printer option button and finish with OK. The printout gives the account number, name and figures under the headings Debit and Credit. There should be figures for the accounts 1100 Debtors Control, 2100 Creditors Control, 9998 Suspense Account, and possibly 2202 VAT Liability. The trial balance will show which of your accounts have a figure, so set all accounts listed to zero. In order to cancel these figures you will have to make reverse double entry postings. That means that if an account is in credit by £1,000 you will have to make a journal entry giving a debit balance of £1,000.

How do I make reverse double entry postings?

Select Nominal from the Toolbar then Journals from the Nominal display to see a box headed Journal Entry. Start with the debtors control account by filling in 1100 under the heading N/C and Debtors Control will appear under Name. Type Reversing Journal under Description and T9 under T/c. The exact amount which appears under debit on the printout should be added to the credit field so that it will be cancelled out. Do the same for the Creditors Control account. Here the existing credit balance on the printout should be typed into the debit field to be cleared. The T/c field is the tax code and this is always

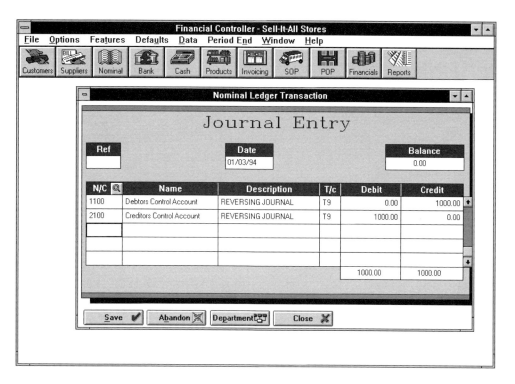

T9 for opening balances. When you have finished, try printing out another trial balance from the nominal ledger. There should be no amounts for any of the accounts - they should all be at zero. If there are any figures you must have forgotten some reverse journal, so make a journal entry to clear them.

Tip

Remember to print out the trial balance or view it, by selecting Financials from the Toolbar and then Trial. Don't select Nominal and print out the balances as this will list all accounts whether or not they are set to zero.

Once this is done you can enter the opening trial balance. It's best to ask your accountant to provide this information (see the Business Guide at the end of the chapter if you want to do this yourself). Select Nominal from the Toolbar, then Record. Fill in the reference code for each nominal account you want to enter an opening balance for then press the Setup button. On the next screen enter the balance whether credit or debit. Once you are happy with the information click on the Save button and the figure will be posted. Enter the opening balances for bank accounts in a similar way: choose Bank, highlight each record then press Records and finish with the Setup button. Instead of debits and credits you will fill in the opening balances as payments and receipts. Alternatively, you can enter the opening balances for bank accounts along with other Nominal accounts. Press nominal, then Record, enter the nominal code for the bank account and press Setup.

By this stage all of the opening balances should have been entered correctly. If you print a trial balance the suspense account should have a balance of zero as all the debits and credits should be equal. Look at the suspense account to check if this is true, because any amount showing in the suspense account balance means you have forgotten to include some of your opening figures.

Products

After sorting out the nominal ledger the opening balances on products for stock control purposes should seem easy! This procedure is slightly different as it's important to start by using the Setup option because it won't function once you start to use other features. Select Products, then Record, enter the product code then click on the Setup button. Sage has set the default to O/BAL as a reference for the opening balance and the current date should be displayed. Fill in the quantity in stock for each product and the cost price (the price you paid the supplier, not the price you will sell the goods for) then click on Save. To make sure the true value of stock is recorded it's important to do a thorough stock take and give reduced prices for items that are damaged and will have to be sold cheaply. It's important to get the value right for your opening stock as this will later be used together with other figures to work out accurately the profit made from sales for the year. The value for your opening stock also has to be recorded in the nominal ledger as this is not updated automatically from the product files. Enter your stock value as the opening balance for the nominal account 5200 (Opening Stock).

With all the opening balances entered, Sterling +2 can now help you keep updated information on your business. You are ready to start doing your daily work with the software set up to cope with your company's specific requirements.

Selecting records

Now that you have a complete database, Sterling +2 will display a list of current records each time you choose Customers, Suppliers, Products or Nominal from the Toolbar. Look at your list of customers to try out different methods of choosing records. Click on Customers, then scroll through the list and click on the desired customer to highlight the line. If you now click on Invoice, the software will present an invoice with this customer's details filled in. Close the invoice and return to the main Customers screen and list. Select a number of customers by highlighting two or three. When you move on to work on these records you will be able to choose the Next button to go through them in order, or the Prev (previous) button to return to a record you have already worked on. A variety of records would typically be selected if you wanted to produce a report, or if you were writing a number of invoices or amending the customer information.

If you highlight records by mistake click on them a second time to remove them from your selection. If you want to cancel all of your choices click on the Clear button at the bottom of the screen. Sometimes you will want to select the majority of records. In this case you can highlight the few that you don't want, then press the Swap button at the bottom of the screen to reverse your choice.

The magnifying-glass icon at the end of a field means the software can help you to choose records. For example, if you select Invoice without specifying the customer you will be able to click on the magnifying-glass icon in the account number field and the software will display all the choices. If you know the start letters or numbers for the code type these in first, then click on the magnifying-glass icon and the software will start the list at the right place.

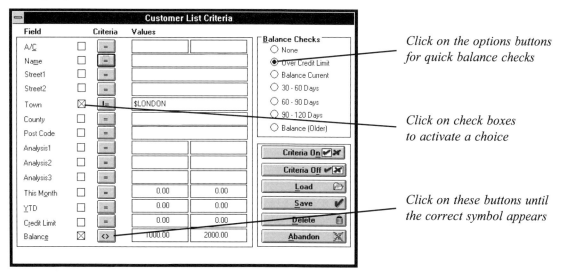

Click on the options buttons for quick balance checks

Click on check boxes to activate a choice

Click on these buttons until the correct symbol appears

For reports it's often necessary to select all records with common features - for example all accounts with a balance of a certain figure. You can also do this to limit the display to a smaller list of accounts you are interested in. This will make it easier for you to find the ones you're looking for. To do this you need to click on the Criteria button on the bottom of the screen. Depending on the function you are using the Criteria button will call up a display with relevant variables and you will be able to fill in the specifications for choosing records. For example, select Customers then click on Criteria to see the various selection methods. On the Criteria screen you could fill in any of the fields, perhaps clicking on the Over Credit Limit check box to display all customers who need to be reminded to pay before receiving any more goods.

Perhaps you want to be more specific, giving the customer name, address or town ranges. Click in as many check boxes as you want to tailor your choice of customer. Then, in the boxes headed Criteria you can use mathematical symbols to show how you want the calculations performed. For example, by Balance you could specify all customers with a balance greater than 100. The symbols are:

> greater than   < less than

= equal to   != not equal to.

<> within a set range of values (i.e. greater than one and less than another)

The Criteria fields are just for the mathematical symbol and work together with the Values fields. The boxes headed Criteria are actually buttons with the = sign set as default. Just click on them until the symbol you require appears.

In the fields headed Values you put the figures or letters to finish the calculation for sorting. For example, if you have activated the check box for Post Code, put an = sign under Criteria and fill in the letters WC1 under Values to find all records with that post code. Use the asterisk as a wild card, e.g. WC* to have all postcodes beginning with the specified letters but ending with any other character. If you have clicked on Balance put > under Criteria and 100 under Values to find all customers with a balance greater than £100. Specify customers with balance between £200 and £300 by using the symbol <> followed by 200 and 300 in the Values boxes.

The $ can be used to find all records with a string of characters anywhere in the field. To do this put = under Criteria for the relevant field followed by $XYZ to choose all records with the specified characters. Mark out records you don't want by specifying a string of characters that show the record is not required: put != under Criteria followed by $XYZ.

If you change your mind about the criteria, just click on Abandon. You can also use this to remove criteria once you have no more use for the selection specifications. The criteria you set may be useful for standard reports, in which case you can save it for future use, by pressing Save and filling in a file name when the dialog box appears. To use it again click on Criteria, then click on Load to see a choice of files, highlight the file you want and press OK. Finish by clicking on Criteria On to see the list of selected records displayed. When you have no further use for criteria files stored in this way, click on Delete then highlight the unwanted file from the Delete Criteria box and press OK.

Tip

When you want to see a full list of records and not the ones selected using Criteria, just click on the Criteria Off button. Press Criteria On to limit the selection again.

Try using each of the Criteria options to sort your records as it's worth getting plenty of practice on this feature. You can use the Criteria facility to set up quite complex analyses of your data and it's surprisingly simple to use. Later you will learn how to use the report generator to produce more sophisticated analyses (see Chapter 10), but in the mean time the Criteria method is particularly useful. The variety of ways in which Sterling +2 can manipulate your records for reports and enquiries is impressive - make the most of it. Remember to press Criteria Off when you don't need to limit the selection on your main display. Otherwise, you may continue to work with Customers/Suppliers and other records removed from view.

BUSINESS*guide*

The opening entries for your business are particularly important. It's vital to get the balances right whether you are just starting up or if you have already been running a different accounting system. Even if your business is new, you will have invested some money in the bank account and also purchased goods such as stationery and larger items such as computer equipment. The money spent on these goods can be included in your expenditure and will entitle you to tax allowances. It's important to keep all the receipts for purchases made, starting in the months before you actually begin to trade. To keep all the receipts in order simply number them so that you can use this code as a reference on the Cash or Bank payments options.

If you are just starting out in business the opening entries are to record all of your assets and liabilities - these figures must balance. For example, a simple business run by a sole trader to offer desktop publishing may only need a computer system for £3,000, stationery for £500 and a car for £4,000. On the liabilities side of the balance sheet would be any bank loans and money invested in the business by the owner. If the owner asked for a bank loan of £5,000 to start the business he must also record his own invested capital, which should amount to £2,500, in order to balance the assets and liabilities. When you look at the balance sheet you will see all the assets and liabilities clearly listed (check the Balance Sheet available from Financials on the Toolbar).

If you are moving to Sterling +2 from a manual system or another type of software, you will have a greater number of assets and liabilities to record. Assets fall into two categories: fixed assets which last for years and current assets which include short term items and also investments. Fixed assets include property which may appreciate in value and other items which depreciate (this is recorded in the nominal ledger as described in Chapter 9). The fixed assets which depreciate might only be sold, once they are of no further use or finally scrapped. Typical fixed assets which will need to be recorded include property, office equipment, vehicles and any other types of machinery. Current assets will include any stock you have as well as debtors and money in the bank/investments.

Liabilities also fall into different categories, namely current liabilities and long-term liabilities. A long-term liability is one which will take more than a year to pay back and would include bank loans and mortgages. Current liabilities are those which will be paid back in less than a year, for example to trade creditors. Bank overdrafts, PAYE, VAT and similar items (NI, SSP and SMP) are also current liabilities.

If you are entering your own opening balances without the help of an accountant you can take the figures from your last trial balance in your previous manual or computer system (the trial balance includes all your recorded transactions for the year to date). The long-term liabilities will go into the nominal ledger in the section of the chart of accounts called Financed By (code numbers 3000-3200). As well as long-term bank loans and shares sold to investors this is also where you should record any accumulated profits (under the heading Retained Profit and Loss).

Directors of limited companies will have taken out salaries if the company has been trading for more than a year. Sole traders and partners will have taken out drawings (the correct name for the wages they allow themselves). This will be an amount they calculate to be less than the annual profit. For limited companies the amount of profit remaining after salaries, corporation tax and dividends have been paid is carried forward to the next financial year. For sole traders and partnerships the same is true for the amount remaining after drawings and tax have been paid. The remaining profit is automatically recorded in the Retained Profit and Loss Account. This is your retained profit for the year and will be carried forward into the next year's capital.

Current liabilities will be recorded in the purchase ledger using the opening balance technique described earlier in the chapter. Any short term loans are also classed as current liabilities and would be recorded by the code 2300 in the current liabilities section of the chart of accounts (numbers 2100-2330). Money in the bank account will be recorded as a bank receipt - use this to enter the amount received as a loan and also the amount put into the business by the directors or owners (see the Question and Answer section later for more detail).

The current assets section of Sage's chart of accounts runs from 1001-1230. These include stock (1001) for which you have already entered an opening balance. Look through the list by pressing Nominal and scrolling through this section of the chart to see the other current assets such as money in the bank, petty cash and debtors.

The opening balances for fixed assets will have to be recorded in the nominal ledger. These include property, vehicles and equipment. The codes run from 0010 to 0051 so find the correct accounts to enter opening balances on each of your fixed assets. Depreciation also plays a part in the valuation of each fixed asset, so set a fair value on these items allowing for age, wear and tear. In Chapter 9 you will set the rate for future depreciation, so forget about this for the time being.

These four categories - Financed By, Current Liabilities, Fixed Assets, and Current Assets - make up the balance sheet section of Sage's default chart of accounts. It's important that if you add any account codes they should be in the correct section numerically so that the balance sheet reports will be able to extract and use the data accurately.

Money spent on fixed assets is called capital expenditure. Correct valuation and depreciation settings will help you to prepare capital allowances for tax purposes - it's best to take advice from your accountant. There is another type of expenditure which is more short term and this is called revenue expenditure. Revenue expenditure is added up and the total is subtracted from your profit before tax is calculated. Revenue expenditure includes money spent on stock, stamps and stationery. This type of expenditure is recorded in the profit and loss section of the chart of accounts. At the end of the year, the total revenue expenditure will be added up to show the expenses recorded in this section of the accounts.

The profit and loss section of the chart of accounts has four categories. Sales run from 4000 to 4999, while Purchases run from 5000 to 5299. The other two categories are Direct Expenses (6000-6999) and Overheads (7000-8299). It's worth looking at the full list by choosing Nominal on the Toolbar and scrolling through. The direct expenses in manufacturing and selling goods include wages to factory staff, sales commission and publicity. Overheads include all other salaries, electricity bills and stationery. To get a true idea of your actual profit, the profit and loss section of the accounts will deduct the Purchases, Direct Expenses and Overheads from the total Sales. Payments for Overheads and Direct Expenses will be recorded as bank payments when setting up opening balances.

It's vital to get the opening balances right, as incorrect working methods will only mean that your accountant will have to re-enter all the figures at year end. If in any doubt about this task get professional advice at the beginning to start you off in the right way.

Q&A

I've just started out in business with a bank loan of £10,000 and £5,000 of my own money. How do I record this invested capital in the opening balances?

You will need to start by recording these two figures in the Financed By section of the chart of accounts. Although they could fit into the general category of Reserves it will make more sense if you create two new nominal accounts. Choose Nominal then Record, give a number of 3120 to fit into the Financed By section and the name could be Directors Capital or Owners Capital depending on your status. Create a second account with the number 3130 and give it the name Bank Loans. There is no need to enter opening balances for these accounts as the software will update these records automatically when you record them as bank receipts. Finish by pressing Bank, choosing the bank account where you have placed the money, then click on Receipt. Fill in the nominal codes 3120 and 3130 and the amount of money received both from the bank loan and your own investment, a tax code of T9 and press Save. If your business is a partnership the only difference is that you must create separate Directors/Owners Capital accounts for each partner to record the amounts invested by each partner. It's also important to decide early on how you and your partners are going to divide the net profits at year end and have the percentages put in writing by a solicitor.

CHAPTER 5

Basic Ledger Work and Communications

On Sterling +2, sales and purchase ledger transactions are dealt with by selecting Customers or Suppliers from the Toolbar. As the screens have been designed to look like standard forms to be filled in, the software is quite straightforward to use. Most transactions are posted as invoices or credit notes - this is done by selecting Customers or Suppliers then clicking on the Invoice or Credit Note button.

If you are posting invoices and credit notes this way it will also be necessary to print out the documents and to update the product files as this is not done automatically. The information is posted only to the sales, purchase and nominal ledgers. This is the only option if you have Bookkeeper or Accountant. There is a second way to produce invoices if you have Accountant Plus or Financial Controller. Select Invoicing from the main menu - this option links to the product files for a more integrated approach. It's important not to produce invoices through the Customers Invoice option and also via the Invoicing option as the information will be duplicated. If you have Financial Controller the best method is to start by choosing SOP (sales order processing) from the main menu and to generate an invoice for further processing using the Invoicing option. The sales order processing technique is the most integrated as it lets you update the stock files, create an invoice and post the transaction to the nominal ledger.

Tip

Find out about Invoicing in Chapter 8. If you are using Financial Controller you can enter details on changes to stock levels and create invoices at the same time when working on sales and purchase order processing (see Chapter 7).

Customer and supplier invoices

To enter an invoice, choose Customers or Suppliers from the Toolbar then highlight the desired customer or supplier from the list on the opening screen and click on Invoice. Alternatively select Customers/Suppliers and click on Invoice then click on the magnifying-glass icon in the A/C field to see and select the correct account. The Customer Invoice screen has a familiar look, even to those using a computer for the first time.

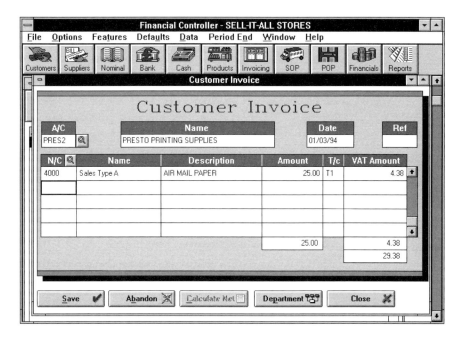

The software will automatically enter the customer/supplier's name in the next box. If this is a new account, click on the magnifying-glass icon in the A/C box then click on New in the Customer/Supplier Accounts window to fill in a complete record. The software will not allow you to progress with the invoice unless you fill in a record, if the account code is not already on file. If you know the start of the account reference put the initial letter or first number in the A/C field then click on the magnifying-glass icon to start the search in the right place alphabetically or numerically.

Sage displays today's date as default, but change this to the tax point date of the transaction, if necessary. Under N/C put the nominal ledger reference to show which nominal account will be used to analyse this transaction, and again the magnifying-glass icon can be used to display all available codes with descriptions. The Sage default nominal accounts for sales are Sales Type A, Sales Type B and Sales Type C. Perhaps by now you have changed these descriptions to make more sense for your specific business dealings.

Tip

If you use SOP or Invoicing on the Toolbar, the software will be able to provide more details on the products automatically (Accountant Plus and Financial Controller versions only). This includes the stock code and default nominal code you entered in the product record. For more details see Chapters 7 and 8 - don't enter your invoices using the Customers facilities which are for users with Bookkeeper or Accountant.

The Description field on customer/supplier invoices allows up to 30 characters although you can only see 19 at a time - read the whole field by using the directional arrow keys. This field lets you specify what the invoices is for by describing the product being sold or purchased. In the Amount field you should put the net amount of the invoice if you want the system to analyse VAT liability. It is possible to enter the gross amount but you must then finish by clicking on the Calculate Net button at the bottom of the screen, to let the system calculate the VAT and change the Amount field accordingly.

When you filled in the supplier and customer records, each was given a default department, but if you want to allocate the invoice to a different one click on the Department button to get the full list. When the Department box appears click on the down arrow at the end of the field, highlight the desired department from the pull-down list and finish by pressing OK.

To edit and amend the details on the invoice use the standard Windows or Sage techniques. Moving from field to field is done by pressing TAB or by pointing and clicking on the required field with the mouse. The handy F6 key now comes into use - press it when the cursor is in a field you want to delete and all the information in the field will be removed.

Once you are happy with the data, click on Save to post all the details to the relevant ledgers. Although the Invoice screen only has a few lines you can keep entering transactions and the display will scroll down until you have finished. The Abandon button will cancel all the transactions without posting any data to the ledgers. Once you have finished entering invoice details you can click on Save and then Close. Alternatively, press Save then close this function using the standard Windows methods.

Tip

Closing windows can be done quickly by double-clicking on the Control-menu box in the top left-hand corner. Alternatively choose Window from the menu bar and Close All from the pull-down menu to clear the Desktop completely. Always choose Save first.

Warning

Don't choose File from the menu bar and Exit from the pull-down menu simply to close the invoice display - this will close Sterling +2 completely. Be careful to double-click on the Control-menu box in the correct window, as double clicking on the Control-menu box above the Toolbar will also close down the whole Sterling +2 system.

What is the difference between entering net and gross amounts, and how do I enter these figures?

Put the correct rate of VAT in the T/c field first. Then, if you want to enter the net amount, enter this in the Amount field. If the T/c field specifies the standard rate of VAT with the code T1, then the system will calculate the figure for the VAT Amount field automatically, by adding VAT calculated at the standard rate to the figure in the Amount field. Alternatively you can enter the gross amount and Sterling +2 will calculate the net amount. Fill in the VAT code under T/c then enter the gross amount in the Amount field. Keep the cursor in the Amount field and click on the Calculate Net button so that the system can subtract the VAT amount from the figure you have entered. The VAT Amount field will be calculated and displayed automatically. Some transactions may only consist of VAT, in which case don't fill in any figure in the Amount field, but fill the figure directly into the VAT Amount field.

Credit notes

Credit notes are issued in the Customers option when customers return goods to you or need to be credited with money for other reasons. The credit notes in the Suppliers option are for goods you have purchased and returned to the supplier. Customer and supplier credit notes are entered by selecting Customers/Suppliers from the Toolbar then Credit Note. The screen display is identical to the invoice entry display as is the method for filling in each of the fields.

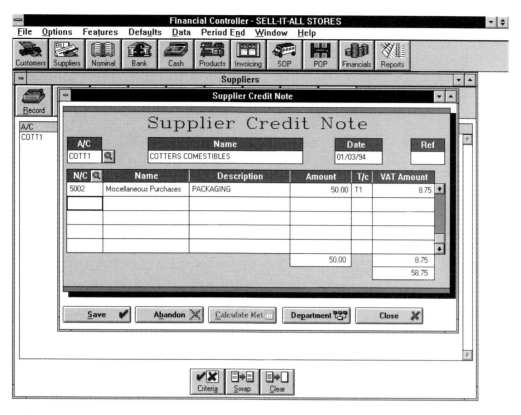

Checking your work

Once you have started posting transactions to the sales and purchase ledgers, it's worth checking to see that you are working correctly and the amounts are being processed by Sterling +2. From the main menu select Reports and then highlight Audit Trail to see a full list of all the transactions you have posted. Choose Display or Printer as the method of output by clicking on the correct option button and press Run. Are some of the transactions missing? First scroll down the list - not everything can be displayed on the screen at once. If this is not the reason that transactions are missing, you are probably forgetting to press the Save button before closing down the invoicing and credit note entry screens. Start again! If you choose to display the audit trail on the screen, it appears on a Windows display. You have to close it by double-clicking on the minus sign in the corner. If you choose Window from the Sterling+2 menu bar and Close All from the pull-down menu the audit trail won't be cleared away as it is not on the Sterling +2 Desktop. This happens with a variety of Windows applications which link into Sterling +2. They have to be closed down individually otherwise you will find a few of them are still on the screen as you exit from the system.

The audit trail report gives a full list of every single transaction you have posted using Sterling +2. You can also choose other fixed transaction reports to view specific types of postings you have made. Do this by pressing Reports then scrolling down through the list. All of the fixed transaction reports listed on this display take their information from the audit trail but contain more specific information. For the transactions you have been posting so far you will want to check the different customer and supplier reports listed (invoices and credit notes). There is also a useful EU sales list which includes all the postings relating to European Union customers. Find out more about the Reports options in Chapter 10.

Tip

Wide reports can be printed in landscape mode to fit onto standard printer stationery. Choose the Audit Trail report by highlighting it, press the Printer option button and then Run. Press Setup on the Print screen and then click on the Landscape option button in the box labelled Orientation on the Print Setup screen. Finish by pressing OK on each screen to return to the Report display and press Run.

Warning

How long is it since you backed up your records onto floppy disk and stored them in a safe place? Now that your supplier and customer invoices and credit notes are on file you risk losing valuable business information - especially if you are starting to rely totally on the computer. Keep copies of the disks away from the office or in a fire-proof safe in case of disaster.

You will not be automatically informed when entering transactions if a customer or supplier has passed the credit limit you set during configuration. Get in the habit of checking balances to see if individual accounts are marked out as owing too much money. Select Customers or Suppliers from the Toolbar, then Report and highlight Balances in the list. Choose Display or Printer as the method of output by pressing the appropriate option button before clicking on Run. Erring customers and suppliers will be singled out and given a tell-tale asterisk. You can see a full aged debt analysis for each account - scroll right to see the full report by pressing the scroll arrow at the bottom right of the window. Check regularly for asterisks between the Turnover and Credit Limit columns on the aged balances report to keep a careful watch on customers exceeding their limits.

Warning

Sterling +2 only automates the following procedures if you are using the standard VAT accounting method. Those using VAT cash accounting should refer to the Questions and Answers section in Chapter 6 which describes how to make the necessary adjustments manually using the payment and receipts facilities in the Bank option. It's vital not to use the wrong technique if you do use VAT cash accounting or your VAT liability will not be calculated correctly.

Q&A

What should I do when I need to make a refund to a customer, or when suppliers give me a refund?

Sterling +2 lets you make a complete refund for paid invoices via a simple menu option and will amend the figures in all ledgers accordingly. If you are only refunding part of the total figure on the invoice, the software can't handle this automatically. If you are

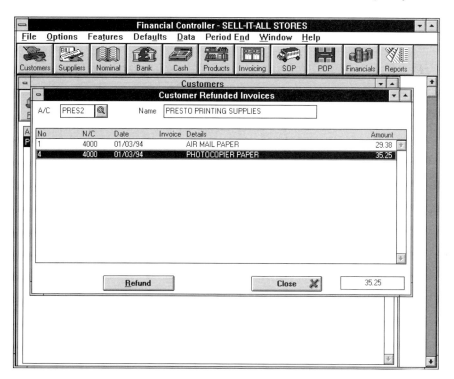

refunding part of the invoice, it's best to produce a credit note for the refunded amount. Once a refund has been made using the menu option, the Sage records treat the invoice as if it had never been sent.

Choose Customers or Suppliers from the Toolbar, then click on the relevant account in the displayed list to highlight it. Select Features from the menu bar, choose Customer or Supplier Features from the first pull-down menu then Invoice Refunds from the second pull-down menu. If you forgot to choose the supplier or customer, select them now by filling in the account code reference or click on the magnifying-glass icon for the list.

Once an account has been selected Sterling +2 automatically lists all paid-up transactions which could potentially be refunded. Click on the correct transaction to highlight it, then click on Refund and respond to the prompt confirming that this amount should be refunded. The figures will be posted to the appropriate ledgers.

What can I do when a cheque bounces?

The software can automatically adjust the figures in all the ledgers should a cheque be returned by the bank. Select Customers or Suppliers from the Toolbar and highlight the required account. Then choose Features from the menu bar, Customer or Supplier Features from the first pull-down menu then Cheque Returns from the second pull-down menu. The software automatically displays all transactions which have been paid by cheque, if there are any. If there is no information on this screen perhaps you forgot to select a customer/supplier. You can fill the code in now in the A/C field or click on the magnifying-glass icon for a list. Click on the relevant transaction to highlight it, then click on the Save button and respond to the prompt asking you to confirm this choice. The necessary postings will be made by the software.

How do I enter credit card payments?

See the Questions and Answer section in Chapter 6 as you will need to be able to use the Bank option on the Toolbar to record these transactions. You will also have to create bank account records to deal with credit card payments and receipts.

These days I find some of my customers and suppliers are going out of business. How do I write off the amount owed?

The best way to do this is to write off all the outstanding invoices in one fell swoop. Sterling +2 can do this quickly and adjust all the ledgers accordingly. Select Customers or Suppliers from the Toolbar and highlight the account. Click on Features on the menu bar, choose Customer/Supplier Features from the first pull-down menu, then Write Off Account on the second pull-down menu. You can also choose the account by filling in the account code or clicking on the magnifying-glass icon to select it. The display shows the customer account details with individual outstanding transactions and the total amount outstanding. Click on the Write Off button and confirm this choice to have the figures cleared from the system. This method can be used to write off all outstanding transactions for a customer or supplier when they go out of business, or if payment is definitely not going to be made for any other reason.

What should I do if I write off an account and then the customer pays some or all of the monies?

You should not allow this to happen. You mustn't write off a debt until you have exhausted every possible method of calling in the payment. See the Business Guide on credit control in Chapter 8 which shows each step, from tactful letters through to court action, which you need to use before writing off a bad debt. If you use the standard VAT accounting method you may have already paid VAT on the debt. You are entitled to claim back the VAT element of bad debts. Take all the necessary steps to make sure there is no chance of payment then act as quickly as possible. Refer to the Business Guide in Chapter 9 to find out how to claim a refund. Debts should not be written off in a casual way - usually your accountant asks at year end which ones should be written off and checks that there is no chance of payment. If you have mistakenly written off a debt and then get paid, some or all of it, you will have to produce another invoice. This will duplicate the VAT liability which will then automatically be added to the amount you have to pay on the VAT return. To find out how to cancel the VAT element of the bad debt see the Questions and Answers section in Chapter 9.

Warning

None of the bad debt write off features can adjust the VAT liability. Once an invoice has been raised on the system you will have to pay the VAT regardless of whether or not the debt is paid. It is your responsibility to reclaim VAT from HM Customs and Excise, so keep a manual record of bad debts and remember to ask for the VAT element to be returned to you. You are permitted by law to write off bad debts and the VAT liability six months after goods or services have been provided if you don't want to wait until year end for professional advice. Find out how to keep a record of the VAT liability you have incurred through bad debts and what to do about it in Chapter 9.

I don't want to write off the whole amount a customer owes me, but there are some small amounts that just aren't worth collecting. Can I clear these petty figures, often just pence, from the ledgers?

This is done by writing off individual transactions from the customers accounts. Again, be careful to keep a record of the VAT element which you can reclaim later. Select Customers from the Toolbar and highlight the account. Then press Features on the menu bar followed by Customer Features and Write Off Transactions on the pull-down menus. If you didn't highlight the required account in the Customers window, enter the account code on the Write Off Customer Transactions display. You will be asked to fill in the maximum amount you would like to write off for individual transactions and the software will display all transactions which fit into this category. If you don't want to write off all the transactions click on individual ones to highlight them and mark them out to be removed. The display will show the total amount you have chosen to write off. If you're happy, click on the Write Off button then confirm this choice when prompted. This option is also available for writing off amounts owed to suppliers - choose it through Supplier Features on the Features pull-down menu.

Are there any other ways to remove invoices posted in error?

Instead of using the Features options to post reverse transactions and cancel the invoices you can use the Disk Doctor Error Correction routines. These are described in Chapter 12.

Some of my customers are also suppliers and we usually match up the figures we owe each other and cancel these debts. Can I continue to do this with Sterling +2?

This procedure is called making contra entries by accountants and the software can handle it. Choose Features from the menu bar, then Customer (not Supplier) Features and finally Contra Entries. Although you must select this option from the Customer Features pull-down menu the Contra Entries screen lets you enter the account codes you use for this company both as a supplier and as a customer. As there are no headings remember that the left-hand box shows the transactions for the customer account, while the right hand box shows the supplier's invoices. Highlight the transactions from both boxes that you would like to offset and a total amount will appear at the bottom. The two totals have to match before you can click on the OK button. Remember that if you use VAT cash accounting the transactions must also have the same VAT codes. If the totals don't match you will not be permitted to offset the invoices against each other without changing your selection or adding extra invoices.

Can't I make contra entries if the amounts we owe each other aren't equal?

This can be done using a method described in the Questions and Answer section of Chapter 6.

I'm not sure if I'm filling in the tax codes correctly. How important is this?

Sterling +2 fills in the VAT return automatically using the tax codes from the correct fields on each transaction. It's vital to get the codes right, otherwise the software won't get the figures right and you won't be able to reconcile your VAT return. If you take the trouble to fill in the correct codes, Sterling +2 makes the VAT return quick and simple to complete.

Communications

Not many Sterling +2 users are taking full advantage of the communications facilities offered via the software. Even if you don't have all the necessary add-ons there should be at least some features to help you contact customers and suppliers. If your company already has a fax machine then it's unlikely you would want to buy a fax card to use this option. However, a modem to make quick automatic calls to your contacts would be helpful - especially in busy departments such as telesales. If you don't want to use telecomms equipment, take advantage of the handy ways to arrange letter and label printing using information from your records. If you want to buy any of the telecommunications equipment later, always double-check that the device you buy is compatible with Sterling +2 and Windows.

Phone calls

To use the automatic dialling facilities you will need a Hayes-compatible modem. This must be set up for use with your Windows software. To do this load Windows and click on Accessories in the Program Manager Window. Next click on the Terminal icon. The first time you use this option you may be prompted to choose the default serial port for the communications equipment. If you are prompted to select a Port, return to the Program Manager window, then select Main. Choose Control Panel then ports to make your selection. Once you have selected the port (this should be marked on your computer and is the place your modem is connected), choose Settings from the

Terminal menu, then Modem Commands. The next display lets you specify the type of modem you are using. The check box beside the name Hayes should be activated - if not click on it and then on OK to save the settings. The only other box you may need to change is labelled dial and has the default ATDT which means tone dial. If you need to use pulse dialling this will have to be changed to ATDP.

Once the modem is set up the software will be able to dial your customers and suppliers automatically using the telephone numbers listed in their records. Choose Customers or Suppliers from the main menu, then highlight the record in the list either by clicking on it or moving the highlight bar with the cursor keys. You don't need to load the record - just click on the Phone button and the number will be called. While you wait, a dialog box will appear showing you the name of the company, the contact name and the phone number. This reminds you who to ask for and you can check that you haven't selected the wrong account. If you have made a mistake or suddenly need to hang up simply click on the Cancel button. The Time Remaining box will give a countdown starting at 30 seconds while the phone rings until a connection is made or the default delay time runs out.

Letters

Letters can be created using Windows Write and then sent to customers or suppliers selected using the Criteria button or by highlighting. If you are sending letters to customers to remind them to pay overdue debts there is a standard letter set up by Sage which will extract all the necessary information from the records for each individual debtor. Choose Customers or Suppliers from the Toolbar and highlight the ones who should receive the letter (or use Criteria to specify all accounts which fit the requirements). Press Letter on the Customers/Suppliers menu then choose the output method (click on Preview if you just want to see the layout of the letter on screen, or Printer to have the letters printed out). Press Browse to see the list of available letters - at first there will only be the standard ones written by Sage. Highlight the required letter then press OK to select it. If you are printing the letters, check that you have the correct paper loaded in the printer and finish by clicking on Run. To stop printing in mid-flow press Cancel.

Tip

Browse lets you view the old and new document design layouts and the one you choose becomes the default. Preview displays the document layout and lets you make changes to fonts and colours - you can also add your company logo (find out how in Chapter 10).

To see the letter as it appears to customers/suppliers highlight it on the Browse display and press OK, click on Preview and then Run. To see the letter with all the variables to extract data from the customer records press Edit instead of Run. The Preview/Run buttons will display a miniaturised version of the letter, so press Options on the menu bar followed by Zoom In on the pull-down menu to enlarge it. The only active button on the top right of the screen will also enlarge the letter - the next button will decrease its size (or you can use Zoom Out from the pull-down menu).

The two standard letters set up by Sage for communications with Customers are called OVERDUE.SAL and FAX.SAL. The first is to inform customers that their payment is overdue. You can inform them when their balance is 30, 60 or 90 days old. The FAX.SAL file is a standard layout for faxes to be sent to customers selected using highlighting or Criteria. You can create more standard letters but make sure they all end with the suffix SAL, so that they will appear in the list for you to select via Customers and the Letter button.

The only standard letter for suppliers provided by Sage is to notify them of changes to your business address (the file name is ADDRESS.PUR). You can use the customer fax layout for faxes to suppliers as well. Any of the text on these documents can be altered to suit your exact methods of working. Choose Letter from the Suppliers menu, press Browse, then highlight the letter you want to change and click on Edit. The letter will appear on the Windows Write display for amendment. You will see that the letter includes text and also information which will change (the supplier's name and address on the change of address letter, and the amount owed by debtors on the Customers overdue letter, for example). Don't change these parts of the letter as they have been set up using codes called variables which enable the software to find and fill in this information from the files.

During configuration you set up a simple connection to Microsoft Windows Write (if you look on the Company Preferences Defaults screen this is how the function key F12 has been allocated). If you choose Letter from the Customers/Suppliers menu, then New, the screen will display the Write window for you to type the letter in free text. All letters to customers have the suffix SAL, so, for example, the overdue letter is called OVERDUE.SAL. Supplier letters, on the other hand, are identified with the letters PUR, so the one giving change of address details is called ADDRESS.PUR. All letters for customers and suppliers must have these suffixes or they won't be identified correctly by the software and displayed for selection on the Letter/Browse screens. When you finish writing a letter, select File on the menu bar, then Save on the pull-down menu. When the software prompts for a file name fill in a name which makes the letter easily identifiable, followed by a full stop and the correct suffix SAL or PUR. Check that it has been added to your list of letter files and select it for printing or further editing.

If you want to create letters using variables, either press F12 or choose Customers/Suppliers from the Toolbar, then Letter, and press New. This will load Windows Write - so long as you load it through Sterling +2, you can choose Edit from the menu bar and the final option will be Variables. Click on Variables to see a full list of variables which you can put into your letters and other document designs. Use the scroll bar to see the full selection. Wherever you insert a variable in a document, Sterling +2 will automatically find and include the information from the fields specified. For example, you will need to put the variables for your business address lines at the top of the letter, together with your company name.

Before changing a letter take a copy of the standard Sage document, in case you have problems and need to go back to the original version. Then type the letter using free text and include variables wherever the software needs to supply data from the records. The variables are identified by the software as they are enclosed in curly brackets. For example, if you want the letter to have the system date inserted just put the cursor in the correct place on the document and select the variable SDATE3 from the Variable List display. You can also choose the correct justification by clicking on the check box. Press the Insert button to have your selection included in the document design. Experiment with a few letters but make sure you keep at least one copy of the standard Sage letter as you know it will work!

Tip

The Variable List display lets you choose variables and justification to the left and right margins or centre, it also lets you specify the type of document you are working on whether for sales/purchase ledgers, invoice, remittance note or other format.

Warning

When you want to get rid of unwanted letters you have created highlight them and press Delete. Be careful not to delete any of the standard letters by mistake - you won't get much warning as you erase them and they are difficult to retrieve!

Faxes

Don't be confused into thinking the fax function actually sends faxes - it just creates fax files for sending. You will need your own fax card to complete the transmission. To write faxes, you need to select Customers or Suppliers from the Toolbar, then Letter, then New. This lets you write out your fax using the methods described for writing letters - you can use free text and variables and end by giving the file a name. Sage has provided a default fax layout file called FAX.SAL and you can use this to provide the heading information - just write your communication underneath. To do so choose Customers, then Letter, then Browse to highlight and select the FAX.SAL file. Choose Edit instead of New to add your communication under the variables. To send the fax, you need to use your fax card software to send the file FAX.SAL, or any other files you have created. You can create your own fax format by choosing Customers/Suppliers from the Toolbar, then pressing Letter and choosing New. Just type the fax in free text as you would prepare a letter document and insert variables using the techniques already described. It's worth looking at the FAX.SAL layout before trying to create an improved standard document. You can use FAX.SAL as the basis for your new design. Edit it as described above, then press File on the menu bar and Save As on the pull-down menu to give your file another name.

You can also use Sterling +2 to highlight the customers/suppliers to receive the fax. Alternatively, use Criteria (see Chapter 4 on record selection) to specify all the types of customers/suppliers who should be faxed - perhaps all the customers in a certain part of the country, or with the same salesman. Finally, choose Customers/Suppliers from the Toolbar, then Fax. Press Browse and Sterling +2 will display a list of letter files: choose the one you have created by double-clicking on it or just click once and press OK. If you are using the supplier option you will have to press Fax, then Browse and, at the bottom of the screen, click on the arrow at the end of the List Files of Type field. Choose All Files *.* and then scroll down through the list to highlight and select FAX.SAL or any other file you have created. Finish by clicking on OK and the file FAX.SAL (or any other document file you have selected) will appear on the Customer/Supplier Facsimile window. Press OK and the software switches you over to the Windows screen headed Save As. Click on the arrow at the end of the Save As File Type field and select Write

File by highlighting it. In the File Name field type FAX.WRI and press OK. Now you can check that you have prepared the fax correctly for transmission by pressing F12 to load Windows Write. Choose File from the menu bar and Open from the pull-down menu, then select FAX.WRI from the list and click on OK. The fax file contains the fax for each customer with their details inserted at the top. Each separate fax is on a different page but in a single document. To send it you will have to use your fax card software to separate these pages using the option to transmit a page (or a specified number of pages) at a time.

Tip

The steps for preparing a fax to transmit are slightly fiddly because at the moment there are many different types of fax card software. However, with emerging standards Sage is currently preparing a more easy to use link to Windows supported fax software. If you have any problem with the Fax option on the Customers/Suppliers menu you can use Windows Write. Press F12 and load your fax file as described earlier. Choose Save As from the File menu and call the file FAX.WRI. Send it using your fax software.

Designing your own documents

Sterling +2 allows you to redesign many of the standard accounting documents using Windows Write facilities. This will be necessary if you want to use your own stationery, as the default designs are for the Sage range of documents. The letter and fax options automatically transfer you to Windows Write, but you can also load Write when you start Windows. Select Accessories and then Write (this will not give you access to the Variables option). The quickest way to transfer to Write is by pressing the F12 key from any Sterling +2 screen - this does give access to the Variables option on the Edit pull-down menu.

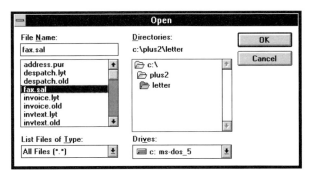

To find the document design files, load Write by pressing F12 or by selecting Customers, then Letter, then New. Press File and choose Open from the pull-down menu. At the bottom of the screen there is a box called List Files of Type. Click on the arrow to see a complete list (you will have to scroll down to the end as not all the options are visible). Select the line All Files [*.*]. All of the document designs will appear in the list on the left so you can highlight the one you want to edit and press OK to see it on the Write window.

In the list you will see the files for many types of document, not just letters and faxes. The invoices for stock are in the file INVOICE.LYT, invoices for services are in INVTEXT.LYT, the remittance advice is REMITT.LYT, the statement is STATMENT.LYT, the despatch/delivery note is DESPATCH.LYT, the sales order acknowledgement is SAORDER.LYT and the purchase order copy is PUORDER.LYT. There are also two designs for labels - LABEL.SLB for customer address labels, and LABEL.PLB for supplier labels - these are used together with automatic methods of selecting contacts and addresses for large mailshots. Any of these can be amended to suit your own stationery and methods of working, but take care by keeping copies of the originals as a backup!

Tip

You will see from the list that there are more file names and certain documents have more than one design. This is because the software offers both the old and new document layouts.

If you want to change a layout, perhaps for the invoice, use the method described earlier to find the file INVOICE.LYT. Highlight it and click on OK so that it will be loaded onto the Write display. Press File on the menu bar then Print on the pull-down menu and respond with OK to the next prompt to have the standard document printed out. Use this standard layout to help you create a new design.

Tip

Make printouts of the standard documents before altering them and copy the files to a floppy disk in case you want to revert to the originals. Make copies by choosing Main from the Windows Program Manager then File Manager. Press File on the menu bar and choose Copy from the pull-down menu. In the From field put C:\PLUS2\LETTER*.* and in the To field put A: to have all the files copied to a new floppy disk. You can practice on the floppy disk version by pressing F12 to load Write, pressing File then Open and choosing All Files *.* in the List of File Types box and the A drive in the Drives box. Highlight the required document and press OK to work on it.

Labels

If you have produced a number of letters or other communications using the Criteria button, make sure you save the set of criteria specified (refer back to Chapter 4 if you can't remember how this is done). The criteria you saved to select names and addresses for the letters can then be used to produce the address labels for the envelopes. It's important to start by filling in details on the label stationery so that the printer will position the addresses in the right place.

Choose Customers/Suppliers, then Labels and Browse to choose the correct file by highlighting it and pressing OK (at first there will only be one file listed). Next click on Preview and press Run to see a depiction of your label layouts with the contact names and addresses included, if you have selected the accounts correctly. The labels are too small to read as the preview gives a miniaturised version of the whole page. So press the small button to the right of the box stating Page 1 (there are a variety of buttons but only one is dark and therefore active). This button enlarges the labels so that you can read them. Scroll down through the whole page using the vertical scroll bar. To miniaturise the page again press the next button which has now become active. This function is also available from the menu bar - choose Options then Zoom In or Zoom Out from the pull-down menu.

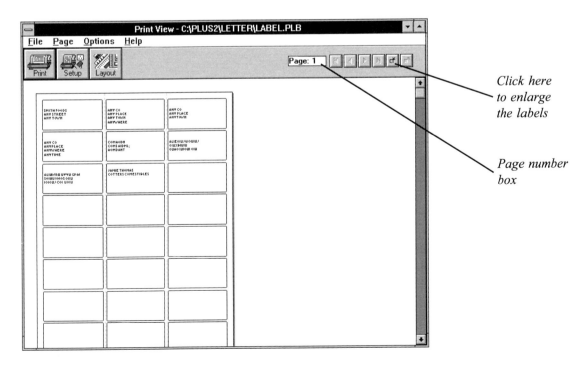

Click here to enlarge the labels

Page number box

Press Layout and click on the check box for laser labels if this is your method of printing. Be careful to measure the label stationery accurately to fill in the remaining boxes. In the Labels section, fill in the Across and Down boxes with the number of label rows there are on your stationery. In the Margins box, fill in the size of the margin in inches/centimetres from the left and right-hand edges and click on the option buttons to specify inches or centimetres. If you're unsure about the details, abandon the setup procedure by pressing Cancel, but to continue with the printout choose OK. Finish by pressing the Print button and you will be offered default options which should be suitable for your label printout and won't need changing. The software offers to print out all records and only accept this if you have selected the appropriate customers or suppliers in advance. Press the Setup button if you need to change the default printer. Click on the arrow at the end of the printer name field and highlight the required equipment. Click on OK to print out the labels.

Tip

Once you have set the layout for your first print run of labels you will be able to simply select the customers or suppliers to be contacted for future mailshots. Press Labels, select the label file (by using the Browse option), then click on Printer and Run. If you make a mistake in your label layout specifications, you can revert to Sage's default settings by pressing Layout and then the Default button.

I've deleted my overdue debt letter by mistake. How can I get it back - can't I just copy it from the Sterling +2 master disk from the A: drive to the C:\PLUS2\LETTER subdirectory?

Sage has compressed the files to fit them all onto one single master disk. If you copy the letter it will appear on your list of letter files but will be in compressed form so you won't be able to use it. This is true of all the Sterling +2 master files, so anything you delete is difficult to copy onto your working system. The only method is to install Sterling +2 again. You can only do this if you have a bureau licence allowing you to run more than one copy. Make sure you specify a different subdirectory for all the files during installation. You could then copy any of the files, including the letter, from the new subdirectory to C:\PLUS2\LETTER. To copy files choose Main from the Windows Program Manager, choose File Manager, click on File on the menu bar then Copy on the pull-down menu. Fill in the directory where you have temporarily installed Sterling +2 (e.g. C:\TEMP\LETTER\OVERDUE.SAL) in the From box and C:\PLUS2\LETTER\ in the To box. It would be best to copy all document files onto a floppy disk, as described earlier. This way you have a copy of all the standard layouts in decompressed form and these could then be copied easily from the A drive to C:\PLUS2\LETTER\. If you have any problems make sure you have all the correct letters and backslashes to let the computer find your files and transfer them to the right place.

Warning

Don't attempt to install Sterling +2 a second time just to copy files unless you have a bureau licence - the system will stop you running either version of the software.

BUSINESS*guide*

Sales ledger

Keep a clear documentary record of all sales by providing customers either with a receipt or an invoice. This not only ensures a professional image for the business but also helps you prepare your final accounts and provides evidence of your takings for the Inland Revenue and HM Customs and Excise. Apart from initial investment to start up the business, the sales recorded in this ledger are the only finance coming in to pay for the day to day running costs including salaries. The total sales figure is called turnover and is easy to keep an eye on using Sterling +2 reports to see just how well the business is performing.

Tip

See the Business Guide in Chapter 12 to find out how to prepare your final accounts for submission to the Inland Revenue.

To work out the profitability of the business, you will need to consider not only the turnover figure, but also how much you have had to pay out in overheads and how much you will have to pay in VAT. To work out the actual profit you make from sales you need to start by deducting the cost price (the amount you paid to suppliers) for each item from the selling price to see how much extra you have earned. This calculation tells you the gross profit made from sales. However, the gross profit doesn't take into account all the overheads involved, so a more complex calculation needs to be performed to subtract the overheads from the gross profit so that you will be left with the net profit. The net profit is the amount you have actually earned after all the expenses are subtracted. Fortunately Sterling +2 performs all the necessary calculations so you can check the results in the Profit and Loss Report (choose Financials then P & L to see the gross and net figures).

Wherever possible try to get immediate payment from customers by cash or cheque. If they need credit, it's worth offering different credit card options so that you pass the responsibility for extracting payment over to the credit card company. For some businesses, invoices are the only acceptable way of requesting payment, in which case the customer receives the goods or services before settling the bill. It's important to keep an eye on bad debts both for credit control purposes and also to check your VAT liability. Once you raise an invoice, the VAT can't be written off, even if payment is not received. You will have to pay HM Customs and Excise and then reclaim all the VAT paid on bad debts. More powerful software would handle this automatically but with a small business package, the VAT liability from all sales transactions will be added to your liability on the VAT return. You will have to keep track of the amounts you can reclaim due to bad debts.

Purchase ledger

Traditionally, the purchase ledger was used only to record goods bought from suppliers to be resold to customers, so it didn't include goods and services such as consumables, insurance, or capital items such as computers and vehicles. All purchases apart from those intended for resale were recorded in the nominal ledger. However, as the software is integrated you can keep details on all types of suppliers in the same place, regardless of the types of goods or services they provide. Fill in details on all suppliers, including the computer dealer or insurance company, in the purchase ledger records and the code can be used when making payments through the Bank and Payment options.

When goods arrive, the documentation to accompany them should include the purchase invoice and a remittance or advice note listing the items despatched. Check the advice note carefully to see that all the goods are included in the delivery and inform the supplier as soon as possible of any errors. You will generally be asked by the delivery driver to sign for receipt of the goods - be careful how you deal with this. Usually you have to sign quickly, in which case it's best to write a few words to indicate that you haven't checked the consignment before signing. If possible check the goods to see that they are all included and not damaged before signing.

Keep the documentation for each transaction clipped together, in this case the purchase invoice and advice note. These are necessary backups to your computer records to provide proof of your VAT liability. The supplier should send statements if you are a regular customer, giving amounts and due dates for payment. Sterling +2 helps by recording terms and discounts agreed for early payment, so take advantage of these offers.

Stocktaking

The gross profit is calculated by deducting cost of goods sold from sales, but another important figure in the equation is the value of stock. Always set the value of your stock at the cost price (the price you paid the supplier for it) unless it is damaged or unsaleable for some other reason. Set the price you could realistically ask for damaged goods if this is lower than the cost price. In order to work out your gross profit accurately, you need to add the total purchases for the year to the value of your opening stock and then deduct the value of stock you have left on your shelves, called closing stock, at the end of the year. The result will be the true cost of your sales, which you can deduct from your total sales figure to find the gross profit. Sterling +2 helps by keeping a record of stock levels and values according to the recorded transactions, but you will still have to take stock regularly to count the items and check for damage. There may be differences between the computer records and actual stock levels due to theft, loss or damage and it's important to record losses as soon as possible. To do this, you will need to use the Adjust-In and Adjust-Out facilities, accessed via Products on the Toolbar (find out how in Chapter 7). A basic accounting rule is to admit loss quickly as you may be compensated for it, but record profit only when it is definite (such as when payment actually arrives) as you will be taxed on it! The value of your stock appears on the balance sheet which the Inland Revenue requires at year end to see an overall picture of your business' performance (refer to the Business Guide in Chapter 12). Sterling+2 doesn't automatically update the stock accounts in the nominal ledger as the products are purchased or sold. See the Question and Answer section in Chapter 11 to find out how to make manual adjustments.

CHAPTER 6

Banking - Payments and Receipts

Now that you have entered your company's invoices and credit notes, the next step is to learn how to handle payments and receipts. The Toolbar offers two selections for these tasks: choose either Bank or Cash depending on the transaction. Sterling +2 boasts quite an impressive range of banking facilities for a small to medium sized business package and these can be used to keep a careful watch on all transactions and invested finance.

Petty cash

If the payment or receipt just involves petty cash then select Cash from the main menu followed by either Payments or Receipts and watch the pictures move! Sage has included a default account in the nominal ledger for petty cash, but remember to add one if you have set up your own chart of accounts before continuing. The Cash Payments and Receipts screens are similar and resemble familiar forms to be filled in.

Warning

If you're setting up your own chart of accounts remember that the petty cash account must be specified in two places or you can't post cash transactions. It must be included as a nominal account (choose Nominal then Record) and also on the Control Accounts screen (press Defaults on the menu bar then Control Accounts on the pull-down menu).

The Ref field can take up to six numbers and this should be the code from the paper documentation relating to the transaction. Change the default date if necessary, then put the nominal account code under N/C. There is a magnifying-glass icon so you can search

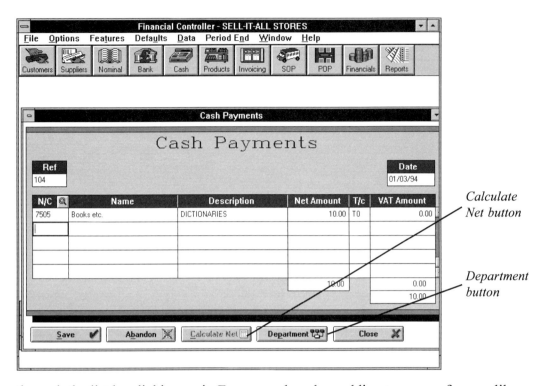

Calculate
Net button

Department
button

through the list by clicking on it. For example, when adding to your reference library you could put 7505 as the nominal code (this is for books), and then under description some detail about the transaction (such as Dictionaries). In the Net Amount field put the net price and the system can analyse the figures over different nominal accounts and calculate the VAT. If you put the gross figure you will have to press the Calculate Net button so that the software can deduct VAT and show the net amount. To make sure that the VAT is correct put the relevant code in the T/c field using the table set up during configuration. The VAT field will automatically display the correct amount, but this can be amended independently of the other fields. If you enter more than one transaction the running totals can be seen at the bottom of the display.

You might want to link this transaction to a specific department, in which case you should click on the Department button. In the dialog box that appears, click on the arrow at the end of the Department field to see the list you set up during configuration. Highlight and select the required one. If payments are to be allocated to different departments, fill in a different record for each transaction - they can share the same reference code. Remember to click on Save to post the information.

When altering details on a petty cash record you must first highlight the line you want to work on and then alter the incorrect field. Highlight the line and press F6 to remove the whole entry, or press Abandon to delete all the information you have input. If you want to save the record with amendments click on Save to be presented with a clear record card. Then click on Close if you want to leave the Petty Cash Payments/Receipts screen.

Banking

Bank payments and receipts are more complicated than petty cash - it's important to get the procedures right. First of all you need to decide whether the payments and receipts relate to outstanding supplier/customer credit notes and invoices. If so you will want to automatically adjust the sales and purchase ledgers accordingly. Perhaps the payment or receipt is not to be allocated to a transaction in the sales or purchase ledger, in which case you will only want it posted to the nominal ledger. When you select Bank from the main menu Sterling +2 will present a list of all the available bank accounts. Start by highlighting and selecting the correct one for the transactions you need to process.

Nominal ledger payments

If you wish to record a payment, which is not linked to an outstanding supplier invoice, select Bank from the main menu, highlight the correct bank account then click on Payment. Sage has made the entry screen simple to use. At the top of the screen there is a cheque to be filled in, then at the bottom you must input extra information for nominal ledger analysis. The cheque is headed with the name of the bank account you have chosen, so make sure this is the right one before proceeding.

Fill in the cheque by putting the supplier's account code in the Pay To box and the full name will appear on the line. There is also a magnifying-glass icon so you can click on this to see all of your supplier codes - or put the first letter if you know it, then click on the icon to start the search at the best point in the list. Although you have given a supplier code remember that this method does not automatically match the payment to any outstanding invoices. Use the method described later in this chapter (in the Purchase ledger payments section) to automatically match up payments to invoices in order to avoid mistakes in the records.

Tip

Use the supplier code to link payments to suppliers on your database. For other suppliers you can skip the Pay To line and start with the date and cheque number fields.

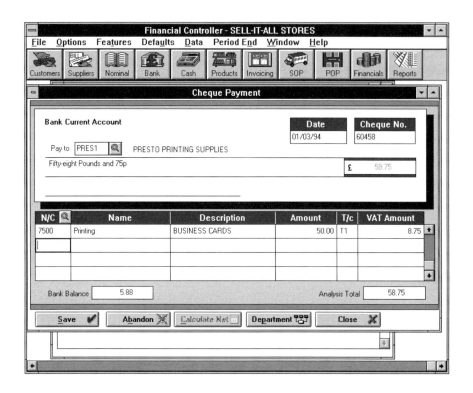

Warning

These procedures are for payments and receipts which only need to be recorded in the nominal ledger. They mustn't be used for payments and receipts which relate to invoices and credit notes in the sales and purchase ledgers. This method should only be used for straightforward payments of expenses - these are normally for services where no credit is given.

The software displays today's date on the cheque (this can be changed) and you should copy the cheque number from your cheque book. Fill in the amount in numbers after the £ sign and watch your bank balance at the bottom of the screen decrease accordingly. You only need to type in the amount in numbers and it will be written out automatically on the second line of the cheque. It's not necessary to fill in the amount on the cheque at this point. The next step will be to enter details on your purchases in the bottom part of the display and the cheque amount will be calculated and displayed automatically. If you do enter the cheque amount make sure it is the gross amount (i.e. it includes VAT).

In the bottom half of the screen, fill in the details for the nominal ledger, starting with the nominal code under N/C. This could, for example, be 7505 for Books and this description would appear automatically in the Name field. Put the details, such as Software Directories under Descriptions. Either put the net amount in the Amount field and the system will calculate VAT across different accounts using the code you enter under T/c, or you can put the gross amount and press the Calculate Net button. Remember there is a difference between zero-rated items purchased which have the code T0, and payments which have nothing to do with VAT, such as salaries, which have the code T9. The VAT amount will be displayed automatically. The total amount is displayed at the bottom in the Analysis Total box.

Click on the Department button if the payment should be analysed according to department. You can click on the arrow at the end of the field to see a complete list of choices to highlight and select. Edit the details on the record entry screen, if necessary, by highlighting the line to be changed and altering it, or press F6 to delete it. Click on Abandon to remove all the details on the screen, or click on Save to post the transaction. If the Save button has faded to grey and you can't make it work, check that the amount on the cheque matches the analysis total - these two must be the same before you can continue. When you press Save a new record entry screen appears. Click on Close if you have no more transactions to post.

Nominal ledger receipts

When you receive money to be banked which does not relate to an outstanding customer invoice you should select Bank, highlight the desired type of bank account and then press Receipts. Don't confuse this with the method of banking money received as payment for an invoice. In that case use the technique described later in this chapter (in the Sales ledger receipts section) so that the sales ledger will be updated automatically.

The Bank Receipts screen is headed with the name of the bank account you have chosen (such as current account or deposit account) and updates the nominal ledger. Fill in a reference number in the box labelled Deposit No (this could be the number on the cheque to a maximum of 6 figures). Change the default date if you need to, then fill in the Amount box if you know the exact figure. You don't need to fill in the Amount box at the top of the display. This will be calculated by the software when you enter details on the receipt, or receipts, in the lines underneath. If you start by filling in the Amount box, make sure you enter the gross figure (i.e. including VAT). The bank balance box at the bottom of the screen will automatically increase.

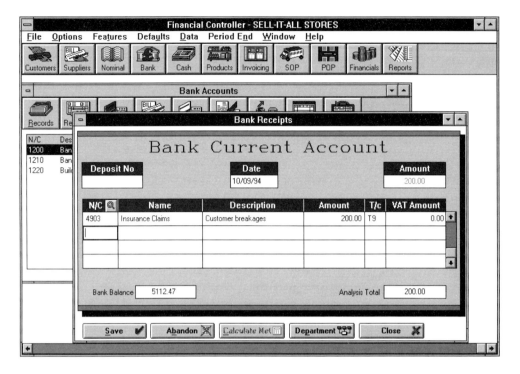

Under N/C enter the code to show which account should receive this income. For example, this could be 4902 for commissions received. This description would appear automatically in the Name field. Add a further description in the next field to identify this transaction in the audit trail. The Amount field lets you enter a net amount if you want the system to calculate VAT, or put the gross amount and press the Calculate Net button. Make sure you have the correct VAT code (look at your configuration settings) so that the amount will be calculated correctly and displayed.

If the receipt should be linked to a department, press the Department button. Click on the arrow at the end of the Department field, then select the appropriate one. Click on Save to post the information or Abandon to delete it, then click on Close when you have no more receipts to post.

How can I transfer money from my current account to my deposit account?

To record money transferred from one bank account to another, choose Bank from the Toolbar then Transfer from the Bank menu. The next screen prompts you to fill in the nominal ledger codes of the two banks involved. Although it displays the account you selected on the main Bank window you can overwrite this. Press the magnifying-glass icon at the end of the Account from and Account to boxes to see a full list of your bank accounts. Highlight the one you want to select and it will be entered automatically. Perhaps you are transferring money to a newly opened bank account, or one you haven't yet recorded in Sterling +2. In this case you should click on the magnifying-glass icon, then press the New button at the bottom of the list of available accounts. Fill in a new bank account record card for the nominal ledger. The software automatically enters information in the Ref and Details fields to indicate a transfer of money but you can overwrite these. Then fill in the Amount field with the total to be moved between the specified bank accounts. You can change the default system date if necessary, then finish by pressing Save followed by Close when you have no more transfers to record. If in any doubt, press Abandon to exit without recording the transfer details.

Purchase ledger payments

When making a payment which needs to be matched to an invoice sent by one of your suppliers don't press Payment on the Bank menu. From the Toolbar select Bank, highlight the correct bank account and then press Supplier. Don't confuse this screen with the one described previously for processing receipts, even though it looks similar. In the top half of the display is a cheque and the heading Supplier Cheque. The bottom half

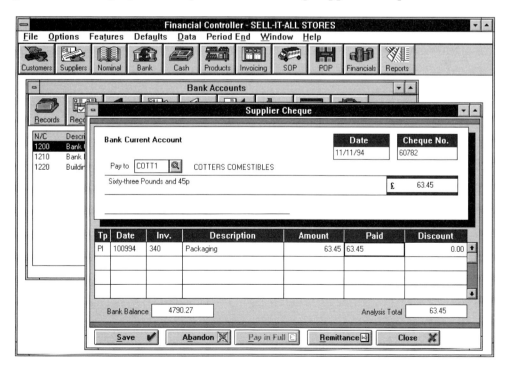

of the screen takes details to update the purchase ledger and clear the outstanding invoice.

On the cheque, use the magnifying-glass icon to select the relevant supplier account code and the full name will be displayed. Fill in the date or leave today's date which appears by default. Then put a reference number, which would normally be the cheque number, in the next field. If you want to fill in the amount at this stage, put it in the box after the £ sign in figures. It will automatically appear in writing for you to check. The Amount box may be left blank and the software will later calculate the figure for you using the information you supply in the bottom half of the screen. The software automatically displays all outstanding invoices from the supplier you have selected, just choose the ones you want to pay. If you don't fill in the Amount box before selecting invoices to settle you won't be able to alter the amount which appears automatically on the cheque without cancelling the chosen transactions.

The payment may be the complete amount for one or more invoices, or perhaps you only want to pay part of the total invoice amount. The software automatically displays the invoices (these have the code PI in the first field) and credit notes (PC). There are two methods to be used, depending on whether you want to pay the invoices in full or in part.

The first method is only for transactions which should be paid completely. Select the transaction you want to pay (it should have PI for purchase invoice under the heading Tp). Place the cursor in the field headed Paid on the required transaction line and click on the Pay in Full button. The Paid field will then be filled in automatically. Check the Analysis Total field at the bottom of the screen for the cumulative payment figure. If the supplier has offered a discount put the amount in the Discount field and the outstanding invoice figure will be adjusted for you.

When you only want to make a part payment, select the relevant invoice and type the amount you want to pay in the field headed Paid. Be careful not to put the part payment figure in the Amount field which should still have the total requested on the invoice. Don't fill in the Discount field or the software will change the figures and automatically allocate the total payment. This time finish by clicking on Save to make the part payment.

Tip

Use the scroll bar on the right to see all the outstanding invoices and credit notes so that you can allocate the payment being made against the full list of transactions. If you can't see the scroll bar use the Windows techniques described in Chapter 2 to maximise and move the windows so that the whole display is visible. If you don't want to change the size of the window use the scroll bars on the Desktop to see the hidden parts, or resize the windows by using the mouse to position the pointer on any of the boundary lines and dragging them to a new position.

Warning

Don't get confused by the multitude of similar Windows symbols on the complete display. Perhaps the Control-menu box is not visible on the window you are working on, but don't press the Control-menu box on the main window or you will exit from Sterling +2. A variety of open windows can make the screen look cluttered and confusing. It can appear difficult to exit from part of the system if the methods of saving and closing are out of sight. Save the transactions you are working on then clear away the build-up of windows from time to time by pressing Window on the menu bar and Close All on the pull-down menu. Be careful not to close active windows with unsaved transactions.

If I have credit notes and invoices from the same supplier can I clear the invoices with the credit notes while working on this screen?

It makes sense to clear outstanding credit notes with invoices when working on the supplier payments option. To do this, select credit note transactions (these have the code PC under the heading Tp), place the cursor in the Paid field and click on Pay in Full. Check the analysis total which should increase giving you the extra money to allocate to the payment of invoices. Select the invoices you want to settle and pay them as described earlier.

Warning

Always remember to finish by clicking on the Save button in order to post transactions (if it's not easily visible use the different Windows techniques to find it). It's tempting to click on the Close button when the work is complete - the software will confirm that you want to exit, but it will not allocate any of the payments or update the ledgers. You will see that your supplier's balance has not changed and the work has been completely wasted. Click on the Save button each time you post transactions. Only click on Close after you have saved the final transaction and want to exit.

The software checks that the amount you have allocated to different invoices and credit notes matches the amount on the cheque. If the cheque is for a greater amount this will be pointed out to you when you click on Save. At this point you have two choices: respond to the prompt to click on Yes and store the excess figure as a payment on account to be allocated to invoices in the future, or choose No to go back to the transactions display and make more payments.

The other choices at the bottom of the Supplier Cheque transaction screen are Abandon to completely cancel all the details, or Remittance. Choose Remittance if you want a remittance note printed out giving a list of all the payments allocated to supplier transactions. Remember to do this before clicking on Save otherwise Sterling +2 can't provide the information. Once you press Save, a clear supplier payment screen appears. Press Close if you have no more payments to record.

Sales ledger receipts

When a customer sends you a cheque, you can allocate this receipt to one or more outstanding debts. Do this by selecting Bank from the Toolbar then Customer. Put the customer's account code in the A/C box and the software will display details on all outstanding transactions. Change the default date if you need to and put a reference

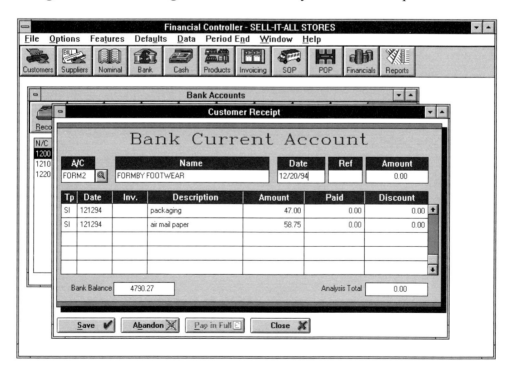

number such as the cheque number. If you leave the Amount box at the top of the screen blank, it will be calculated for you as you select the transactions you want to settle. You can enter the exact amount received at this stage. Any excess can then be stored on account for the customer.

To allocate receipts, place the cursor in the Paid field and you can scroll through all the outstanding transactions one by one. If you want to pay the transaction completely click on Pay in Full, then if there is a discount put it in the Discount field. If the customer has only paid part of the invoice total put the amount received in the Paid field (not the Amount field which is for the total debt). Don't put any discount as the software can't make this calculation and will alter the figures to show complete payment. Look down the codes in the Tp field to see which transactions are sales invoices (SI) and which are credit notes (SC). If you want to, you can allocate credit notes against invoices by placing the cursor in the Paid field of any line starting with SC and pressing Pay in Full. The figure on the credit note will then be added to the amount in the analysis total which is available to pay off outstanding invoices.

Remember to click on Save to post the transactions. The Close button will ask you to confirm that you want to exit, but will not post the changes to any of the ledgers and the customer balance will not be updated. On pressing Save, you will have the chance to enter transactions for other customers. Press Close when you have no more receipts to enter. If you entered the amount received in the Amount field and the transactions add up to a lower figure you must decide what to do. Respond to the prompt to keep the excess as payment on account to be used for the payment of invoices in the future. Choose Yes to select this option, or No for another opportunity to allocate the receipt for outstanding invoices.

Overseas customers and suppliers

Perhaps some of your customers and suppliers are in other countries. This can mean problems due to the constantly rising and falling exchange rates. The amount on the original invoice might be quite different to the amount actually paid or received and you will have to adjust the figures accordingly. It's important first of all to create a nominal code to handle these descriptions. Choose Nominal from the Toolbar, then Record and put in a free code number (for example 9996), give it the name Exchange Rate Variance, then click on Save. If you are not using the Sage default chart of accounts make sure you use a free number. When you create a new nominal record, Sterling +2 will display a message confirming that this is a new account code.

If the payment received or paid is less than the amount on the supplier or customer invoice you will have to write a credit note for the difference. Select Customers or Suppliers from the Toolbar, then Credit Note. Fill in the amount of difference together with the tax code T9 and the nominal code for the Exchange Rate Variance account. Process the transaction as normal, paying the invoice with the cheque amount and the credit note.

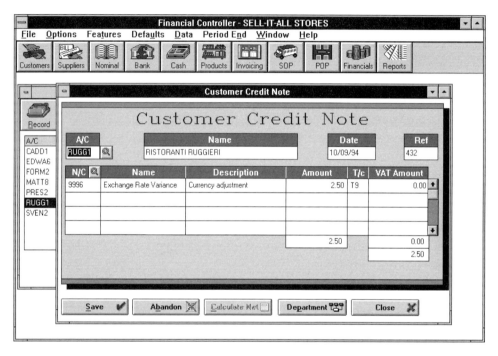

Should the payment made or received be more than the figure on the original invoice you need to create an additional invoice for the extra amount. Select Customers or Suppliers from the Toolbar followed by Invoice. Fill in the amount which has been paid in excess, put T9 as the tax code and fill in the nominal code for Exchange Rate Variance. Finish by processing the transaction in the normal way, paying the invoices with the cheque.

Standing orders and direct debits

Some of your customer and supplier accounts will be paid by standing orders or direct debits. The software lets you set up recurring credits or debits to reflect the changes this makes to the balances in bank accounts. It's important to keep a check on this recurring entry information as it will need to be amended from time to time. It also provides useful information on the exact amount you are spending on various goods and services. It's far too easy to use standing orders and direct debits to save time and effort on making payments but you can easily lose track of money being spent on items that are no longer required. The bank doesn't supply this information as a standard service, so it helps to be able to refer to your accounting software.

The recurring entries can be processed at any time - the software will automatically process all the ones with dates up to and including the system date. All the accounts are updated and marked accordingly to show that they have been paid. When you run periodic functions such as the month end procedures, Sterling +2 will ensure no recurring entries have been left unprocessed. It's possible to process recurring entries as often as you like as the software knows which have already been done and there is no risk of repeating a transaction. At month end, all the recurring entries which have been processed and marked will be cleared so that the next period's payment will be processed correctly.

Select Bank from the Toolbar, then choose Recurring and fill in all the necessary details in the table displayed. Under Tp put a code for the recurring entry: BP for bank payments, BR for bank receipts, JC for journal credits and JD for journal debits. A typical line would have BP for bank payments, then the relevant nominal code (for example 7200 for electricity - click on the magnifying-glass icon for the complete selection), the date

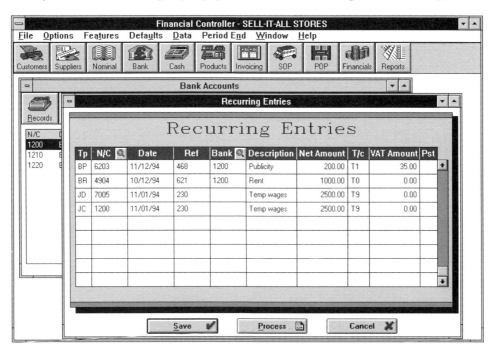

when the payment should be posted (this must be in the current period and will be repeated each month), a reference number of up to six characters you want to use to identify this entry, the code for the bank account (use the searcher to see the available types of bank account), a description in free text of up to 30 characters to describe the goods or services paid for, and the net amount. Enter the VAT code in the T/c field by referring to the table you set up during configuration and the correct amount will be displayed. The field headed Pst is system-maintained and is used to indicate if the posting has been made for the current period. If it has been posted this will be a Y, otherwise a N.

If the recurring entries are credits or debits relating to a bank account the procedure is straightforward. For journal entries, however, make sure that the credits and debits balance or Sterling +2 will not let you continue. A typical journal entry for a recurring type of transaction would be to record regular transfers from one nominal account to another so you would balance the figures by crediting one code and debiting the other. This can be complicated as you will often need to credit the account giving value and debit the account receiving value, so check the description of double entry bookkeeping in Chapter 1 and the full description of nominal ledger processing in Chapter 9 before attempting the procedure.

You can edit the information on recurring entries in order to correct mistakes or to alter the figures at a later date. Just click on the line to highlight it and type the changes - if you want to remove the whole line highlight it and press F6. However, the software will not let you change the marker which indicates whether or not the transaction has been processed. System-maintained information including this Pst field, which indicates whether or not the amount has been posted, can't be amended by the user as this would create inconsistencies in your accounting data files.

Make sure you finish by clicking on Save each time you add or amend recurring entries or your work will be lost. If the software refuses to save your work check that journal entries balance - if not you will have to amend them. The recurring entries will all be processed and updated at month end. Any time you're working on this part of the system you can click on the Process button and the software will indicate which transactions have already been dealt with by the bank.

Checking bank and credit card statements

It's all too easy to lose control of the bank account when you have put all the information on computer - the sheer volume of transactions makes it difficult to check the figures. At this stage you might begin to trust the software and the bank statements without questioning interest charges, but any shrewd businessman needs to keep a careful watch on the bank balance. Even banks make mistakes, so use Sterling +2 to ensure you don't give away more money than you have to.

Tip

As already mentioned, a national Daily Mail survey showed that more than 95% of businesses were incorrectly charged interest on their bank accounts. Sage's own research showed that 80% of small businesses were affected. There is a high likelihood your bank charges are wrong, so check your statements carefully as you can ask for compensation for all stopped cheques and excessive charges due to bank errors.

When the bank or credit card statement arrives, select Bank from the Toolbar, highlight the appropriate bank account in the list, then click on the Reconcile option. A screen appears headed Bank Reconciliation plus the name of the bank account - check that you've selected the right account. Sterling+2 will display a window, listing all the cheques posted to the bank account which have not yet been reconciled. This window brings together information on cheques posted through the Bank and Invoicing options, as well as taking all details affecting the bank account which have been processed by the nominal ledger.

At the top of the screen you can see your balance, then the transactions are listed by type, date, reference, cheque number and description (such as customer deposit or cheque payment) as well as amount. At the bottom of the screen are three important boxes. The Statement Balance amount will change as you reconcile individual transactions being dealt with by the bank. The Uncleared Items amount shows the balance of outstanding debits and credits recorded in your books and waiting for bank reconciliation. The Book Balance amount shows your bank balance as it has been recorded in the nominal ledger (this acts as if all outstanding debits and credits have been paid immediately).

Warning

Before completing the reconciliation process check that the final figure in the Statement Balance box matches that sent on the bank statement. If there is a difference find out where the error has been made. Adjust the figures otherwise the next time you start to reconcile a statement the opening balance will be wrong.

Start by clicking on transactions in the list which also appear on the bank statement, taking care not to add any which are not on the statement. Remember that if most of the transactions appear on the statement it might be easier to highlight the transactions you don't want. Then press the Swap button to choose all the un-highlighted lines. If you do use the handy Swap button, double-check to see you are only leaving transactions un-highlighted which are on the bank statement. Find out if the figures are right by checking that the Statement Balance on the screen is the same as the balance on the bank statement. Click on the Save button to update your records and reconcile all the transactions cleared by the bank.

If the figures don't match, check that you have included all the transactions on the statement and no extra ones. Then see if there are transactions listed on the bank statement which you have forgotten to record in Sterling +2 - you can add these extra payments and receipts by clicking on the Adjustment button. The Adjustment option is also used to record details on any bank charges which affect the overall balance.

Warning

Any adjustments made will automatically change the nominal ledger as soon as they are made, even if you later decide to cancel the reconciliation option. If you decide not to process the reconciliation you will have to reverse the adjustments to the nominal ledger if they were made in error. To do this you will have to make reverse journal entries. It's easier to calculate your figures first to avoid mistakes.

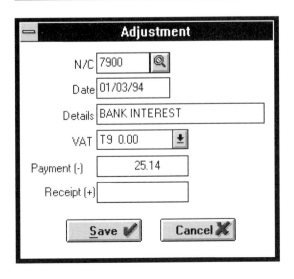

Once in the Adjustment screen, fill in the display to record the payment or receipt. The adjustment will automatically amend the correct bank account in the nominal ledger, so don't put the bank account code in any field. In the A/C field the code required is not the bank account but the nominal account relating to the transaction (for example 7900 for bank interest - click on the magnifying-glass icon for a selection). Change the default date if necessary and fill in a description of the transaction of up to 30 characters if you want to. Click on the arrow at the end of the VAT field to choose the correct tax code from the ones you set up during configuration. Be careful about where you enter the amount - the Payment field is for money you are paying out and will decrease your balance, while the Receipt field is for money paid to you and will increase your balance. Put the gross amount for the appropriate field and the software will work out the VAT element. Only click on the Save button if you are sure you will be able to continue with the reconciliation process. Work out all the calculations beforehand to see if you can match the bank statement to your own on-screen Statement Balance. If not you should click on Cancel and find out where the error lies.

Tip

Press F2 and use the Windows calculator to check your figures.

When you have managed to adjust all the figures so that the bank statement and the display show the same balance it's time to click on Save to reconcile the figures and post the information to the nominal ledger. Now when you look at the Bank Reconciliation screen for this bank account only the uncleared transactions will be displayed. If you can't get the two balances to match you should select Abandon to cancel the reconciliation. Remember that any adjustments you have made will affect the nominal ledger and will have to be reversed.

Q&A

How do I reconcile my petty cash account?

Print out reports to check all cash receipts on the system. To print out the reports choose Reports from the Toolbar and use the scroll bar to move down through the list. Find and highlight the Cash Receipts and Cash Payments files. Click on the Printer option button and press Run. Another handy way to find file names in this long list is to press Reports on the Toolbar then position the pointer arrow on the bottom boundary of the window so that it becomes a double arrow, then drag the boundary to the bottom of the screen. The window lengthens and the cash reports become visible. It's good business practice to check your actual petty cash balance against the Sterling+2 cash account on a regular basis. Use the reports to analyse the cash accounts in more detail.

Can I print a bank statement of my own to check all the payments and receipts I have posted to each bank account?

There is an option which allows you to print out all transactions which have been recorded on Sterling +2 since the date of the last reconciliation. This provides a useful check on your bank account between statements. Select Bank, highlight the desired account in the opening window, then click on the Statement button. You will be prompted to choose between Preview to see the information on screen, Printer to print it, and File to store it in a file to be used later. Click on the option button beside the desired method of output and then choose OK. The Cancel button lets you abandon the statement option - it will also stop the printing if you change your mind in mid-flow. If you choose Preview to see the statement on screen it may appear in miniature form. You will need to enlarge the display twice to make it big enough to read - do this by pressing the enlarge button on the top of the screen. Alternatively choose Options from the menu bar and Zoom In from the pull-down menu. Repeat this procedure to keep enlarging the display. The page number is also given at the top of the screen - the buttons beside it let you move page by page backwards and forwards through the document or to skip straight to the end or beginning.

What is the best way to record transfers of funds between the petty cash and bank accounts?

These transfers need to be recorded directly into the nominal ledger as journal entries and it's important to debit and credit the correct codes. To transfer £100 from the bank to petty cash choose Nominal from the Toolbar then Journals. Under N/C put the bank account code (1200 in the Sage default chart if it's the current account), type Transfer to petty cash under Description, put T9 under T/c and fill in 100 under Credit. On the next line put the petty cash code under N/C (the Sage default is 1230), type Transfer from bank under Description and put 100 in the debit column. It's important to understand that you have debited the account receiving the money and credited the account giving it (remember the rule credit the giver and debit the receiver). This also fits in with the rules described in Chapter 1 - the cash account is an asset and any increase in the value of an asset is recorded as a debit. To record a transfer of funds from petty cash to the bank follow the same steps but credit the cash account and debit the bank account. In this case the cash account is the giver and should be credited. Alternatively, you can view the transaction as decreasing the value of an asset and therefore to be recorded as a credit as described in Chapters 1 and 9.

What is the best way to deal with customer payments by credit card?

Start by creating separate bank accounts for each credit card company you use. Choose Bank from the Toolbar then Record. Fill in a new record card remembering to give it a nominal code in the same range as your other bank accounts (this will be a four figure number starting with 12 if you're using the Sage default chart). If you want to record transactions directly into the nominal ledger you can do so by pressing Bank, highlighting the correct credit card company, then using the Receipts option as described earlier. You will fill in the nominal code for the appropriate credit card company bank account under N/C followed by details of the transaction.

Warning

Be careful to highlight the credit card company before recording the receipt, otherwise you will mistakenly enter a receipt into your bank current account which is the default selection.

If you also want to update customer accounts you can't use the Bank option for nominal receipts and payments option. Instead you should choose Customers then Invoice or use the SOP and Invoicing options (see Chapters 7 and 8) to produce an invoice. Next press Bank and be sure to choose the correct credit card company by highlighting it before pressing Customer to record the payment using the same technique described earlier for standard bank accounts. It helps if you put the credit card name on the customer receipt screen. For example, enter VISA in the Ref box.

How do I record money received from credit card sales in my bank account records?

Press Bank then Transfer and fill in the correct credit card account code in the From box and the bank account in the To box. Fill in the amount and finish by clicking on Save.

Tip

You can reconcile your credit card statements in the same way as bank statements by highlighting the account and pressing Reconcile. Credit card companies impose charges for dealing with the transactions and you will need to use the Adjustment button to add these figures - put the nominal code 7905 (Credit Charges) together with the amount.

How should I record payments I make by credit card?

The easiest method only works if you pay your credit card bills on the due dates and in full. When the statement arrives select Bank, highlight your bank current account and press Payment. Enter each item on the statement on a separate line giving the appropriate nominal codes (for example 7505 for books). It's important to keep all the documents relating to the transactions so that you can fill in the correct amounts for VAT. For payments that you want to allocate to outstanding supplier invoices you would have to choose Bank then Supplier, select the transactions listed on the display which are also on the statement and use the Pay in Full button.

What if I don't pay the full credit card bill immediately and often pay just part?

In this case you need to treat the credit card company as a supplier by creating a supplier record (press Suppliers on the main menu then Record). This has the added advantage that you can record each credit card transaction immediately as a standard purchase invoice. When the credit card statement arrives check that there are no extra or missing transactions. If there are then add them in as purchase invoices or credit notes. If you pay the bill in full choose Bank then Suppliers, put the supplier account code for the credit card company and press the Pay in Full button for all of the transactions displayed on the screen and listed on the statement. Should you only part pay the bill, you can either press Pay in Full for just some of the transactions and make a part payment, if you wish, for some of the other items. Any interest charges should be recorded as an invoice. Give these transactions the nominal account code 7905 (credit charges).

Tip

The manual warns that the automatic feature to handle refunds and similar transactions don't adjust VAT liability. If you use VAT cash accounting use the following techniques instead. They are similar to the steps taken by the automatic features except that you can manually enter the VAT codes from the original transactions. The software just enters T9.

I'm using VAT cash accounting. How do I refund payments to customers?

You can't use the menu options to do this automatically. Instead you will have to make the refund by adjusting the figures manually. Start by creating a credit note - select Customers then click on Credit Note. If you're using the Sage default chart of accounts for the nominal ledger there is an account set up for mispostings (number 9999). Make sure you have created one if you have set up your own codes. On the credit note, enter the nominal code, amount and VAT code as on the original customer invoice (the VAT amount will be filled in automatically). If it's a part-refund, put the partial amount instead. Next create a sales invoice by selecting Customers from the Toolbar then Invoice. Fill in the mispostings code (the Sage setting is 9999) as the nominal ledger code and copy the amount and VAT code from the credit note.

Follow the customer receipts options described earlier: choose Bank from the Toolbar, then Customer. Fill in the customer code under A/C and fill in a cheque amount of zero in the Amount box. In the list of transactions you will see the credit note and the invoice you have just created. Allocate the credit note to the invoice by putting the cursor in the Paid field for both the credit note and the invoice and pressing Pay in Full.

Finally create a bank payment record by selecting Bank and then Payment. Put the nominal code for mispostings (default 9999), and copy the amount and VAT code from the invoice. It's a good idea to check the changes to nominal accounts to make sure you have taken all the necessary steps. Before starting choose Nominal from the Toolbar and check the figures in the Debtors Control and Mispostings accounts. When you finish the refund these figures should be exactly the same as when you began (Mispostings is normally set to zero).

Warning

Adjusting the figures manually for refunds is slightly complicated. Test out the procedure before working on your actual records by using a demonstration company if you have installed Multico, or by using demonstration data which you can set up and store separately from your working files (see Chapter 2 to find out how).

How do I process refunds from suppliers if I'm using VAT Cash Accounting?

Write out a credit note by selecting Suppliers from the main menu, then Credit Note. Copy the nominal code, amount (or partial amount for a part-refund) and VAT code from the original invoice. If you are not using the default Sage chart of accounts with 9999 set up for mispostings, remember to create a mispostings account before proceeding. Create a purchase invoice by selecting Suppliers from the Toolbar, then Invoice. On this you must put the code for mispostings (default 9999) as the nominal code, then copy the amount and VAT code from the credit note.

Next follow the steps for supplier payments by selecting Bank from the Toolbar, then Suppliers. Put in the code to identify the supplier. In the Amount box of the cheque put a value of zero. The credit note and invoice will be listed and allocate them to each other by placing the cursor in both Paid fields and clicking on Pay in Full. Remember to click on Save before closing this screen. Lastly create a bank receipt by choosing Bank from the Toolbar and then Receipts. Put the code for mispostings under N/C (default 9999),

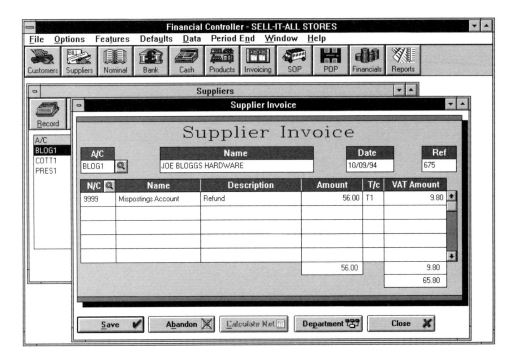

then copy the amount and VAT code from the invoice. Save and post this transaction as for normal bank receipts.

Once you have finished, you can double-check your work by looking at the figures in some of the nominal accounts. These should be checked both before and after posting all the necessary transactions. Choose Nominal from the Toolbar and make a note of the figures in the Creditors Control and Mispostings accounts before you start making adjustments. When you finish look at these figures again - they should not have changed.

How do I deal with bounced cheques from customers as I use VAT Cash Accounting?

Create a new invoice (select Customers then Invoice) and fill in the code for mispostings (9999) under N/C. Then copy the amount and VAT code from the original invoice. Make a bank payment by choosing Bank from the Toolbar then Payment. Under N/C put the code for mispostings, under description put 'returned cheque', then copy the amount and VAT code from the original invoice. If you want to check your work make a note of the figures in the Debtors Control and Mispostings accounts in the nominal ledger before and after to see that they don't change.

What if I cancel a cheque I have sent to suppliers?

If you use VAT Cash Accounting you can't use the automatic features for this procedure. You need to produce a new invoice (select Suppliers and then Invoice) with the nominal code for mispostings in the N/C field. The amount and VAT code are the same as on the original invoice. Then choose Bank followed by Receipts and fill in the nominal code for mispostings. Copy the amount and VAT code from the invoice. Finish off by checking the Creditors Control and Mispostings accounts in the nominal ledger - they should be unchanged by the transactions.

Tip

Most of these tasks can be handled automatically by Sterling +2 if you're using the standard VAT accounting method. See Chapter 5.

Contra Entries

There are quick and simple ways of making contra entries as described in Chapter 5, but there are some transactions which are slightly more complicated. A contra entry is any transaction which is posted in order to reverse another transaction. It's the technique you need to use to cancel invoices and credit notes in the sales and purchase ledgers, cash book receipts and payments, or nominal ledger journal entries. Making a contra entry to reverse the unwanted transaction will clear the transaction as if it had never existed.

Tip

You can also reverse transactions using Error Correction on Disk Doctor (see Chapter 12).

Cancelling sales invoices and receipts

If you need to cancel a sales invoice before it has been paid the contra entry will involve creating a credit note for the same amount. Select Customers, then Credit Note and copy all the details from the Invoice. Next go into the customer receipts procedure by choosing Bank from the Toolbar then Customer. Fill in the details from the original invoice but put a cheque amount of zero in the Amount box. The original invoice and the new credit note will both appear in the listing as uncleared items. You can position the cursor in the Paid field for each of them, then press Pay in Full to offset them and clear the unwanted transaction.

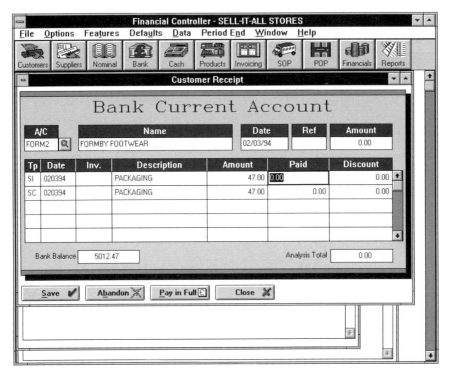

Cancelling customers' credit notes

To cancel a credit note in the sales ledger choose Customers then Invoice and write out an invoice with the same details as on the credit note. Then choose Bank from the Toolbar followed by Customers. Put the customer's account number and a cheque amount of zero. The details on both the invoice and credit note will appear - cancel them both by putting the cursor in the Paid field and pressing Pay in Full.

Cancelling invoices from suppliers

To remove an unwanted invoice, reverse it by producing a credit note of the same value. Choose Suppliers from the main menu, then Credit Note and copy the exact details from the original invoice. Select Bank from the main menu, then suppliers and fill in the supplier code and a cheque value of zero. Both transactions will be listed - position the cursor in the Paid box and press Pay in Full.

Cancelling credit notes from suppliers

Select Suppliers from the Toolbar, then Invoice and create an invoice, copying all the details from the unwanted credit note. Next choose Bank from the main menu followed by Supplier and fill in the supplier's account code and a cheque amount of zero. Locate the credit note and invoice in the list. Cancel them by putting the cursor in the Paid field and clicking on Pay in Full.

Petty cash adjustments

If you have entered payments and receipts by mistake, simply reverse the transactions using a similar contra entry technique. For receipts entered in error, select Cash from the main menu and then Payments. Fill in the cash payment display by copying the unwanted receipt and under Description explain the transaction as a cancellation. To cancel a cash book payment select Cash from the main menu and then Receipts. Fill in the information from the original payment with cancellation as the explanation in the Description field.

Warning

Don't confuse making contra entries to cancel transactions with the steps described for making refunds. Although many of the steps are the same, refunds also involve posting information to the nominal ledger to update the bank balance.

Is it possible to make contra entries when the amount I owe to suppliers is not equal to the amount they owe me?

This is not possible using the automatic features but you can do it manually if you are not using VAT Cash Accounting. To do so, you need to create a nominal account for contra entries. Choose Nominal then Record and give a code in Profit and Loss (for example 9900) and the name Contra Entries. Next choose the smaller of the two amounts owed and produce credit notes for this amount for both the supplier and customer accounts. For example, imagine that you owe a supplier £300 and, as customers, they owe you £200. Produce credit notes for both the supplier account and the customer account using Suppliers and Customers on the Toolbar, followed by Invoice. Give the nominal code 9900 for contra entries, the amount of £200 (the smaller of the two) and the tax code of T9. Next select Bank followed by Customers. Fill in the customer code and allocate the invoice against the credit note on the display by pressing Pay in Full for both. Finish by choosing Bank then Supplier and filling in the supplier code to post the amount you actually owe (the remaining £100). The display will show the original invoice and the credit note you have just produced and again you need to press Pay in Full for both of them. The cheque will automatically display the figure you owe - £100. If you have problems perhaps you forgot to put the tax code T9 on the credit notes, or you didn't make your calculation using the full amounts owed including VAT. Try it out on your demo data. Check that the Contra Entries account has a balance of zero to be sure you have taken all the right steps.

BUSINESS*guide*

The banking facilities on Sterling +2 are among the strong points of the software, so take full advantage of all the features on offer. Sage was the first accounting software company to offer bank account interest checking on a PC on their DOS version. Although users with the first release of Sterling +2 Version 2 don't have this feature it will be available as an upgrade. All businesses should be concerned about the possibility of bank error. Companies with an overdraft should check the figures carefully, as the larger the overdraft the more dramatic the excess charges will be, should the bank make a mistake.

The bank reconciliation procedure is also extremely important because comparisons of records kept by two organisations - the bank and your business - are sure to highlight any errors. The business will not know about any changes to direct debits until the statement arrives and it's vital to check that these are correct. The bank may have also made a computer error which could lead to extra money being credited or debited. The statement will also point out any input errors on your own system such as duplicated or missing records. Ask the bank to explain any transactions which are not on your records. Remember that if the bank has credited your account with too much money you will be guilty of an offence if you use these funds.

Ask the bank to send weekly statements as you will need to reconcile the account regularly. Then keep the statement as documentary evidence for your transactions. If you use funds incorrectly credited to your account, you could be found guilty of theft in court. You are responsible for checking the statement, so it's important to watch out for too much money in the bank! Sterling +2, fortunately, takes over the most complicated part of the work which is the reconciliation. Businesses without computers have endless problems with this task because of the time difference between writing and receiving cheques and having them cleared. Other transactions, such as direct debits are also extremely difficult to keep track of.

Once you have checked the statement, it's time to contact the bank if there are any errors. Double check the figures first and ask the bank for an explanation. Don't rely on the bank to put the figures right. Banks can make errors and correct them so that the final statement you receive tallies with your own records, but they may not offer compensation for any losses you have made due to the mistake. If you point out an error the bank will put it right but you need to know exactly how much compensation you are entitled to.

To work out the amount you can rightfully claim from the bank, find where errors have been made and see how much interest has been charged in excess. On the first release of Sterling +2 Version 2 you have to do this manually, when the bank interest checking feature is added, you will be able to key in the agreed rate of interest and the software will point out places where errors may have occurred. The software will also use this feature to calculate the correct amount of interest on a daily basis and as an overall total.

Should you detect excessive bank charges or interest due to bank error you can ask for this money back. You can also claim compensation transaction by transaction, for example if incorrect bank charges led to any of your cheques being bounced. The new bank interest feature will provide you with all the ammunition necessary to negotiate with the bank, and it's worth checking manually although most businesses are put off by the complex calculations involved.

The National Association of Banking Customers (NABC) ran an independent review of the bank interest checking on Sterling software and recommended it for accuracy and ease of use. The NABC is a non-profit making organisation which provides a wide range of services for a minimal annual subscription (about £10). Subscribers can use a telephone advice line for help with professional, legal and financial problems dealing with banks, building societies, credit card companies and similar businesses. If you aren't sure about how to reclaim money from the bank the NABC has a bureau service which can handle this for you.

Good banking habits

Make sure that all takings are paid into the bank as soon as possible (this should be a daily practice if you have regular takings) so that excess cash goes into the bank account immediately together with cheques and credit card vouchers. Pay credit card vouchers into the bank by adding together the total value and writing it on a single paying in slip (ask at your local bank if you want details on how to start handling credit card sales and want full instructions and all the necessary documents). Retailers shouldn't leave too much cash in the till. If it can't be banked immediately it should be kept secure in a safe overnight. Use the software to record details on cheque number and the customer involved in each transaction so that you can ask for another cheque should the first one be lost in the clearing process.

Order Processing and Stock Control

Basic stock control is handled by choosing the Products option from the Toolbar. This allows you to update the number of products in stock and maintain figures when stock is transferred in groupings to make up sets. It is important to remember that, if you have Financial Controller, the stock levels are amended automatically when you work in the sales and purchase order processing modules. When you process customer orders using SOP, stock will be allocated and then the level will, finally, be reduced when the items are sent out for delivery. Orders to suppliers using POP will increase the level of stock expected to arrive. The actual stock level will be increased when the goods are delivered. The sales and purchase order processing options are two of the most integrated parts of the system, so it's a good idea to create your invoices through sales order processing (SOP) as described later in the sales orders section. Once orders have been entered using SOP, you can use Invoicing from the Toolbar to process the invoices generated. You shouldn't produce invoices in the Sales Ledger if you want to work this way as the figures will be posted twice. The invoicing option is explained in Chapter 8.

Tip

Use the Products option to amend the figures manually after a stock take to correct errors, for example if returned items have not been recorded on the system or if stock has been lost or damaged.

Adding and removing products

If you want to add stock, select Products from the Toolbar then click on the Adjust-In button. To remove them click on Adjust-Out. On the Adjustments In/Out display leave

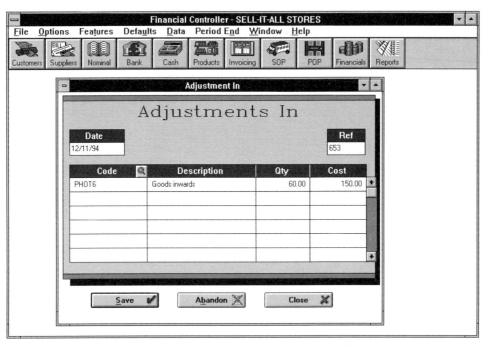

the default date (today's date) unless you need to record a different day for the amendment. The Ref field is optional, so only record information if you want to - perhaps you use documents to record stock movements and if so put the document number. In the Code field type the code number for the product; use the magnifying-glass icon to search for this if you don't know it. In the Description field enter an explanation for the adjustment, such as 'damaged' or, more generally, 'stock adjustment'. When you enter a number of transactions for the same reason this field will help by automatically retaining the description (up to 30 characters). Under Qty put the number of products to be added or removed and under Cost put the total cost price. If the price you enter is different to that on the product record this new figure will update the old one throughout the system.

Tip

If the Description field fails to copy information automatically use the Windows 'copy and paste' method. Put your cursor in the Description field you want to copy and press Control and C simultaneously. Next put the cursor in the field you want to copy into and press Control V.

Use the standard Sterling +2 methods to alter the details if you've made a mistake: move between fields by pressing TAB or point and click on the required field. To delete a whole field click on it and then press F6 to have the entire line removed. Once you're happy with the details, click on the Save button. The software will make the adjustments and a new screen will be displayed for more transactions. When you have no more adjustments in or out, click on the Close button or close the display using the standard Windows techniques.

Warning

Always click on Save for the last transaction before clicking on Close, as you will not be reminded that you are losing your work.

Transferring products

For businesses which put together products to make complete sets, the software can calculate a total cost price for the assembly. These products can then be moved either as sets or component parts. Select Products from the Toolbar then click on Transfers.

Accept the default system date unless you need a specific day for the transfer. Then enter a reference, under Ref, if you have documentation relating to the transaction (this is optional). Under Code you should give the code for the set and not the component part, unless you are recording a part which is also an assembly made from other products. Under Description, explain the posting in not more than 30 characters. Then fill in the quantity of complete sets to be added to stock. If there is a lack of component parts to make up the requested quantity, the software will recognise this and give a warning. Click on the Save button to transfer the stock and a screen will appear for more entries. When you have finished, click on Save and then the Close button. Should you have problems with the transfer click on Abandon instead and take time to recalculate the figures.

Links between stock control and other options

The information you have input on products will soon become particularly useful as you move on to sales and purchase order processing (Financial Controller only). As you start to process orders from customers, you will be able to allocate stock. As the stock levels fall you will be able to process orders to your own suppliers and keep a careful watch on the movements of products in and out of your company. Sterling +2 is a totally integrated system, so that information from each option automatically updates all the other parts of the software. From the sales order processing module you will be able to produce invoices using the customer and product records.

Tip

Remember to look at the report on customer balances from time to time to see when customers are exceeding their credit limit. You may decide to keep trading with customers who have overdue debts, but when they want to place new orders you are in a strong position to ask for payment.

Note

See Chapter 10 to check the full range of reports available to analyse your product records.

Sales and purchase order processing

Businesses with Financial Controller can use the sales and purchase order processing facilities by pressing SOP or POP on the Toolbar. These two options help keep records on customer and supplier orders for products from the time the order is placed right through to delivery. All of the records on file will be updated automatically. Select SOP to see the features available, or look at POP - most of the functions in these two options operate in the same way.

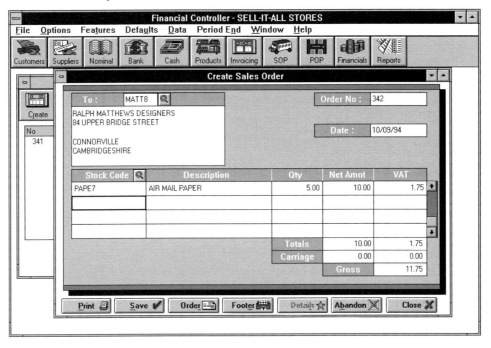

The first stage is to enter information on the order by clicking on Create. This also lets you print out the details - for your own records or to be used as a despatch note. At this stage the software can allocate items in stock to customers placing orders, so the order will update the product files for your own stock level information. It's not necessary to update the files immediately and print out the order details: you can store the record and do the update as a batch, later. You might need to delay printing out a delivery note, if you don't want to despatch all the items on order immediately. In this case there is another method (the Despatch option) which lets you specify the quantity to be sent out.

The Despatch button on the SOP menu enables you to see which orders are complete (with all the items despatched) and which have been partially delivered. This option is also used to keep a watch on outstanding orders. It lets you amend the quantities sent out so that you can try and satisfy the complete order as soon as possible. You can produce invoice records from this part of Sterling +2 - changes here will update the whole system.

Tip

When you have despatched orders, or if you need to cancel them, they can be deleted from the system (use Delete on the SOP/POP menu). To free this disk space use the Disk Doctor to compress the data files (see how in Chapter 12).

Creating orders

Choose SOP or POP from the Toolbar and the system immediately displays a list of all order records on file. The orders each have a number, creation date, account name (for the customer or supplier) and the gross amount. There is also a final field which shows the status of the order which is abbreviated in SOP to:

PART U (part despatched/unallocated)	PART (part allocated)
PART P (part despatched/part allocated)	FULL (fully allocated)
PART F (part despatched/fully allocated)	PART-CAN (part cancelled)
CANCEL (Cancelled)	COMPLETE.

For POP the status field shows:

ON ORDER	PART O (part delivered/on order)
PART-CAN (part cancelled)	CANCEL (cancelled)
COMPLETE	

Next click on Create to enter details on new orders, or highlight an existing order in the first window before clicking on Create to amend details. Make sure no unwanted existing orders are highlighted in the opening window (press the Clear button if there are any) before choosing Create. First enter the customer or supplier's code number, or click on the magnifying-glass icon to see a selection. Full details will appear if they are already on record. If you are creating an order for a new customer or supplier, fill in an unused code. Sterling +2 will display a list of existing accounts and you can complete a new record card for the sales or purchase ledger by clicking on the New button. This means you won't have to leave SOP/POP to add a new account.

The first time you create an order, it's possible to set the starting figure in the order number field. This can have up to six digits, but from then on the software will allocate a number automatically. The default is 1 - you can leave this unless you have a special reason for needing to start at a particular number (perhaps to follow on from your previous accounting system). Change the default system date if necessary, then give the stock code for the item from your product records. If you make a mistake with the product code, Sterling +2 will show you a list of existing records. You can enter an unused code then click on New to produce a new record card for the products file.

You may want to enter details on a non-stock item and Sage has set defaults for this. In the Stock Code field put S1 for non-stock products with a taxable price, or S2 if the item in non-taxable. If you only want to put text put the letter M. The next window lets you fill in all details on the ordered product. If you have put in the code for a product which is in stock, this same window appears but with the details already filled in.

If you are entering details on a non-stock product put the name of the item in the Description field, the way it is bundled for the price (e.g. single, six-pack) by Unit, any optional comments by Comment 1 and 2. You can leave the default Quantity as 1 or change it for individual orders. Enter the cost price (the price the item sells for) by Unit Price. In the Discount field put the percentage to be deducted from the net price before adding VAT. Make sure the correct VAT code is entered as this is mandatory. When placing orders for items in stock the steps are the same but many of the details will be filled in automatically.

It's important to fill in a nominal code for the product because you can generate invoices from this part of Sterling +2. You need to make sure the figures will also be posted to the nominal ledger for processing. Put the relevant account in the Nominal field (the default is 4000 or Sales Type A). You may want to analyse the order by department, in which case put the code by Department (e.g. sales department).

Tip

When entering a number of orders which all relate to the same nominal account and/or department you can use the Footer button described later in this chapter to enter this information once instead of on every record.

When you have filled in these details, the Net and VAT boxes will be updated automatically and can't be altered. Check the record and click on OK to go back to the main order screen. Your order will be added to the list on display and you are ready to fill in the next order on the following line. Enter all the orders for this customer/supplier. At the bottom of the screen the total figures for the net and VAT amounts appear as well as the overall, or gross, amount. The cost for carriage will also have to be added later using the Footer screen.

Once all of the orders have been entered, click on the Order button at the bottom of the screen. Sterling +2 lets you add extra useful information. The next window is headed Order Details. Start by giving a Customer Reference or Order Number for this particular transaction. The Phone No. field will be filled in from the records, but you can enter a different contact number for this individual order together with the person's name in the Deliver To field and the address for delivery. Fill in the expected date in the Due Delivery field, and the name of the person contacted in the Order Taken By field. There are three lines for extra notes. These can be used for any information, such as terms or even sales points, you would like to send to your customers and suppliers. Perhaps you want to tempt them to buy your latest products, in which case use these fields to advertise. When the details are all complete click on the OK button to return to the main order screen.

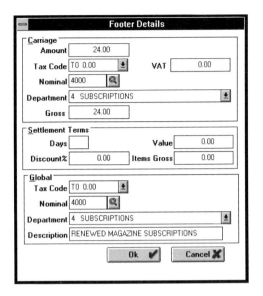

The final details for the order are entered by clicking on the Footer button at the bottom of the screen. A window appears called Footer Details. In this display fill in the cost for post, packing, transportation and insurance in the Amount box. This will appear in the Carriage column of the main order screen to be added to the gross price of the order. The figure you enter in the Amount box should be the amount for carriage before VAT. Then put the VAT code in the Tax Code box to have the overall figure calculated by the system. Fill in the nominal code and department code for analysis of the carriage amount.

In the Settlement Terms section, the Days box should only include the number of days which entitle the customer to a discount for early payment. The Discount box specifies the percentage for prompt payers. On POP these boxes should contain the settlement terms suppliers have offered you. For both SOP and POP the software will take these details automatically from the customer/supplier records.

Warning

Early settlement discounts will alter the VAT calculations.

The Global box (SOP only) is for information which is true for all the items on order, so that you don't have to repeat the same input on each order record. This is useful for orders to be analysed by the same VAT, nominal or department codes. You can put the codes here, the overall figure for the order will be posted and just one line will appear on the audit trail. It's also possible to write a description for the order in the Description box and this will be displayed on the audit trail as well as in the customer history files.

Tip

Make sure now that the nominal account code has been entered on individual order records or on the Footer screen in the Global box.

When the Footer details are complete, click on OK and return to the main screen to decide how you want to progress with the order. If you want to store the details on the order but don't want to progress any further with it for the moment, you can put it on hold by pressing Save (this is the Batch button for users of version 1). This will let you update the records throughout Sterling +2 and despatch the order together with a number of outstanding orders later on. All of the orders stored as a batch can then be printed out later - the stock levels will only be amended and allocated when this is done.

Warning

Don't press Close to exit from this window. First you must choose Print or Save, otherwise the whole order will be ignored. Press Abandon if you want to cancel the whole order.

If you want to progress with the order immediately, press Print to produce a despatch note or acknowledgement. Then you will have the opportunity to allocate stock to satisfy each order. As soon as the order details are printed, respond to the prompt to update your stock records: this will be Allocate to mark out your stock for customers, or On Order to show the levels of new products expected from suppliers. Before closing this option you can press Reprint for another copy of the order, or press Cancel to stop the process.

Tip

If you don't have enough stock to satisfy an order, the system will only allocate stock for part of the order. You will be warned as you enter the order quantity.

Sterling +2 will display a clear order entry screen each time you select Save. Only click on Close once you have completed all the above steps for each order and want to exit from this option.

Despatch and Delivery

When the process of recording orders has been completed, the software allocates stock to customers or indicates expected deliveries of new items from the suppliers. However, the actual stock levels will only be changed once you enter details on products actually despatched to customers or received from the suppliers. To do this, choose SOP or POP from the Toolbar, then select the customer or supplier by highlighting them on the list displayed and click on Despatch (SOP) or Deliveries (POP). This also lets you make enquiries into any of the orders to see how they are progressing.

Sales orders

Pressing Despatch in the SOP option will display the chosen customer's details together with all the products on order. If the screen is full, check by scrolling through to see if

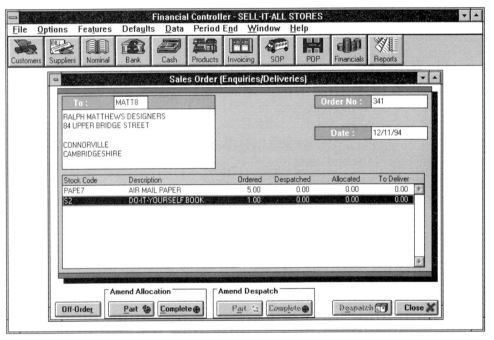

there are more items than the display can show. The products are listed by Stock Code and Description, then the window shows the total quantity Ordered, the quantity Despatched so far, the quantity of stock Allocated to the customer at the time of the order and the remaining number yet To Deliver. This screen is useful for enquiries into the order's status.

At each stage in the allocation and despatch process you will need to amend and process the information on this screen using, the buttons at the bottom. Perhaps the stock levels have changed since the date of the original order and you can allocate a different number of products - check by selecting the buttons in the Amend Allocation box. If you press the Part button a box appears showing the quantity of stock currently allocated to the customer. If you want to change this figure, do so at this point. The Allocate Stock box shows the quantity already allocated under Previous, and the total amount available for allocation is given as the default under New. Select the total to satisfy the order to the best of your ability from current stock levels, or choose a lower number, if the stock is also needed elsewhere. Click on OK to return to the main deliveries screen and press the Complete button in the Amend Allocation box to update your products files with the new allocation details. The software will prompt you to confirm your choice.

If the quantity despatched to the customer needs to be specified or later amended (check the figure in the Despatched column), click on Part in the Amend Despatch Box to see the Stock to be Despatched window. The figures here sometimes need to be changed - perhaps you want to give priority to another customer ordering the same products, or to share out scarce items between customers. Fill in the quantity in the Quantity box, then click on OK to return to the deliveries screen. Press Complete in the Amend Despatch box to send out all the allocated items to this customer.

At this point the software will prompt you to print out the delivery note. There is a second option to update your stock and invoice records. Start with the delivery note by pressing Print Delivery Note, clicking on the Printer option button and finishing with OK. If you want to look at it on screen before printing, press the Preview option button and click on OK. The delivery note will appear in miniature form, so choose Options from the menu bar and Zoom In once or twice to enlarge it (otherwise use the active buttons on the top right of the display to make the delivery note more legible).

Next choose the Stock/Invoice Update button to have your stock records adjusted. This will also generate an invoice which you can process using Invoicing from the Toolbar. The software returns you to the main sales order screen and you can see the new stock quantities in the Despatched, Allocated and To Deliver columns. At the bottom left of the screen is a button which switches between Order and Off-Order. Use this button when it is labelled Off-Order to remove any remaining items on a highlighted outstanding order - this will cancel the amount to be delivered. If part of the order has already been despatched this will cancel the remaining items to be delivered.

Tip

Just press the Despatch button at the bottom of the screen if you don't need to amend the allocation or despatch details.

The remaining two buttons are Despatch and Close. Select Despatch to arrange for the order to be delivered (if you choose Complete in the Amend Despatch box this has the same effect). The screen again offers two choices: decide if you want to print a delivery note and update the stock. You will also be given the chance to send the information to your invoicing records. Click on Print Delivery Note if you want a printout which will include the quantity of stock sent out, then press Stock/Invoice Update to transfer the information to files throughout Sterling +2. If you choose to update the stock figures the software will automatically reduce the amount of allocated items and mark them out for despatch. This button also generates an invoice and you will have to use the Invoicing facilities to print it (see Chapter 8). Once all the steps are completed click on Close, or choose Cancel if you change your mind and want the software to ignore the whole despatch record.

Purchase orders

Deliveries from suppliers are handled in a slightly different way. Start by selecting POP from the Toolbar. Then select the required supplier account by highlighting it and click on Deliveries. The items on order from this supplier are listed by Stock Code and description, then the quantity actually requested under Ordered, the quatity received so

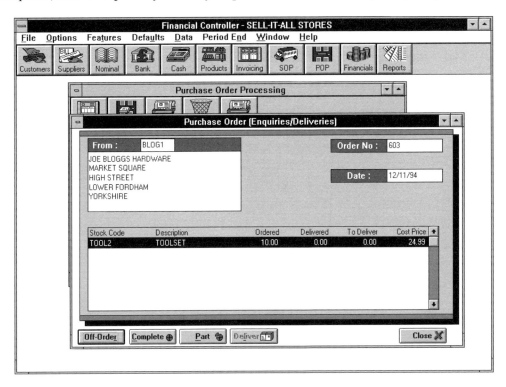

far under Delivered, the remaining number expected under To Deliver and the Cost Price.

The order can be amended using the buttons at the bottom of the screen. Press Order to change the number of items on order and the next two buttons will become functional - Complete and Part. Choose Complete to show that all the items have been delivered, or Part if only some of the order has been satisfied. When you click on Complete, a dialog box appears prompting you to confirm whether or not you want to continue and record receipt of all items on order. If you press Yes, the stock quantity on the order record goes back to zero for the To Deliver column, while the stock quantity in the Delivered column will balance the Ordered column. On the main POP screen this order will have COMPLETE in the status column.

If only some of the ordered items have arrived, you need to highlight each product line and press Part. A window headed Part Deliveries appears and you only need to alter the fields in the box headed New Deliveries. Under Quantity enter the quantity which has arrived and the software will automatically update all the other fields. When you are happy with the details, click on OK to update your records. Press Cancel if you are in any doubt and want to rethink the whole delivery record. Finish by pressing the Deliver button on the main purchase order screen.

Tip

When the Order button switches to Off-Order you can highlight an order line and press this button to cancel all remaining items to be delivered. The main screen will show CANCEL or PART-CAN as the order status.

Batch updating

If you chose to create orders and store them using the Save button, you can now print out all the details and update stock records for all of them at the same time. From the main SOP or POP screen, select the orders you want to include and then press Print Batch. If some orders are highlighted that you don't want to include, press Clear to remove all highlighted lines or click on the highlighted line to de-select it. If you want to select most of the orders then highlight the ones you don't want and press Swap to reverse your choice. Remember that the Criteria button can be used to let you specify records so that the software will automatically select the right ones (see the selecting records section of Chapter 4). To print out all orders stored via Save, don't highlight anything and the software will find and process them all.

When you press Print Batch the software will print out your order acknowledgements (SOP) and order copies (POP) using the standard Sage stationery layouts or any new designs you have created. At this point you may want to update stock records and the software will prompt you to do so. In POP the prompt will ask if you want to put any outstanding stock on order. If you choose Yes, the On Order field in your product records will be updated. In SOP the prompt will ask if you want to allocate any outstanding stock. So choose Yes if you want to update your stock files with this new order information. Choose Despatch from the main SOP display, or Deliveries from the main POP window to finish processing the orders. There is also a Reprint option for a second copy of the order details. You can also escape without processing the orders by selecting Cancel.

Removing orders

The main SOP and POP screens have the popular Windows dustbin as the fourth choice. This is the way to get rid of unwanted order records. Perhaps a current order needs to be cancelled, or perhaps the goods have been delivered and you want to delete the information. To do so you must first select all the relevant orders in the main display then press Delete and reply to the system prompt confirming that these records should be removed. The window will then appear with the reduced list of orders.

Warning

If you're using the Swap and Criteria buttons to select orders make sure no wanted records are mistakenly deleted.

Tip

Keep the records tidy by deleting unwanted orders regularly. Then compress the data files using the Disk Doctor to free disk space (see the compress files section Chapter 12).

Standard reports

Choose SOP or POP from the Toolbar followed by Report to see a list of the standard reports available to analyse your sales and purchase order processing records. For SOP the choice is Back Orders, Despatched Orders and Outstanding Orders. Choose by highlighting the required one, pressing the option button for Printer, Display, Preview or File and finishing with Run. Back Orders shows all the orders on record which still have outstanding items which can't be satisfied by your current stock levels. Despatched Orders gives information on orders which you have processed using the Despatch facilities, and Outstanding Orders lists all sales orders which include items awaiting delivery processing. The POP reports include Delivered Orders which shows all orders you have already processed using the Deliveries functions and Outstanding Orders which lists all orders with items not yet delivered.

Q&A

What can I do if I mistakenly delete orders?

It's important to keep regular backups of data so that you can retrieve this type of vital business information should it be lost by accidental deletion or computer error. Backup and Restore are explained in Chapter 11 and you should use them to back up your accounting data at least once a day. Keep printouts of all documentation produced through SOP or POP - you will be able to copy order details back onto the computer, if the work was done after your last backup. Should the computer fail you will also be able to keep working using the printouts until you can access the software records again.

I like to use my own business stationery. Can I do this for order processing as well as for standard documents like invoices and letters?

All of the business forms used on Sterling +2 can be redesigned to suit your own stationery layouts and particular business requirements. Refer back to Chapter 5 to find the right file for each type of document and to see how to redesign layouts using Windows Write.

Do I need to keep the documents produced through SOP and POP as the information is all stored on computer anyway?

It's essential to keep all the related documents together. They provide the evidence you need in case of legal dispute with your customers or suppliers. Make sure customers sign for products when they are delivered. When you receive goods from the supplier only sign for receipt if you have checked that everything on the delivery note is included and not damaged. If you have to sign quickly, add a note to say the goods have been signed for unchecked.

What is the best way to keep an eye on my stock levels to see when I need to re-order products?

If you have Accountant Plus or Financial Controller, the number of reports available to keep a careful check on stock is impressive (choose Products from the Toolbar then Report and scroll down through the full list). The Reorder Levels report is one of the most useful for your needs as it tells you the current stock level, the quantity allocated to customers, the quantity on order from suppliers and the last quantity purchased. At the top of the list is the Details report which gives the quantity in stock, the quantity on order and the quantities allocated. Choose the products you want to look at using the standard record selection techniques described in Chapter 4. You can also use Criteria to find out of stock products by specifying an amount equal to zero for the Qty In Stock Field. Use these reports together with analysis reports available from within SOP and POP to get a complete picture of your purchasing needs. Choose SOP, then Report and choose Back Orders to see how many outstanding items have been ordered by your customers. Then press POP, Report and Outstanding Orders to find which suppliers you can contact to speed up delivery of the required goods.

How can I find out which products have been selling badly?

One quick method is to use Criteria to select the relevant products (see the section on selecting records in Chapter 4). Specify criteria to select products with a last sale date old enough to indicate they are no longer worth stocking. In Chapter 9 you will find more details on how to generate your own reports for customised analysis of the records.

Note

Sterling +2 doesn't automatically update the opening and closing stock accounts in the nominal ledger. The stock value on the balance sheet will not be updated unless you make manual adjustments. See the Questions and Answers in Chapter 11 to find out how.

Credit Control and Invoicing

One of the main benefits of computerising the accounts for businesses which sell on credit is that it's much easier to keep a close watch on debtors - to make sure they pay their bills as quickly as possible. For the credit controller there are many ways in which Sterling +2 can help to identify and remind late payers. It's a good idea to take a look at each part of the system that facilitates credit control, to see how you should be making constant checks on your debtors. The main methods to remember are: checking the account histories which list all transactions, printing out the balance report which will show the age of the debts and making on-screen enquiries to see the analysis of aged debts. Once the culprits have been singled out, the standard overdue letter can be sent as a reminder. Generally letters are sent in three stages showing increased urgency as more time elapses. There is also the option to print out statements to ensure customers are always aware of their responsibility to make due payments.

To make sure the whole credit control function works well you should start the process each time you input details on a new customer. At this point you should fill in the customer record with the correct credit limit. Perhaps you want to offer no credit at first but start to offer a growing level of credit as time passes and confidence increases. So long as you put all of this information in the customer records, the system will be able to point out when credit limits are being exceeded. It's also important to enter the correct date for transactions for aged debt analysis. This will only be possible for all debts if you input each transaction separately when you start working on Sterling +2. Make sure that the customer has been told about the credit limits on offer before you start to trade. Good customer relations require that both sides are aware of the conditions and have agreed to abide by them.

Reports and enquiries

Account balances can be checked by choosing Customers from the main menu, then Report, highlighting Balances in the box, clicking on Printer or Display, and pressing Run. Users of Version 2 onwards can also press Preview and Run to see the report as it will appear on the printout. Press Options on the menu bar and Zoom In to enlarge the document and make it legible. The balances report option is available from Suppliers, Nominal and Customers on the Toolbar. To avoid having to send out reminder letters make sure you are sending statements so that customers know exactly what they need to pay - these can be sent monthly or at different periods to selected customers or to all accounts. With Sterling +2 you can also attach a remittance advice note to the statement and this can then be returned with the payment. The remittance advice is also useful as it shows which transactions are included in the statement and relate to the customer's payment.

For the credit controller the aged debt analysis enquiry screen provides the most useful information. View it by choosing Customers from the Toolbar, Activity on the Customers menu, then the Aged button. A full list of customers appears with the balance and the amount for debts which are 30, 60 and 90 days old with a column for older debts. This

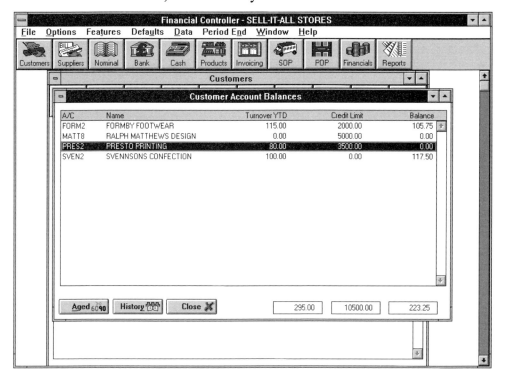

fits neatly onto the screen with no need to scroll across, so it's a better on-screen enquiry than the balances report. The credit limit for each customer can then be checked by choosing Customers and then Activity as this display shows the Turnover, Credit Limit and Balance for all accounts.

The aged debt analysis is a quick on-screen enquiry which can't be printed out. To take a closer look by producing a printer report, you should choose the balances report described earlier. This includes all the details on the aged debt analysis screen. If you choose to view this report, remember to scroll right to see the parts which don't fit on the display by pressing the scroll arrows. Single out the tardy payers on both the on-screen enquiry and the balances report by checking for asterisks between the Turnover and Credit Limit columns on the balances report, or after the account code and name on Activity screen displays.

If you don't want to look at all the customer accounts, use the Criteria button to select the ones you wish to check before clicking on Report, Balances, Printer and Run. This might be useful, for example to select customers with a specific balance. If you already know which customers you want to look at in detail it's best to highlight them before running the report so that the information given is limited to just what you need.

Statements

To produce a statement, choose Customers from the main menu, then click on Statement. This will let you fill in the specifications for statements which can then be sent straight away or stored for future use. The standard design works perfectly with Sage stationery, so choose this unless you want to design your own documentation. Again you can specify the accounts using Criteria or other record selection techniques (unless you want to include all the customers on file) before you click on Statement.

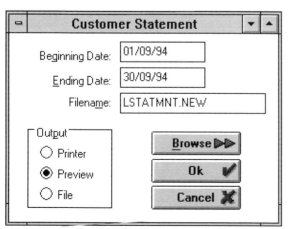

The Customer Statement box is quite simple to use - just fill in the start and end dates for the statement and choose the method of output. Select Printer (making sure you have put in the correct stationery) to print out the statements. Choose Display to view them first, or click on File to store them until later. Version 2 added the extra Preview option which is set as a default to prompt you to look at the documents as they will appear on paper, before printing them out. The default start date is the beginning of the financial year - as you continue to send statements each one will print out the brought forward balance up until the date of the current statement. The default end date is the system date (today's date) which you may leave or amend. Click on OK to produce the statements, or abandon the whole process by pressing Cancel. Press Browse to choose a different layout - the one you select here by highlighting and clicking on OK will become the default.

Tip

The statements are designed to fit window envelopes, but keep the Criteria used for selecting accounts and use them to produce labels if you're using plain envelopes (see the labels section in Chapter 5).

Reminder letters

In Chapter 5 you looked at the standard letters available by choosing Customers then Letter, then Browse. The main one for credit control is called Overdue. Highlight it in the box and press OK to select it. Next click on Preview and press Run to take a look at it as it appears to customers (you will need to enlarge it by pressing Options and then Zoom In or the active button by the page number box). The letter states that the customer owes an amount of zero - this figure will be automatically calculated on the actual printed document. You will probably want to alter this letter to suit your particular needs, and to do so click on Edit instead of Run. This time it will appear with all the variables enclosed in curly brackets, including the customer's address and the amounts owed. Notice that the amount owed is taken from the 30-days column. You will want to change this to 60 or 90 days for older debts - alternatively create extra letters for these older debts as described in Chapter 5. Remember that you can insert variables automatically by choosing Edit from the menu bar when the document is displayed and selecting Variables from the pull-down menu.

Warning

Before editing the standard letter, take a copy of the text and all variables, in case you need to revert to the original. Don't accidentally delete the original letter when deleting other letters of your own creation - it's irretrievable and easily lost!

Use the Criteria option or other record selection methods to choose the customers to receive reminder letters. Then choose Letter and Browse, highlight the standard letter or one you have created in the box and press OK. Check your letter-writing stationery is loaded in the printer, click on the Printer option button and press Run. Use the Criteria set up to select customers to print out labels, if this is how you address your envelopes.

Invoicing

Accountant Plus and Financial Controller have an option called Invoicing on the main menu. This may seem slightly confusing if you are already familiar with the sales and purchase ledger method of entering invoices and credit notes. These are alternative methods of doing exactly the same thing. It's particularly important not to use both methods of entering invoices as the data will be duplicated. The Invoicing option is the best approach as it lets you print out invoices on plain or pre-printed stationery. It is more integrated with the whole system in that it automatically updates the stock levels. Invoicing also updates the sales and nominal ledgers, so it provides the most complete approach. If you have Accountant Plus, it's best to enter invoices using Invoicing on the Toolbar. If you have Financial Controller, use the SOP first (as described in Chapter 7) because this integrates invoice generation with stock control and order processing. If you are using sales order processing (SOP on the main menu) to enter details on orders from customers, you will have already typed in the data which will be used to generate invoices. Alternatively (if you have Accountant Plus) you can use Invoicing to type in all the details - the customer's name and address, the products with their prices and the total amount being charged. Finish by printing out the document. Although the default settings fit Sage stationery you can, with practice, design your own layouts as described in Chapter 5. Print out the invoices as you create them or save them to print out as a batch later.

There are a variety of ways to produce invoices and credit notes using the Invoicing option. It's possible to use invoice items in stock and also products which are not recorded in the files. Sometimes you might just want to put text on the invoice rather than a product name, for example when charging for a service. This can also be done. For Financial Controller users this has been covered in Chapter 7 on order processing, as you will have generated invoices already using the SOP facilities and will only need to print them using Invoicing. To produce invoices from scratch using the Invoicing option Accountant Plus users will employ similar techniques to those offered by the SOP functions.

The Invoicing option can also be used to amend invoices and credit notes so long as the postings haven't yet been made to the ledgers. Those created during sales order processing using SOP from the Toolbar can't be changed in this way, as they will have already been posted. If you already have a set of numbers for invoices prior to using Sterling +2, you can start the sequence of numbers for invoices and credit notes to follow on where your old method left off. Just change the default start number of 1 and the software will then automatically number subsequent transactions. When entering details on an invoice or credit note, you will also be able to create a new customer record (if this is the first time you are entering a transaction for the account).You can also add memo information such as the address for delivery and other useful facts about the trading arrangements.

The Invoicing option lets you enter all the invoice details, including the customer and list of goods/services on order. There is also a Payment button on the Customer Invoice screen to record when the transaction has been settled. The invoices may be analysed for tax, department and nominal codes. If all the items on the invoice you are about to enter are for the same codes then enter these once on the Footer screen (described later) to save repetitive input.

Creating invoices and credit notes

To enter invoices select Invoicing from the Toolbar. The first screen will list all current invoices and credit notes held on file by number, date, account name and total amount. At the beginning of each line is a code to show the type of transaction involved. These comprise stock invoices (Inv), credit notes (Cre) and service invoices (Ser). If you want to look at an existing invoice or credit note, you need to highlight it. To create a new one make sure all the records are de-selected (press Clear if any are highlighted).

The Invoicing menu gives three options for entering transactions: Invoice for products in stock and non-stock goods, Credit Note for returned goods, or Service to produce an invoice for services rather than products. The Invoice option will help by taking details automatically from the product files, filling in the information and performing many of the calculations for you if the item is recorded in stock.

The Invoice button is used to enter invoices, but press the Credit Note button to see an identical screen for the reverse transaction. Both use the same techniques - when the transactions are posted to the ledgers, the software will automatically find out if there are enough stocks to meet the demand. Sterling +2 doesn't post the invoices if the stock level is too low to satisfy all the orders. You will be warned that there is not enough unallocated product when you fill in the quantity field.

Tip

After entering a number of invoices and pressing Update or Print Batch, check your audit trail to see that all of the transactions have been posted.

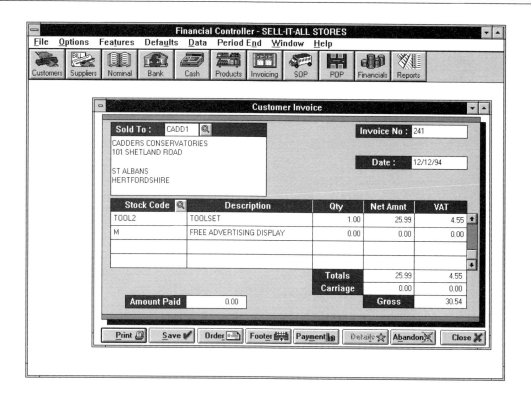

The Invoice button method of entering invoices helps you - in that you just put the customer code, the Stock Code for the product and the quantity ordered and the software will fill in all the amounts using the details set up in the product records. However, you can change any of the data filled in automatically. For example, amend the cost if you notice the price has since changed or want to alter it just for this invoice. If the price has changed remember to alter the product record as well because this won't be done by the software. Products not yet entered on the system can also be included on invoices using this option; just enter a new product code and the software will prompt you to fill in a new stock record card. There are special codes which you can enter if the product is non-stock and you don't want to add it to your records. Once the invoice or credit note is complete, the product records can be updated and marked with 'goods out' or 'goods returned' information. This may be done after each invoice or credit note is produced, or save the transactions to update the stock records as a batch at the end.

To fill in the invoice/credit note, put the customer account code in the Sold To field (or Credit on the credit note display). The name and address will be filled in for you. If unsure use the magnifying-glass icon to search for the correct account. By Invoice No or Credit No leave the default of 1 or put the next number following on from your pre-Sage days. After the first transaction, the software automatically provides the subsequent number each time you create an invoice - try not to change this number manually. This field allows up to six digits, but unless you have a reason to set a new number just leave the default. Today's date will appear as a default and can be changed - remember that this is also the tax date for the transaction.

Tip

You will be warned if a customer is over the credit limit, and by how much, when you start entering a new invoice.

Next, fill in details on the products ordered by typing the Stock Code for each item - again, if unsure, click on the magnifying-glass icon to see a list. Once a stock code has been entered the software will automatically provide the details for products recorded in the files - you only need to fill in the quantity. To add a new product to the files at the

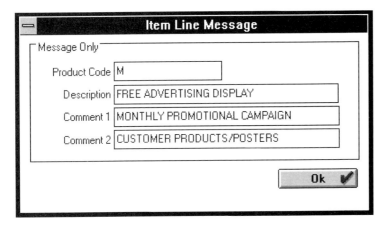

same time, enter the new code and respond to the prompt to fill in a stock record card. If you want to enter text then put the letter M as the stock code (this lets you type in a message). For a non-stock product type S1 if it is taxable, or S2 if it's zero rated. In all cases a pop-up window prompts for more information.

If you want to amend the product details for stock items on this invoice click on the Details button. A pop-up window appears with the heading Product Item Line and all the recorded data for the product code you have chosen. This same window appears with blank fields for you to complete, if you entered the codes S1 or S2. You can change the details for items in stock by altering the fields on this display. Add any comments which you want to appear as free text to complement the description. Put the total quantity of products (the default is 1) and see the amounts fields at the bottom change accordingly. The Unit Price will be taken from the product record. You can change this for individual invoices, but if you want to amend all the files you will also have to change the product files from product options. The Discount field lets you give a reduction on this one item on the invoice. VAT will then be applied to the price after the discount is taken off.

The fields for the VAT, Nominal and Department codes can be filled in individually or using the Footer screen later. The Footer screen lets you analyse all items on an invoice to the same code for each of these areas. If each item has a different code then fill in the VAT field (click on the arrow at the end of the line to see the choices and refer to your configuration settings in Chapter 3 for a full explanation of the codes). The nominal code taken from the product record can be left unchanged, or use the magnifying-glass icon to select another one - if you need separate codes for each item. The department field can also be changed, even if there is a default department on the product record. You can click on the arrow to see your complete selection.

The Net and VAT amounts are calculated by the software and can't be changed. Once all the details are entered correctly, click on OK to return to the invoice/credit note. At the bottom of the invoice/credit note screen the totals will be added up as you enter transactions. These include the Net and VAT amounts after discounts and the amount paid if there has been a prepayment. The Carriage field will be filled in once you complete the Footer screen and this will be added to the other amounts for the overall Gross figure.

Once all the items on the invoice/credit note are complete, click on Order and fill in the pop-up window with further details on the customer. In the Order No field, accept the default. The customer order number which you have been quoting for their use in relation to this transaction goes in the second field. The customer's phone number will be taken from customer files if they have provided one. You probably need to fill in a name and address for delivery of the goods as this can vary. Three lines of free text can be entered by Notes 1, 2 and 3 to keep your customers informed about your latest products and services or agreed terms. Press OK to go back to the main screen.

The final details need to be input by choosing Footer and this displays another pop-up window. This screen lets you type in the all-important Carriage details. Put the amount excluding VAT as this will be added by the software. Put in the Tax code (click on the arrow to see a list) - the amount will be calculated and appears in the VAT box. Then enter the nominal code for carriage, using the magnifying-glass icon to help search for the relevant account. If you also want to analyse the carriage by department you can fill in this field - there is an arrow to click on for a complete selection.

The Settlement Terms box is for those customers who have been offered a discount for early payment. Enter the percentage on offer in the Discount % field. In the Days field enter the length of time which counts as early payment. The Global box lets you fill in tax, nominal and department codes just once so that all items on the invoice/credit note will be analysed to the same code in each of these areas. In this case you should also fill in the Description field as an explanation, because this will appear on the account histories and audit trail to help you make sense of the figures. Finish by pressing OK.

If the customer has made a prepayment on account you can also record this by choosing the Payment button. A small pop-up window prompts for the details so fill in the amount being paid against the invoice in the Amount Paid field. The Reference should help you link the transaction to the actual payment, so it could be the cheque number (but only up to 6 characters). Press the OK button and the prepayment details will be posted at the same time as the invoice. The amount will be allocated to the invoice automatically if it is a full payment, otherwise it will only be part paid.

Warning

Don't try to post a prepayment which is greater than the amount of the invoice. When you try to save the invoice you will not be able to without changing this field.

Printing invoices/credit notes

As already mentioned, all of the invoices and credit notes you are creating can be stored in a batch to be printed out later by pressing the Save button - this also means you are delaying updating the ledgers. When you decide to print out the stored documents, select them on the main Invoicing window (or make sure none are selected to have all outstanding invoices and credit notes printed), then press the Print Batch button. If you want to print out all invoices/credit notes immediately and have the chance to update the ledgers then press the Printer option and OK. Whether you print the invoices as a batch or individually the software will always prompt you with a dialog box to see if you want to update the ledgers and the stock levels - if you want to, choose Yes.

When you press Print Batch, there will be an opportunity to change between different invoice layouts, if you click on Browse and select a different file. The file you choose will become the default. In this way you could also select an invoice layout you have designed using the techniques described in Chapter 5.

Tip

Use the Abandon button to cancel all the details on the invoice you are entering, if you are unsure, so it won't be saved or printed.

Invoicing services

If your company offers services you will need to write invoices with more textual explanations - perhaps the message facility on the standard invoices is not enough. Even if you do generally sell products you may also need to invoice for repairs, time or labour. In this case you should use the service invoice option which will let you write up to five lines of 30 characters in free text. For each textual description you will have to give a price, a nominal code and a VAT rate. Alternatively, the nominal and VAT codes can be set at the end - if all the services on an invoice are to be analysed to the same ones.

From the main menu choose Invoicing then select Service and fill in the customer account code in the same way as you did for stock invoices. Fill in the services you are charging for under Details. These fields will take up to 150 characters of free text although not all of the text appears on screen when you move to the next line. Put the price in the Net Amnt field and the software will use the default setting for tax, nominal and department codes. If you want to change any of these settings later, you must press Save to put the invoice on file, then on the main Invoicing window choose it and press Service to process it further. Now the Details button is active, so press it to alter the settings for tax or nominal codes or department for each line on the invoice. Finish off the invoice from the Footer box, by entering the payment and order information in exactly the same way as on stock invoices. Print the invoices and update ledgers as you did for stock invoices.

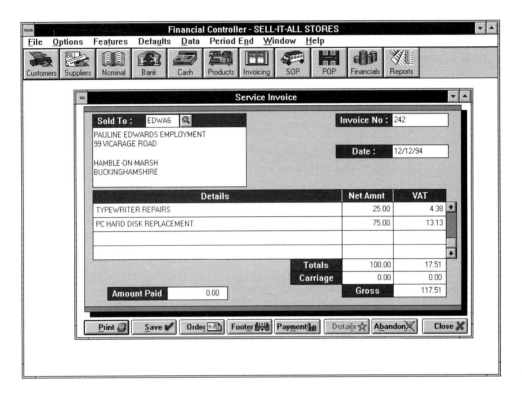

Q&A

I want to use my own invoice stationery. How can I do this?

It is possible to design your own invoice layouts and perhaps miss out some of the information included on the Sage default designs. The Sage files including the default designs are called INVTEXT.LYT for service invoices and INVOICE. LYT for stock invoices (the new layouts are LINVTEXT. NEW and LINVOICE.NEW). Make sure you keep a copy of the original files before amending them or creating your own so that if anything goes wrong you can always use the Sage designs. Refer to Chapter 5 for full details on redesigning documents and copying Sage's original files.

How do I post transactions recorded on the invoices to the ledgers? I printed them out but chose not to respond to the prompt and update the ledgers immediately.

From the Invoicing option you can update the sales and nominal ledgers by selecting all the invoices and credit notes which need to be processed and then clicking on the Update button. Highlight the invoices and credit notes from the list by clicking on them or using the Swap and Criteria selection methods, or press Clear to make sure no records are highlighted and the software will automatically choose all the ones which have not yet been posted if you make no selections. Once you click on Update the posted transactions will be marked with a Y in the Post column in the main Invoicing display window. Sterling +2 will also produce a report to give details on all the transactions so you need to confirm you want to update the ledgers and also choose where you want to have the report output. Keep an eye on the main Invoicing window to make sure outstanding transactions are eventually printed out and posted - there should be a Y in both columns.

Can I remove invoices and credit notes if they have been entered in error? How do I remove them from the Invoicing window once they are printed and posted to the ledgers?

Invoices and credit notes can be deleted, but if they have been posted to the ledgers in error you will also have to adjust the figures manually. To remove unwanted invoices and credit notes simply highlight them and click on the Delete button then confirm your decision. When you delete records in this way remember that you should periodically use Disk Doctor to free the disk space. The Disk Doctor Error Correction facilities can also be used to cancel transactions (find out how in Chapter 12). You can use the Delete button to remove invoices to clear the main Invoicing window, but make sure they have been printed and posted to the ledgers first. If you try to delete an invoice which has not been printed or posted the software will give you a warning before continuing.

I often have to create invoices with exactly the same details. Can I store a model invoice to be re-used time after time?

Sterling +2 lets you 'memorise' invoices and then recall them either to use exactly as they are, or with a few alterations. To use this function you must first load the invoice you want to store, press Features on the menu bar and choose Invoice Features from the pull-down menu. From the next submenu, select Memorise and the software will display a dialog box headed Memorise Entry. In the Invoice Name field put a name of up to seven letters for the file. In the Invoice Description field you can enter up to 29 characters to help you identify the invoice in future. Click on Save to store the invoice file, or Cancel to erase it. When you want to use the model invoice choose Features, Invoice Features and Recall. The software displays all the invoice files by name and description so you can highlight the one you need and press OK. The model invoice will be given the next invoice number and the system date so you can work to amend it or use it as it stands. To remove stored invoices press Features, Invoice Features and Recall. Highlight the invoice you no longer need and press Delete.

BUSINESS*guide*

Sterling +2 offers many facilities to help you with credit control. However, it's important to plan your policy in advance in order to make the system work for you. Decide early on if you want to offer credit and under what conditions, as well as whether or not you want to offer discounts for early payment. Many businesses, particularly retailers, are under no obligation to offer credit apart from the standard credit card option of payment. If, however, your company is competing against others which offer credit it's important to do the same and to plan carefully.

When a customer applies for credit you will need to establish whether or not they are creditworthy. This is done by getting bank and trade references, making a check through the trade protection societies and making your own investigations. Another tactic is to offer no credit at first and then to gradually increase credit as the customer proves to be a reliable payer. When you provide credit facilities you need to also set the length of time and the total amount you are willing to allow.

The best way to establish creditworthiness is to prepare standard letters and forms asking customers for the necessary information. You will need to ask for the banker's name and address together with full details of the accounts. In addition customers should provide two trade references from suppliers who give them credit. The final question should be how much credit the customer requires both as a maximum figure and on a monthly basis.

A typical credit application form should ask for the company name, address, phone and fax numbers, and the nature of business. You should also ask for the company registration number and VAT registration number, how many years the business has been established and the name and position of your contact. At the end of the form, write a short declaration for the applicant to sign which will authorise you to contact the bank and trade referees. When the form comes back, send a copy to the customer's headquarters to make sure your contact is in a position of authority.

Prepare additional forms and letters which you will need to use in order to follow up the customers' applications for credit. You will need a standard letter to your own bank asking them to contact the customer's bank for a reference. The other standard letters are for you to send to the trade referees and then to the customer to inform them whether or not they have been allowed credit. Keep a close eye on these communications. If people don't reply, then phone them - a verbal reference is just as good as a written one. Keep all documents together for each customer and file them in alphabetical order for easy reference.

Until the creditworthiness of your customer is established, you need to decide your terms for payment. These could be cash with the order (best for you but unpopular with customers), cash before shipment, or the more usual cash on delivery. If you are providing customised goods which you can only sell to this customer, you could ask for part payment in advance and the rest on delivery.

For all your customers you will need to work out payment terms and methods. The choices are: net monthly; which lets the customer pay at the end of the month following delivery; net 30 days; which is better for you but you may find most customers work on a batch system and pay at the end of the month anyway; shorter periods if this is common in your type of business; or stage payments; which you can allow for large order values or contract work. Payment can be made by cheque, direct debit or bank transfers (contact your bank for the necessary documentation).

Only offer discounts if you feel they will attract business by making your company more competitive. An early settlement discount is only given for early payment, and this may be attractive to you if you need to improve your cash flow. The discount must make it more appealing for the customer to pay the debt rather than to leave their money in a deposit account, so check the changing bank interest rates. The main problem with offering discounts is that customers tend to pay late and take the discount anyway!

It's important to be efficient at sending out invoices and recording all customer payments immediately so that your customer balances and aged debts reports are up-to-date. If a customer with a good record for paying is exceeding the credit limit, it probably means it's time to extend their credit limit. Watch out for this and don't penalise them too hastily. Sterling +2 lets you send out statements as well as invoices and you should do this monthly. Many customers don't pay individual invoices but wait for the statement to arrive.

If you have used Sterling +2 to the full to monitor and resolve the credit situation and the customer still does not pay, it's time to send reminder statements and the standard overdue debt letters. As the debt ages you will also need to phone to find out the customer's explanation. A visit, if practical, often results in speeding up the payment as it can eliminate excuses such as 'The cheque is in the post'. Debt collecting agencies and legal action are the final resort should all else fail, as these generally mean an end to this particular trading relationship.

Make sure you have all the necessary information to hand when you phone an overdue debtor. At this point you will be glad to have kept all the documentation neatly filed.

Sterling +2 running near the phone will also provide the necessary data for discussion. Be polite and try to establish the reason for non-payment - usually the customer will try to delay by saying the invoice didn't arrive. Use the fax facilities immediately to overcome this excuse then phone back and try to confirm a date for payment. If the excuse is that they are sending cheques which get lost in the post a surprise visit may result in immediate payment.

If you need to keep phoning and excuses are repeated, it's time to worry. It's best if the customer admits to financial difficulties as you can ask for a part payment (which is better than nothing) and can gain a full understanding of the situation. Perhaps they are waiting for a large payment from one of their main customers, in which case it's worth waiting - if their business is important to you. Any further sales should be on cash-only basis and you need to watch carefully to make sure the remainder of the overdue payment is made up as soon as possible.

Some customers just have a policy of delaying payment as long as possible. In this case you need to chase them for payment and decide if they are important enough to your business. One of the best ways to handle these late payers is to stop fulfilling their orders - this may be unavoidable if the level of the debt is getting too high and you can't risk letting it increase. Inform the customer of the situation, suspend any current orders and make sure all your staff know what is happening. If you then add the word STOP after the contact name on the customer account record you can create a report using the report generator to keep a list of all such customers. Call the report Stop List and have two columns: Account Reference and Account Name. Use selection criteria to find the text STOP in the Contact field (see Chapter 10 to find out how the Report Generator works).

Use a debt collection agency only as a final step as this will definitely mean an end to friendly relations. You can make a small claim yourself through the County Court without paying a solicitor. This is inexpensive and only involves getting a form and sending it to the County Court in the debtor's area. Often, the threat of legal action is enough to encourage immediate payment unless there is serious financial difficulty. For large amounts you will need to employ a solicitor who will arrange a High Court writ. The defendant must pay within 14 days of being served with the writ, or the case will go to court. In the past there was a limit to the amount you could claim yourself by filling in a form at the County Court. Legislation in recent years has changed this. There is no longer a limit, but you may be advised by the County Court to employ a solicitor for large amounts where the case may be complicated.

CHAPTER 9

The Nominal ledger and VAT

At the heart of any accounting system is the nominal ledger which can seem a little awe-inspiring to those without expertise in accountancy. The nominal ledger is the centre of all bookkeeping. Transactions from other ledgers are all recorded here together with every other item of income or expenditure. Debits and credits from other ledgers are given control accounts in the nominal ledger and there are also accounts for assets and liabilities. If you are keeping your accounts correctly, all the debits should come to the same total as the credits. This will be reflected in the trial balance report. Any figures which can't be reconciled will be put in the suspense account - so check this to see that all of your transactions are being processed in the right way. The suspense account should have a balance of zero.

In the nominal ledger all the transactions involving sales to customers will be tidied into one account - the debtors control account. All the payments you need to make to suppliers will be put together in the creditors control account. In this way, the nominal ledger takes the software's calculations on all of your transactions so that you can keep a careful watch on the figures and prepare the final accounts at the end of the financial year.

Tip

See the Business Guide in Chapter 12 to find out how to prepare your final accounts.

At times you will have to work directly on the nominal ledger to enter details on transactions which will not be posted to the sales and purchase ledgers. For example, you might need to make journal entries to record details on depreciation, prepayments and accruals (all of these will be described in detail so don't worry if you're unsure what they mean). You have already learnt how to make journal entries when you set up Sterling +2 and needed to make a reverse journal entry to set all the account codes to zero. Journal entries were also described in Chapter 6 to show how to refund money by making contra entries and recording the information in the nominal mispostings account. Nominal ledger journal entries are also necessary when you have to make adjustments to accounts. At month or year end you may need to change opening or closing balances of stock and other amounts in order to correct mistakes, or to record loss or damage.

Journal entries

From the Toolbar choose Nominal then press Journals and in the Ref field put a meaningful reference number, from your method of working, with a maximum of 6 characters. The system date appears as a default, but it's important to put a date which will make Sterling +2 process each transaction in the correct accounting period. Choose a date which will enable the software to set the journal entry in the right period so that your period totals will be correct.

Tip

When making journal entries remember that a credit must have an equal debit figure. Any number of entries on the credit side can be made to balance the debit amount, i.e. one journal entry as a debit can be made to equal the total from several credit entries or vice-versa.

The Balance box at the top of the display shows the amount you need to add to make the debits equal the credits. Once the journal entry has been made correctly this box should show a zero balance and you should be able to post the transaction. In the N/C field you should put the nominal codes for the accounts you are debiting and crediting. You can use the finder to help you select or create new codes, if you need to set up another account.

Imagine you want to draw some money from the bank to put into your petty cash box. The N/C would be 1200 for your bank current account, the description would be For Petty Cash, the T/c would be the VAT code T9 and the figure would be entered in the Credit box. On the next line enter the N/C of 1230 for the Cash account, enter the Description as From Bank, the T/c T9 and the equivalent figure in the Debit box. The

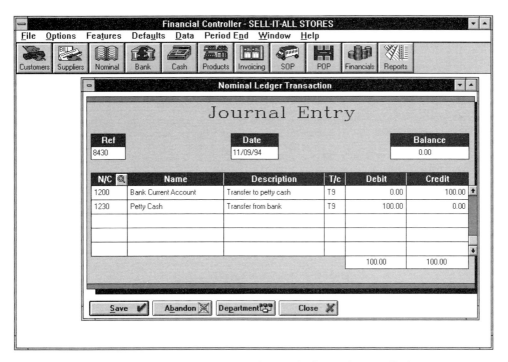

Description field takes up to 30 characters - although these don't all show at once on the screen. The tax code is usually T9 as journal entries record movements of figures between nominal accounts so VAT does not apply. If you do need to enter VAT, you can't do this by entering a different tax code - you can only do this by recording a journal entry for the VAT control account (2202).

Tip

If you want to copy the information in the Description field without re-typing it, simply put the cursor in the field you want to copy and press the Control and C keys simultaneously. Next put the cursor in the field where you want to repeat the information and press Control V.

It might seem strange to non-accountants that the money taken from the bank current account is a credit, while the money put in the petty cash float is a debit. This is because accounting software recognises two types of accounts - credit type accounts and debit type accounts. Debits will actually increase the amount in a debit type account, while credits increase the balance in a credit type account. Debit type accounts include assets and expenses, so when you record a debit for these accounts the figure will increase. Credit type accounts include liabilities, capital and income.

Cash is an asset which makes it a debit type account, so putting a figure in the debit column will increase it's value. The bank account can be an asset or a liability (if overdrawn). In this case (transferring to petty cash) it is giving funds and should be credited - remember the rule of credit the giver and debit the receiver. In Chapter 1 this type of transaction was explained in the following terms: a debit represents the increase in the value of an asset or a decrease in amount of liability; a credit represents a decrease in the value of an asset or an increase in the amount of liability. Assets and liabilities are listed in the balance sheet section of the chart of accounts, so print them out and refer to Chapter 4 to recall which are which. You will notice that the bank accounts and the VAT account are both listed in the assets and liabilities sections as they may have a debit or a credit balance.

To make changes to the journal entry, just click on the line you want to alter and make the necessary amendments. Press F6 if you want to delete a whole line, making sure one of the fields in the correct line is highlighted.

Tip

Ask your accountant to advise you on making journal entries if you're in any doubt.

What can I do if I can't balance the credits and debits and Sterling +2 won't post the journal entry?

Press Abandon to exit and rethink the transaction. If you want to continue, the only way to make the figures balance is to make a reverse posting for the outstanding amount into the suspense account (9998). However, you shouldn't leave figures in the suspense account and must find the correct posting to balance your books as soon as possible. Make sure you get professional advice if you have any difficulty balancing the figures or deciding which accounts to credit and which to debit.

I realise I've made incorrect postings and want to erase them. Can I do this?

There is only one method for removing postings which have already been made and that is to reverse them. To completely cancel a journal entry you should reverse it by posting a journal entry giving a credit of the same amount as the original debit, and a debit for the original credit. If you are only altering the overall figure, post a reverse transaction to change part of the amount, ensuring the calculation is correct.

Once all the figures balance on your journal entry screen, you can complete the posting by clicking on Save. This button will be inactive if your credits and debits are not equal. If you are having trouble with the journal entry it's best to press Abandon and seek expert advice. Once you succeed in saving and posting a journal entry, you will be presented with a new screen to fill in another transaction. Only click on Close once you have posted all the entries and want to finish working on this option.

Adjustments for prepayments and accruals

Prepayments are payments you make in advance for future periods and include expenses such as insurance and rent. Accruals, on the other hand, are amounts paid in arrears such as bills for gas, electricity and telephones. Although you pay for these items in a lump sum for a number of periods, perhaps quarterly or six-monthly, you will want the accounting system to break the payment into separate periods and not allocate it all into the period when the money was sent out.

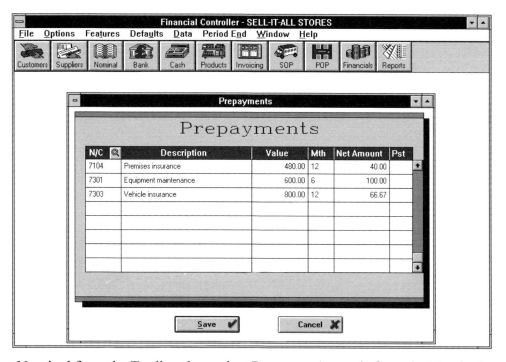

Select Nominal from the Toolbar then select Prepay or Accruals from the Nominal menu. Under N/C, put the relevant nominal code: for example, premises insurance would be 7104 on the prepayments screen, while gas would go under 7201 on the accruals screen, if you're using the Sage default chart of accounts. Take a look through all the nominal accounts and get familiar with them so that you can use them confidently. The Description field is not filled in automatically when you enter the nominal code, as you will want to give a meaningful explanation. Again you can use up to 30 characters, even though they don't show on the display. This description will appear on the audit trail and helps to make sense of the figures, when you look at reports.

In the Value field enter the total amount to be paid. Next, enter the number of months this covers in the field headed Mth (this must be at least 2 months and can't be more than 12). The system automatically divides the total value by the number of months and your monthly payment appears in the Net Amount field. If there is a figure in the Pst field this shows the number of payments made so far according to the system.

Fill in as many prepayments or accruals as you need to. To change any lines click on the relevant field and type your amendment or press F6 to have the whole line removed. Once you're happy with the entries click on Save, but remember that no postings will be made until you run the month end function.

Tip

The prepayments and accruals will only be posted for the number of months you have specified, then they will be cancelled unless you make a new entry.

Depreciation

Most assets need to be depreciated every year because they go down in value. There are two ways of doing this. Many companies choose to depreciate the value of the asset by a fixed percentage of the net asset value (not the original cost) every year. This is called reducing balance accounting. For example, a computer which is worth £10,000 might be reduced by 20% every year. In the first year this would mean a reduction of £2,000 so that a balance of £8,000 would be left to represent the value of the computer. In the second year the figure of £8,000 would be reduced by 20%, i.e. £1,600, leaving a value of £6,400 to be carried on to the third year. In this way the value of the computer is never completely written off. At some stage you will need to use a separate option to write off the remaining value in one posting in order to put an end to the computer's life!

Tip

It's important to get your depreciation figures right to make sure you get the correct capital allowances. Check the figures at the outset with your accountant.

The second method is called straight line accounting and this reduces the value of the asset to a figure of zero over a specified amount of time. To do this you take the value of the computer (£10,000) and divide this by the estimated life in years (perhaps five years) to arrive at an annual amount of £2,000. The depreciation amount would be £2,000 every year for five years. The monthly depreciation figure would be calculated simply by dividing this into 12 equal amounts.

To record the figures for each of your assets choose Nominal from the Toolbar, then select Deprec from the Nominal menu. On the depreciation screen fill in the nominal code for each asset under N/C and use the magnifying-glass icon to see what is available. The computer could be listed under office equipment depreciation (0031) - then enter it's name under Description. Enter the price paid for the item under Value if you're using straight line accounting (or the net book value if for the reducing balance method). Then under Tp, enter the initial letter for your method of depreciation: S for straight line, R for reducing balance or W when you want to write off the remaining balance in one posting. Under % you will need to put the annual percentage of depreciation. Sterling +2 will then calculate the figure for the Amount field depending on which method you are choosing. Then it will divide this into monthly amounts. The Pst column will have an asterisk if the

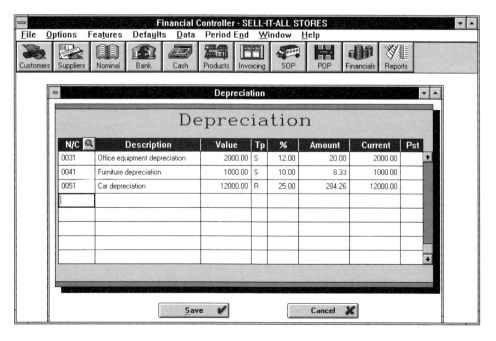

posting has been made for the current period or month.

Once you have filled in all the items to be depreciated, check them. Click on any line you need to amend and make the necessary changes. Again you can use F6 on a line to delete the whole entry. Remember to click on Save when all the details are satisfactory. The postings will be made next time you run the month end procedures.

Note

You must put the correct depreciation account code for each item. For example, 0041 for furniture/fixture depreciation, or 0051 for motor vehicle depreciation.

I need to sell a car which cost £10,000 but which has depreciated by £7,500. Once it's sold I will have £2,500 cash. How can I record these amounts in Sterling +2?

You have to make three double entries to post the figures to the correct sections of the profit and loss and balance sheet accounts. As a fixed asset the car is in the balance sheet - and so is the accumulated depreciation. You need to transfer the remaining £2,500 to the profit and loss section. To do this choose Nominal from the Toolbar then Journals and post the following double entries:

N/C	Details	Debit	Credit
0050	Motor vehicles		10,000
4200	Sales of assets	10,000	
4200	Sales of assets		7,500
0051	Motor vehicle depreciation	7,500	
4200	Sales of assets		2,500
1200	Bank account	2,500	

The outstanding amount of £2,500 will appear on the profit and loss account under Sales of assets. This same technique can be used for the sales of any fixed assets. Remember that if you are selling valuable assets (particularly property) you should consult your accountant as correct valuation is important.

VAT accounting

During configuration you should have set up your chosen method of VAT accounting -

either the standard or cash accounting method - and the VAT codes to be used throughout your Sterling +2 records. Look at the table in Chapter 3 to see the VAT codes and what they mean as you work on transactions and on the final VAT return. If you are using the Sage default VAT codes there is no need to add extra codes. T1 will be set at the present UK standard rate and will have to be changed if this is altered.

European Union customers and suppliers

Sage has set T4 as the tax code for sales to EU countries, and if you have set up a different one make sure it has a Y in the Euro column on the VAT code table. The T4 code must be used for EU sales and on the invoice you must put the customer's country code and VAT registration number. If you don't have a VAT registration number for EU customers you have to put the code T1 and charge VAT at the UK rate then declare it on your own VAT return. When filling in the records for EU customers, remember to put the VAT registration number and the country code (refer to the list in Chapter 3) in the field labelled Tax Id.

EU suppliers may be sending goods which attract VAT (even if they haven't charged you). In this case you should enter the VAT code T8 for the transaction and the suppliers should put your VAT registration number and country code on the invoice. For goods which do not attract VAT, you should still have your country code and VAT registration number on the supplier's invoice, but in this case the code is T7.

What should I do if the supplier hasn't quoted my VAT registration number and country code on the invoice?

This means that the supplier ought to be charging VAT, according to the rates in their country. Separate the amount charged for the product and the amount charged for VAT, then type them as separate lines on the invoice. Put the net amount charged for the goods with a VAT code of T8 if it attracts VAT or T7 if it doesn't. On the line giving the amount charged for VAT in the EU supplier's country put the VAT code T0 (exempt).

VAT returns

The Sterling +2 VAT Return form can be viewed by choosing Financials from the Toolbar then VAT. This display shows the nine boxes which are also standard on the VAT form sent by HM Customs and Excise. All the necessary information should be provided on this screen. The latest EU legislation requires that you provide all of these figures - Sterling +2 will help you do this.

The first box shows the amount of VAT charged on all of your sales, both to UK and overseas customers, with any credit note amounts subtracted. The second box shows the VAT payable on all goods bought from EU suppliers and this is worked out by charging the standard UK rate to all transactions with a code of T8. Box three is the result of the first two boxes, added together to show the total amount of VAT payable.

Value Added Tax Return

SELL-IT-ALL STORES
24 MARKET ROAD
MERRITON
BERKSHIRE

Period from 01/09/94
to 30/09/94

VAT due in this period on sales	1	543.39
VAT due in this period on EC acquisitions	2	0.00
Total VAT due (sum of boxes 1 and 2)	3	543.39
VAT reclaimed in this period on purchases	4	177.45
Net VAT to be paid to Customs or reclaimed by you	5	365.94
Total value of sales, excluding VAT	6	3105.00
Total value of purchases, excluding VAT	7	1025.75
Total value of EC sales, excluding VAT	8	0.00
Total value of EC purchases, excluding VAT	9	0.00

☐ Include Reconciled Transactions

Calculate   Reconcile   Print   Close

Box 4 shows the amount of VAT you can reclaim on goods bought in the UK and from the EU, then this figure is subtracted from the total VAT due (Box 3) to show the amount you need to pay or can reclaim which is displayed in Box 5.

Boxes 6 and 7 show the total amounts for all your UK, EU and non-EU sales and purchases excluding VAT, while Boxes 8 and 9 record the total figures for sales and purchases excluding VAT to EU member countries only.

Tip

The information for the VAT return can only be calculated properly if you use the correct VAT codes at each point throughout the system. Every box uses a specific selection of VAT codes to arrive at the right figure.

VAT return analysis

This VAT return form can be filled in just like the standard VAT return document provided by HM Customs and Excise. If you have entered all your tax codes correctly the calculations will be handled automatically by the software. To calculate and reconcile your VAT start by entering the start and end dates for your VAT return at the top of the screen, or accept the default dates which are set for the current period. Once the dates are correct, simply press the Calculate button to have your VAT analysed. If there are transactions from a previous period which have not yet been reconciled on a past VAT return, you will be prompted to answer whether or not you want them included.

Tip

Choosing not to include transactions from previous accounting periods will mean they are left unreconciled and will still have to be processed at a later date. If in doubt, speak to your accountant or VAT office to make sure you handle the return correctly.

You can also include reconciled transactions by clicking on the check box at the bottom of the VAT return display. This lets you add in transactions during the given date range to make sure they have already been dealt with on a previous return. The first time you use the VAT return options you will not need to worry about previously reconciled transactions and transactions from earlier periods.

Once you have pressed Calculate, respond to the prompts regarding unreconciled transactions. The software will show you the number of transactions found - click on OK to see the VAT return. Next, click on any of the boxes (except numbers 3 and 5) and a window will appear showing you a summary of the figures for that field. For example, click on box 1 to see information on your sales figures. Boxes at the bottom of the screen offer extra transaction details such as invoices, credits and the like. Look through these windows to analyse your VAT return figures and then move back to the main window by clicking on Close.

When you are happy with the calculations, click on the Reconcile button on the main VAT Return screen. You will be prompted to indicate whether or not you want reconciled transactions to be flagged (marked with a letter R) on transaction histories and reports. If you don't choose to flag reconciled transactions, the letter N will appear by unreconciled transactions instead. By setting the flags you can use the prompts on later returns to have previously reconciled figures missed out or included as explained in the first paragraph.

After pressing Reconcile you will be able to print out the return analysis. This will prove useful later if you realise there are errors and need to check the figures. On the VAT Return screen press Print.

Different reports are available to help you check your VAT return. Select the Printer option button as the method of output and highlight Detailed, Summary or VAT Return before clicking on OK. The Summary report just gives the totals by each code for each of the boxes on the form. These figures may be enough, if your figures match exactly and

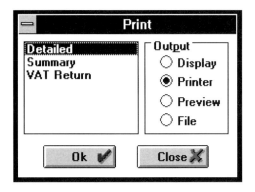

you're using the standard VAT accounting method. The Detailed report gives both the summary information available in the first report plus all transactions used to calculate the figures on the return. The VAT Return printout is a standard document with exactly the same appearance as your main VAT Return screen. These reports are all useful when looking for mistakes in your VAT calculations, to reconcile the figures.

If you're using standard VAT accounting the difference between input and output tax (the figure in box 5) should be the same as the closing balance on your VAT control accounts (2200 and 2201 in the nominal ledger). It's vital to find out the reason for any discrepancy. If the difference between your two tax control accounts is a credit, then that is the amount you need to pay HM Customs and Excise. If the difference is a debit you are owed that amount of money. Should the control accounts show a different figure to your VAT return display, you need to check all the relevant transactions to make sure you have entered the right tax codes throughout.

VAT cash accounting

If you use the VAT cash accounting method make sure that you have ticked the check box on the Company Preferences Defaults screen. Cash accounting means VAT is only calculated on paid transactions in all of the ledgers - if you want to use this method make sure to select it during configuration before you enter any figures. VAT cash accounting is only permitted if your turnover is below a set limit (£350,000 in the 1993 Budget). Check with HM Customs and Excise to see that the rate has not been amended and that you are eligible.

Tip

If you use the cash accounting method you are only liable to pay the VAT office when your customers pay you. On the other hand, you can only reclaim the VAT element on supplier invoices when you pay your bills.

The VAT control account adds up the VAT on all invoices and credit notes. If you are using VAT cash accounting, the balance for the VAT contra account will not be the same as your VAT, which will only give the total liability from the paid transactions. In order to check your VAT return you will have to look at a variety of reports and extract the figures for paid transactions. Choose Reports from the Toolbar then highlight the following reports in the window, click on Printer and press Run: Cash Payments, Cash Receipts, Deposits Report and Payments Report.

If VAT cash accounting is your chosen method, the software will mark all taxable transactions which have not yet been paid. These will not be included on the VAT return. At month end following VAT return reconciliation, you can delete the paid transactions which will be marked with an R (for reconciled) on the audit trail and reports, but carry forward the unreconciled transactions.

Tip

With VAT cash accounting you will often have to adjust the figures manually if transactions are reversed: for example after refunds or when cheques bounce. See Chapter 5 to check that you are doing this the right way and changing the tax figures accurately.

Standard VAT accounting

During configuration you should make sure that the cash accounting method is not chosen if you want to use the standard VAT accounting method. This method of VAT accounting makes the work easier as many of the functions can be handled automatically by the software. You don't need to adjust figures manually following refunds and other mispostings. With this technique, the VAT control account should have the same figure as the VAT return - if it doesn't you will need to find out where you have made a mistake. Although this method makes the software easier to use it does have financial drawbacks for smaller businesses. VAT is automatically calculated on transactions regardless of whether or not they have been paid. If your turnover is below the limit quoted above, it will be in your interest to use the cash accounting method - this just means you will have to take extra trouble in learning how to make manual adjustments!

I use the standard VAT accounting method but I can't reconcile my VAT because the figure on the return doesn't match the VAT control account. What can I do?

Errors can be caused by putting the wrong date, particularly the wrong year, on transactions or due to technical problems (such as corruption) which have altered correctly typed information. If the figures don't match look at various reports to try to find where the mistake lies. Start by choosing Nominal from the Toolbar and highlight two VAT control accounts: the sales tax control account (2200), and the purchase tax control account (2201). Next click on Report, highlight Activity in the list of files then choose Printer and press Run.

More useful information can be taken from the audit trail report - print this out by choosing Reports from the Toolbar, highlighting Audit Trail, then pressing Printer and Run. Use the Reports option to print out all the fixed transactions (they're marked with the word Fixed in the window). Don't change any of the boxes on the Reports screen except the date range - click on the two boxes to enter a start date and end date to match the dates on the VAT return.

Print out the VAT return analysis and the detailed VAT analysis report. Check the fixed transaction reports against the VAT return analysis to see that the figures are the same. On the detailed VAT analysis report the figures at the end should correspond to the figures marked with an N on the VAT control account - make sure none are missing. You also need to check the figures on the fixed transaction reports against those on the detailed VAT analysis report. If you can't find any human error in the information, especially the dates, the only explanation is technical failure such as data corruption.

Warning

The VAT return will only be calculated correctly if you ensure all transactions are entered with the correct tax code.

Keeping the VAT records tidy

There are two tax control accounts: the sales tax control account (2200) and the purchase tax control account (2201). When you look at the figures in these two accounts and the total is a credit balance that figure must be paid to HM Customs and Excise, but when there is a debit, that figure should be paid to you. To keep the files tidy it's a good idea to reconcile your VAT every month and then set the figures to zero in both control accounts. This way there is just one clear set of transactions to calculate each month. The balances in both accounts can then be transferred to the VAT Liability Account (2202) as they must still be kept on record.

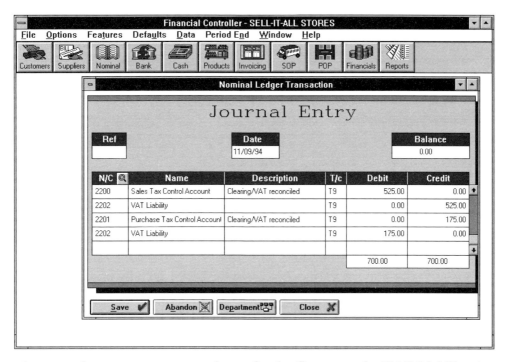

To set the control accounts to zero and transfer the figures to the VAT Liability Account choose Nominal from the Toolbar then Journals. Make sure the VAT return has been reconciled for the month before continuing. Next you can enter all the necessary transactions to clear the control accounts and transfer the figures to the VAT Liability Account by recording the following transactions:

Simply debit the sales control account with the total closing balance and credit the VAT Liability Account with the same figure. As the Purchase Tax Control Account is a debit type account you will have to credit this one with the closing balance and debit the same figure from the VAT Liability Account.

Q&A
How do I know whether or not I need to register for VAT?

You will need to register for VAT if your turnover exceeds the amount set by the Chancellor at the last Budget. The 1993 Budget increased the limit to £45,000, but it's important to check HM Customs and Excise regulations to see that the figure has not been altered. It is vital to register for VAT as quickly as possible if your turnover for a quarter is likely to exceed the limit permitted. It's dangerous to wait until the last minute to register - if your turnover for a quarter exceeds the limit you will be liable to pay VAT which you haven't collected. There are benefits to registering: once you start adding VAT to your prices and charging your customers you will also be able to reclaim the amount of VAT you have paid to suppliers. Ask the local VAT office for a registration form (look under Customs and Excise in the phone book). If you are a retailer ask for details on the special schemes for retailers which are tailored to your particular business needs.

How often do I have to pay my VAT, and how should I record this payment on Sterling +2? How do I record any VAT I reclaim?

When you register for VAT the local tax office will agree with you how often you should pay. Usually businesses pay quarterly, but you can choose to pay monthly, half-yearly or annually. To record the payment, choose Bank from the Toolbar, highlight the relevant bank account and press Payment. Under N/C put the nominal code for the VAT liability account (the Sage default is 2202) and put T9 as the tax code. In the Description field you should enter the period for which the payment is being made, such as VAT first quarter, then enter the total figure in the Amount field. When you reclaim VAT and receive a payment from HM Customs and Excise take the same steps but press Receipts instead of Payments on the Bank menu. You will still need to enter the VAT liability account 2202 as the nominal code and T9 as the tax code.

What if I have written off a debt and also the VAT liability before paying HM Customs and Excise - how do I record this?

See the Business Guide at the end of this chapter for details on when you can write off the VAT liability on bad debts. If you haven't paid the VAT element of bad debts and want to remove it manually from your tax control account you must make a double entry in the nominal ledger. Press Nominal on the Toolbar then Journals. Check your records (as described in the Business Guide) to find the VAT part of the debts you have written off. Next post a double entry. On the first line enter the amount as a debit to the VAT liability account (2202) and give it a tax code of T1. On the second line enter the amount as a credit to the bad debt write off account (8100) and give it a tax code of T9. Make sure each of these instructions is followed exactly, including the tax codes, and your VAT return will be adjusted accordingly.

Can I change between the standard and cash accounting schemes?

On Sterling +2 you can switch over to the alternative VAT accounting method, but only if you reconcile all your outstanding transactions involving VAT first. If you don't do this, transactions using the previous method will create confusion when the return is calculated.

My documentary records are a mess. How will the VAT office know whether or not the figures I give on my tax return are correct?

The tax authorities are likely to send a VAT inspector periodically to check your records - if this is your first year of trading you should expect a call at any time! It's best to keep your records in order (this means documents as well as computer files) and make sure that you throw nothing away for at least six years. Make sure that you only reclaim VAT on business expenses and bad debts (see the Business Guide). Don't be tempted to add in your personal bills as deliberate fraud may lead to a fine. Genuine errors are likely to be made as this is a complicated tax, but don't worry about these as you will not be penalised.

BUSINESS*guide*

Payroll

Sage has a popular software package which handles all the personnel records as well as wages and salaries which is called Payroll. However, if you only have a small number of employees you may choose to tackle this work without buying add-on applications. This will mean putting your knowledge of the nominal ledger to practical use. It's worth trying out the steps on demonstration data first until you gain confidence. Start by printing out the nominal ledger chart of accounts as a reference. Where default Sage settings are given you can substitute your own, if you have set up a new structure.

Start by trying out a simple and rather basic set of payroll data. Imagine that your staff receive a Nett Wage of £4,500, The Employers NI is £600, the Staff PAYE is £500 and the Staff NI is £400. To process these payments as journal entries you will need to enter an equal credit and debit for the amounts. Enter the figures as follows:

For the Nett Wage credit the bank account £4,500 and debit Staff Salaries £4,500

For the Employers NI credit the NI Liability account £600 and debit Staff Salaries £600

For Staff PAYE credit the PAYE Liability account £500 and debit Staff Salaries £500

For Staff NI credit the NI Liability account £400 and debit Staff Salaries £400

If you list the figures in this way you can see that the same nominal accounts are repeated in various postings, specifically the NI Liability account and also Salaries and Wages. Before making the actual journal entry you can add the figures together for these two accounts and post them as single figures. Your final journal entry would then be:

N/C	Details	Debit	Credit
1200	Bank Current Account		4,500
7003	Staff Salaries	6000	
2210	PAYE		500
2211	National Insurance		1,000

The total amounts in the Debit and Credit columns come to £6,000 so the figures balance and you will be able to post the journal. The amount posted to the Staff Salaries account will appear as an overhead in your profit and loss report. The amounts for PAYE and NI will appear as a liability on the balance sheet report for you to pay to the Inland Revenue and DSS.

How do I record my payment of PAYE and NI when the time comes?

You can either enter this as a bank payment using the Bank option from the Toolbar, or as a journal entry in the nominal ledger. Both have exactly the same effect on your records. To use the bank method, choose Bank from the Toolbar then Payment from the Bank menu. Enter 2210 (PAYE) and 2211 (NI) under N/C, then enter the amounts (£500 and £1,000 in the example above) followed by a tax code of T9. This transaction will automatically debit the PAYE and NI accounts and credit the bank account with the amount of £1,500. Alternatively you can post a journal entry by choosing Nominal on the Toolbar, then Journals and posting both the debit and credit amounts. In the first line enter 1200 (Bank Current Account) under N/C and put the amount of 1,500 under Credit. On the second line enter 2210 (PAYE) under N/C and the amount of 500 under debit, then on the third line enter 2211 (NI) under N/C and 1000 under debit. Remember to use the tax code T9 for all entries.

Advanced payroll processing

The payroll described earlier is extremely basic and you will probably want to divide the figures up in a more meaningful way. Perhaps you would like to separate wages paid to directors from those paid to employees, and also to separate payments made to each department. This is all possible using Sterling +2 - you can also separate the gross pay into basic pay, bonus and overtime amounts.

Some of the account codes are already provided in the Sage default chart of accounts, but you will need to create some new ones. Start with the part of the profit and loss section which includes salaries and wages. It's important to create any similar accounts in the same section so that they will appear as an overhead on the profit and loss report. Look at the accounts from 7001 to 7008. The default settings already help you to divide salaries into those paid to directors and staff. You can also divide wages between regular and casual workers (7004 and 7005) instead of putting them all together under Staff Salaries (7003). Perhaps you have a partnership in which case you will need to create a drawings account for each partner. When partners draw funds, you should make a double entry crediting the bank account and debiting each drawings account, just as you did for staff salaries (see the Business Guide in Chapter 12 for more information on partnerships).

Now create some accounts by pressing Nominal then Record and setting four-figure codes beginning with 7 to fit into this same group in the profit and loss report. The existing code 7003 can be used just to record the basic salaries for staff. You will want to create extra codes for additional types of payments. Decide on your own requirements or use these codes: 7009 Overtime, 7010 Bonus, 7011 Holiday Pay.

How do I record amounts for statutory sick pay (SSP) and statutory maternity pay (SMP)?

Sage hasn't included these in the default chart of accounts and you will definitely need to add them in. They need to appear as liabilities in the balance sheet report, so it's best to give them a code starting with the numbers 221. This way they will be neatly grouped together with similar items such as PAYE and NI. Press Nominal then Record and use the following settings: 2214 SSP and 2215 SMP. Post the amounts in the same way you posted NI and PAYE in the basic payroll example earlier.

How do I calculate the figures for PAYE and NI liability?

If you only have Sterling +2 but not Payroll, you will have to do this manually using the tables available from the Inland Revenue and DSS. Payroll +2 can make these complicated calculations automatically. It also handles SSP, SMP and different types of pay. Unlike the DOS version of Payroll, this Windows version lets you scan in photographs of each employee and also uses screen representations of official documents to guide you through the complexities of government employment legislation.

Reclaiming VAT

Every year hundreds of millions of pounds worth of VAT which could be reclaimed under the refunds system are left in the hands of European Union governments. Even the Institute of Chartered Accountants has announced that the refund system in underused and therefore not working. This is partly because many businesses don't realise how much VAT they are entitled to reclaim and because the refund system is too complicated to understand. There are time limits which must be met in order to process a successful claim, there are also regulations you must be aware of.

Businesses can reclaim the VAT element of expenses for business travel across Europe. With some countries charging up to 25% VAT this means they can recover up to a quarter of their costs. The types of allowable expenses vary from country to country and can include hotel and restaurant bills as well as business entertainment. Other areas which qualify are marketing, training, travel and motoring expenses apart from the obvious costs such as fees for conferences, exhibitions and professional services.

A trader established in one country incurring business expenditure in another EU country can't claim a refund from his own government but must recover the money from the tax authorities in the country visited. The claim must be made within six months of the calendar year in which the VAT was incurred, so you must be well prepared to process your claim by June each year. It can take three months to put through a claim so you need to start in March. Although the refund system was introduced to encourage trade between EU member countries it was extended to take in business travellers from all over the world. Just including EU countries was seen as a potential barrier to global trade.

If your business has overseas customers it's worth letting them know that they can reclaim VAT from the UK tax authorities. This is not just a goodwill gesture - it also makes the costs of business trips to the UK more competitive and should increase trade. Non-EU businesses making a claim to HM Customs and Excise have a different deadline to meet - their claims must be made by December 31 each year.

Each claim must be accompanied by invoices to give evidence of each VAT payment, so make sure these are kept in order throughout the year. Remind all staff going on business trips to keep all of their invoices even for expenses they may not believe to be allowable. If you don't have the linguistic skills to contact EU tax authorities to get the necessary forms then use a translation agency or hand this job over to a VAT reclaim bureau. Reclaim agencies charge about 20% of the amount they recover on your behalf.

If you need to reclaim VAT which you have incurred in the UK you can do this on the standard VAT return. It's important to remember that you can reclaim the VAT element of bad debts you have written off after a specific time has elapsed. Many businesses don't realise that recent legislation means they can write off the VAT on a bad debt as early as six months after the date goods or services were supplied. This used to be one year - your accountant may not be up-to-date with the change.

If you use the standard VAT accounting method you will be liable for VAT as soon as you raise an invoice and will have to pay it even if the bill isn't settled. Remember to write off this liability as soon as six months have passed if you have exhausted all the possible ways of calling in the payment (see the Business Guide on credit control in Chapter 8). If you have already paid the VAT on a bad debt, don't forget to reclaim it on the next return. When you write off a bad debt using Features on the Sterling +2 Toolbar, the VAT liability will remain in the control account. You will also need to keep a manual record of the VAT amount you can reclaim.

How do I keep a record of VAT paid on bad debts so that I can reclaim it?

Before writing off bad debts press Customers, select the account, then press Activity. Click on the History button to see a list of all transactions. Find the transactions you are writing off and make a note of the audit trail numbers at the beginning of the lines for each of them (you will need to keep these numbers on file for future reference). Now you can write off the bad debts. When you want to calculate the amount of VAT you can reclaim press Reports on the Toolbar, highlight Audit Trail then click on the option button for Display or Printer and finish by pressing Run. Scroll down through the transactions to find the numbers of the debts you have written off - each has the VAT amount clearly marked. Keep this type of information safely together with all of the documentary records you are storing in preparation for VAT refund claims.

CHAPTER 10

Reports and Enquiries

By now you will have been using the software to make on-screen enquiries and to print out information so you will be aware of many of the reports available on Sterling +2. The reports are accessed via different Toolbar options. Once selected, you can choose whether to output the information to the screen display for enquiries, to the printer for hard copy, or to disk file for later use. The customer, supplier, product and nominal files can be used to produce standard reports. No doubt you have already worked on these by choosing the appropriate Toolbar option, selecting records and clicking on the Report button.

Specialised functions also have their own reports: the chapter on credit control showed how to identify overdue debts, while the chapter on VAT showed how to access a variety of reports to reconcile the tax return. There are two more Toolbar choices which are used to create standard reports - Financials and Reports - and it's worth remembering all these options, to take full advantage of the wealth of information stored in Sterling +2. Apart from Bookkeeper, which only has the standard reports available in each ledger plus the VAT return, all other versions have the powerful report generator facilities.

Tip

Use the Preview option before selecting Printer as the method of output to see the report as it will appear on paper.

Customers and Suppliers

To produce sales and purchase ledger reports on printout or to make on-screen enquiries select Customers/Suppliers from the Toolbar, highlight the records you want to include

and press the Report button. Next highlight the relevant report on the list - choose from Activity, Balances, Customer/Supplier List, and VAT List. You should have printed out the customer/supplier list already when entering your database. It's a good idea to print out this type of information regularly as a hard copy backup to your computer records. Printouts are also useful when you want to check information and search for errors. You can spend longer working through figures on paper - your eyes can become weary after too many hours on the computer and you may begin to make mistakes.

Tip

Use the record selection techniques described in Chapter 4 to highlight records to be included in the report. The Criteria button is especially important.

The Activity report gives the transaction histories for all the accounts you have selected. You can identify the transactions awaiting settlement as they are asterisked. The letter p does not mean the amount has been paid - this is just a part-payment. At the end of this report are the total figures for the amount outstanding, the amount paid this period, the credit limit, and sales for the year-to-date.

For a quicker on-screen enquiry into customer or supplier balances, choose Customers/ Suppliers from the Toolbar then Activity from the Customers/Suppliers menu. The screen display shows the account codes and names with overall balances for year-to-date turnover, credit limit and balance. At the bottom of the screen are two buttons for more detailed on-screen enquiries. Press History to see each transaction listed. Choose Aged to see the total figures for debts which are 30, 60 and 90 days old or older together with the overall balance and current balances for each customer or supplier account. These options do not let you print out the reports, but they do provide the same type of information as on the Activity report accessed by choosing Report on the Customers/ Suppliers menu. Watch out for asterisks after the Name or Value columns as these mean the credit limits have been exceeded.

Warning

Don't confuse the two types of Activity report. Try choosing Report from the Customers/Suppliers menu followed by highlighting Activity, selecting Display and Run;

then compare the on-screen reports accessed by choosing Activity from the main Customers/Suppliers menu.

The aged debts report is particularly important for credit control. The tell-tale asterisk marks out customers and suppliers with balances over the credit limit, according to your record cards. If you need to print it out you will have to choose Report on the Customers/Suppliers menu, highlight Balances then press the Printer option button followed by Run. Only use the Activity button on the Customers/Suppliers menu followed by Aged when you just want to check the figures on-screen. The columns for ageing are headed 30, 60, 90 and older. In fact these columns record debts 30-60 days old, 60-90 days old, 90-120 days old and more than 120 days old respectively.

The final reports accessed by choosing Report on the Customers/Suppliers menu offer straightforward lists. Customer/Supplier lists just give the information you have on your database records without any transaction details. You need to keep a printout of this report (make a habit of producing a new one regularly), together with documentation recording the transactions. In this way you are not totally relying on the computer system but will have complete records on paper should you need to work without the computer at any time - for example during computer or power failure. The VAT List adds details on each customer's country code and VAT registration number, to complete your manual records. If you want to make a simple enquiry on a particular customer or supplier, simply highlight them on the main Customers/Suppliers window and press Record to see their database entry.

Products

To see the reports available for stock control choose Products from the Toolbar then Report. From this option the variety of reports available to help you keep an eye on your

stock is impressive. The reports provide analysis of stock levels and movements, prices and histories. These reports help in purchase ordering: you need to watch the stock levels to check when you need to reorder. You also need to see which items sell well and which are not worth handling. If you just want to check the recorded information for individual products, simply highlight them on the main Products window and press Record to see what you have on file.

Information on products can be viewed in the Details report. This shows everything on record for each item - keep an updated copy of this printout. If you assemble separate products to make up sets, the Explosion report will give details on the components, including where they are stored. The Movements report traces the progress of products with dates, price and textual explanation. The Price List report is useful for enquiries and can also be used to print out a price list for customers or to publish in brochures. The Products report gives summary information on each item - the product code, description, price, nominal account and name.

To see whether a product is selling well (to ascertain if it should be continued), take a look at the Profit report for the month and for the year. It may sell more at one time of the year than at another and a bad month should be taken into account. See how much of the stock has been sold and check the profit gained from the sales - remember to run month end procedures to ensure your figures are up-to-date.

The Reorder Levels report only lists products which need to be ordered - that is, those that are below the levels specified. To help you place the order there may be a supplier reference and price, if this information has been entered.

All transactions for a product are listed in the Stock History report. This is used to trace movements of the products as a result of orders, invoices and credit notes as well as stock transfers. Finally, there is a Valuation report which shows how much stock there is and the total value. When you need to post opening and closing valuations of stock to the nominal ledger, you can use this report for accurate figures.

Tip

Before posting a closing valuation, do a physical stock take and adjust the figures for lost or damaged stock. The true value of stock is vital to work out your profits accurately - see the Business Guide in Chapter 5.

Bank accounts

Checking the balances in your bank accounts is one of the fastest on-screen enquiries. The balances are displayed by account name in the main window, when you choose Bank from the Toolbar. Sterling +2 updates these figures immediately, when you post a transaction affecting the bank accounts. To check the details you entered on the database for each bank account, press Bank then Record. For more information choose Nominal, highlight the required bank account in the list and click on Record. The nominal record for each bank account will show the overall balance together with period balances and budgets.

Even if you don't want to reconcile a bank statement, the Reconcile button on the Bank display is useful. Press it to see all the unreconciled transactions still outstanding, to get a true picture of your bank balance. Calculate the balance when all the uncleared debits and credits have been settled. Highlight the bank accounts and press Recurring to keep a close eye on your recurring entries. Check which payments have been made (they are marked with a Y in the Pst column) and which are imminent. This again gives a good idea of your actual financial position.

Nominal ledger

It is possible to make quick on-screen enquiries to check the balances in the nominal ledger, or to view and print out more detailed reports. For on-screen reports, choose Nominal from the Toolbar then Activity. The next display lists all nominal accounts with their balances, whether debit or credit. This is just the same as the main Nominal window except that the total figure for debits and credits is given at the bottom of the columns. Check particular nominal accounts by highlighting them in the list and pressing History to see the full set of transactions posted to them. The name of the account you are viewing appears in a box at the top of the screen - press the arrow at the end of this field to select a different account without returning to the previous display.

To see and print out more detailed nominal ledger reports, choose Nominal from the Toolbar then Report. Make sure you at least take a printout of your Nominal List report to keep a record of you complete chart of accounts. The other two standard reports are Activity and Balances. The Activity report provides a transaction history for any nominal accounts you select. These can be checked against the audit trail as the audit trail number is given on each line. As this report lists activities it will give an explanation of each transaction, for example 'insurance' together with the date, value and whether it is a debit or a credit. The Balances report gives the amount in each nominal account, whether debit or credit.

Tip

The Balances report is similar to the Trial Balance but lists every nominal account even if they have a zero balance. The Trial Balance and other similar reports are available from the Financials option on the Toolbar. Audit trail reports are found by pressing

Reports on the Toolbar.

Audit trail

The audit trail report sounds slightly complicated to the non-accountant. It is simply a complete list of transactions, grouped together and marked up to help you when you want to check your books. To see the audit trail, or other reports which use the same transaction data, choose Reports from the Toolbar. You will be presented with a list of reports and prompts to specify the necessary transactions you want to check. The ranges

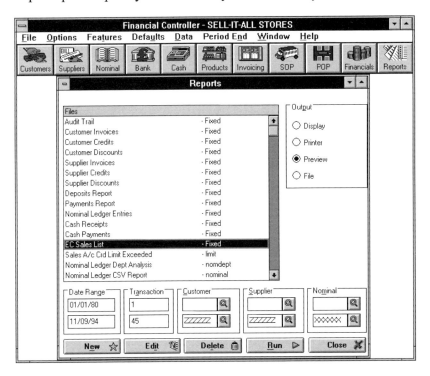

are set at the bottom of the window beginning with a start and end date. The default settings mean that all your records will be included. However, you can specify the start and end numbers for the date, customers, suppliers, nominal codes and transactions.

Note

Bank or cash payments and receipts have the bank or cash account number on the audit trail in the place where the customer or supplier code normally appears. To see these transactions, you need to create a report with the report generator (find out how later). Alternatively, don't set a range - and remember that it will not help if you put the bank or cash account code in the N/C field. For these transactions this code is in the A/C field.

Other reports on the list break down the transactions into separate categories and you can select the type of transactions you want to see. These include all cash payments and receipts; customer and supplier credits, discounts and invoices. The Deposits Report lists all receipts you have entered using the Bank facilities, while the Payments Report shows payments made via Bank on the Toolbar. If you have customers in other EU countries you will need to send details on all their transactions to the VAT office. The EU Sales List Report provides all the information you require, as it groups these customers together and gives the total figures for all trade during the quarter you choose to specify.

When specifying the ranges, you need to start with the Date Range specified and then the Transaction numbers (which are automatically generated by the software). You can see the transaction numbers on the Nominal Activity report and can use these numbers to identify the right transaction in separate reports. The numbers are generated as transactions are entered, so they do not necessarily fit in with the date order as you can give varied dates to each transaction.

All of the reports which use audit trail data are called fixed transaction reports, and are useful when checking the tax return (see Chapter 9 on VAT). The Audit Trail lists every single transaction recorded in Sterling +2 - always check the column headed Paid which will be marked with a Y if the amount has been settled.

What do the letters in the Tp column mean?

These letters show the transaction type and are necessary to help analyse the information. The transaction types are abbreviated to the following codes:

SI sales invoice	SC sales credit note
SR sales receipt	SA sales payment on account
SD sales discount	BP bank payment
BR bank receipt	CP cash payment
CR cash receipt	JC journal credit
JD journal debit	PI purchase invoice

PC purchase credit note

PA purchase payment on account

PP purchase payment

PD purchase discount

Product movements are abbreviated to:

AI adjustment in

MI movement in (by stock transfer)

AO adjustment out

MO movement out (by stock transfer)

GR goods returned (figure taken from credit notes)

GO goods out (figure taken from sales orders and invoicing)

GI goods in (figure taken from purchase orders)

Financials

Some of the most useful reports are available from the Financials option on the Toolbar, as they indicate how the business is doing. These reports let you compare your results against budgets, for example. This is also where you should look for the all-important

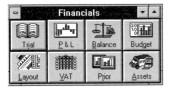

trial balance as well as the profit and loss report, balance sheet and budget report. You can also compare this year's figures for a specific period against the same time last year and find the values of company assets after depreciation.

Trial balance

During everyday accounting you will often need to check the trial balance which shows balances in the nominal accounts, whether credit or debit. It also gives an overall total for the debit and credit columns. To view the trial balance, select Financials from the Toolbar then click on Trial and the figures will be presented on-screen. If you also need a printout, simply press the Print button.

Tip

The following reports take the figures from various categories in the nominal ledger. See Chapter 4 on creating nominal account records, as a reminder on how accounts are grouped together for categories including profit and loss and balance sheet.

Profit and loss

The second choice on the Financials menu is P & L. This report takes data from the nominal account records for the month you specify. Click on P & L then enter the date for the month you wish to view - the default date will appear but you can change it. Click on the arrow at the end of the Financial Month field and scroll up and down to your choice. This time you have to click on the method of output you want: Display or Preview to see the information on screen, Printer to have a printout, or File to store the data on disk. Click on OK to produce the report which shows amounts for the month and year-to-date for each section of the profit and loss sections of the chart of accounts (i.e. sales, purchases, direct expenses, and overheads).

Tip

The default chart of accounts has already allocated nominal accounts to profit and loss categories so that they will appear in this report. If you have set up your own chart of accounts make sure you have grouped profit and loss accounts together. If you set up any new nominal records always add them into the correct group.

Balance sheet

The balance sheet also takes information from nominal accounts grouped together for the purpose. Make sure you have done this correctly, if you are not using the default chart of accounts set up by Sage. Click on Balance in the Financials menu and a dialog box opens prompting you to set the date for the desired month (click on the arrow at the end of the Financial Month field to change the default setting). Choose the output option as on the Profit and Loss report to view, print out or store the data on disk and finish by pressing OK. The report gives the monthly figures plus year-to-date for your assets and liabilities.

Budget report

When you want to see how the business is performing the budget report is particularly important. The statistics highlighted here will also be useful for presentations when you want to prove a point. This report lets you choose a month and compare actual figures against the budgets. These should have been set when you entered nominal account records (if you haven't yet set budgets the report will not make sense). Again the figures are for the month and also year-to-date.

Select Budget from the Toolbar, then set the month and the output option as for the previous two reports. Click on OK to produce the report, which will show the actual balance for each account set against the budget and the percentage of variance. The screen shows the monthly figures. Use the scroll arrow to scroll to the right where the annual figures are displayed.

Prior year

This report is selected by clicking on Prior on the Financials menu and looks similar to the budget report. This time, however, the figures provided are for a specific month and are compared with the results for the previous year together with the percentage and amount of variance. Choose Prior, then fill in the box with the required month and method of output as with the other reports. Click on OK to produce the report.

Warning

These reports take the figures from the profit and loss account category in the nominal ledger. Mistakes in setting account codes for the nominal ledger will mean incorrect reports.

Asset valuation

In the section on nominal ledger processing (Chapter 9) you found out how to set the figures for depreciation on various company assets. This information can be extracted and used to produce a report which shows you the present value of your assets, month by month. Select Assets from the Financials menu and the screen will display all your assets (you may need to scroll down if there are too many). The report shows their present value, the opening value and the amount of depreciation. Print out the report to get extra details such as the type of depreciation method you have specified and the percentage together with how much the value depreciates each month and whether or not this has been posted.

VAT return

Choose VAT from the Financials menu to see a representation of the HM Customs and Excise VAT return with the nine standard boxes to be filled in. Sterling +2 will do this automatically using information on file and you may need to check the figures against a variety of standard reports in order to reconcile the tax return. For details on how to do so, refer to Chapter 9.

Changing the layouts

The reports on the Financials menu take figures from the nominal accounts, as grouped for the profit and loss and balance sheet. It's clear that unless you are using the Sage default chart of accounts, you must make sure you group your nominal accounts together correctly. This is also true of any additional nominal accounts you have created - they will only appear in the relevant reports if they fall into the right category grouping.

The structure of the chart of accounts was described in Chapter 4, but you can also take a look at how it is built up by choosing Layout on the Financials menu. This shows a display with all the groupings listed on the left under the heading Categories. These are: then grouped by Sterling +2 into two separate types - profit and loss and balance sheet. The profit and loss accounts are: Sales, Purchases, Direct Expenses and Overheads. For the balance sheet the accounts are: Fixed Assets, Current Assets, Current Liabilities and Financed By.

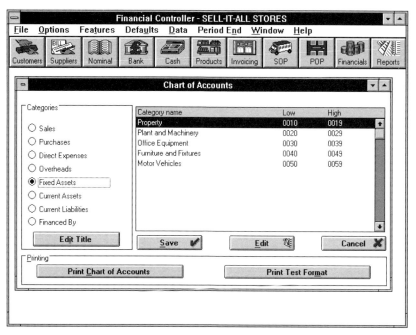

Start by looking at how the codes have been set. Category of Sales has been selected, as the default and the window shows different types of sales - Product Sales, Export Sales, Sales of Assets and Other Sales. Beside each sales type, are the account code numbers set from the lowest to the highest. Before attempting to change the chart of accounts in any way, try clicking on each of the Categories option buttons, from Purchases to Financed By. The account codes and names will appear in the window, to clarify the layout. Use the Print Chart of Accounts Button on the bottom of the screen to see a complete list of the Sage default settings or your own set of nominal accounts. Respond to the dialog box by pressing the Display or Printer option buttons to view or print the chart of accounts.

You can use this option to alter the layout of your reports. For example, you might want to switch the second type of sales with the first type, so that the former appears first on Financials reports. To change any of the lines, just highlight the required one in the window and click on Edit. Fill in the name in the headings field plus the high and low numbers to specify the range of nominal codes covered. For example, if you wanted to switch the first two sales types you would click on the first line, then Edit, and type in the details for the second sales type. Then you would highlight the second line, press Edit then replace the information with the name and account range for the first sales type. Reports take the order from this window, regardless of the nominal code numbers.

You may want to add extra categories within each group, for example extra types of Sales. You can include up to 15 categories (or 45 for Overheads). To do so highlight an unused line and click on Edit to specify the heading and range of nominal codes. If you are only using one nominal account code number put this in both the Low and High field.

If you have changed the layout in any way, click on the Print Test Format button to see examples of your new design for the financial reports. Finish by pressing Print Chart of Accounts to produce a complete listing of all the nominal codes.

Basic report generator

Although Sterling +2 provides a wide variety of reports as standard, including all the ones you need for typical analysis of the accounts, at times you will want to create your own reports. It's possible to do this by designing reports to give exactly the details you require as long as they will take information from your Sage records. There are two types of reports you can produce in this way: simple lists which don't include any calculations and reports which show information on transactions, derived by mathematical commands and resorting records.

Tip

The Criteria button lets you sort the records even for a basic listing report.

What is the difference between listings and reports involving calculations?

You have already been working with both types of report. When you created your databases for the nominal, customer and supplier options you printed out listings by choosing Customers/Suppliers/Nominal from the Toolbar, pressing Report and highlighting the List option for each set of records. This printed out the most basic type of report - a listing of all the records without sorting or calculations on the data. The second type of report is similar to the financial reports you have used, drawing transaction data from the audit trail and producing analyses of the statistics. These are then used to check your accounts, for example when reconciling the tax return.

Tailor-made listings

To design your own listings select the option (Customers, Suppliers or Nominal) from the Toolbar, click on Report and press the New button. The methods for all three options are similar, but practice by creating a new listing report for the customer option. Select Customers, then Report, then New. A screen headed Customer Report Creation displays all the available fields - you can select the ones you want to include in the report by clicking on the check boxes. When an X appears in the check box the information from that field will be added to the report. For example, you could click on the Name, Contact and Fax boxes to create a directory of all your customer fax numbers. When you want to check the credit limits for each customer you could click on the Name and Credit Limit boxes to see if any need to be increased or decreased. The Report Width box at the bottom right shows you the number of columns your design will take, as the software calculates the size of each field included.

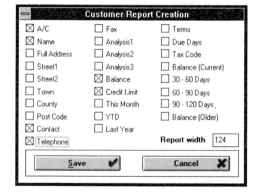

Tip

Check the Report Width field to see if your report will fit your stationery - otherwise create separate reports to include all the fields you want to view.

If the report is not satisfactory, press Cancel to abandon it, otherwise choose Save and you will be prompted to enter a name (8 characters maximum). Choose a name which you will remember easily in future, as it will appear in the list of standard reports each time you click on Report for the Customers/Suppliers/Nominal option. The name should also indicate the type of information it will handle. Type in the name and press OK to save it. If you decide the report is not of any further use, you can remove it later by highlighting it in the list of reports, pressing Delete and confirming that it should be erased.

Once you have completed these steps, your tailor-made report will run just like the standard ones provided by Sage. Select the records you want to include in the report by highlighting them or using the Swap and Criteria buttons (refer to Chapter 4 on choosing records). Press Report, highlight the file name you created, then choose the method of output and press Run to print out, view on screen or store the report on disk.

User defined reports are just like the ones produced by Sage with one difference - your creations can be deleted or amended. If you print out the listing and find it needs some amendments, highlight the report's file name in the Report window (choose Customers/ Suppliers/Nominal then Report) and click on Edit. This gives you the chance to change the fields you selected for the report - remember to save the file with the same name if you want it to overwrite the previous version. Should you need to keep both versions of the report design, simply give the amended version a new name and both will appear in the Report window.

Warning
Don't confuse the Report option chosen by selecting Customers/Suppliers/Nominal from the Toolbar with the Reports option available on the Toolbar.

Advanced report generator

To create reports for analysis of financial information and to include more advanced sorting and mathematical calculations you need to use the Reports option on the Toolbar. Start by choosing Reports then click on New to get a form to fill in with all the layout specifications. This time the title can be longer as the report will need to have a meaningful name - it will be listed together with other financial reports such as Audit Trail, Nominal Ledger Entries and Customer Invoices. Choose a name which fits in with the other transaction reports when you save the finished layout. Type the title into the Report Heading box using up to 30 characters to explain exactly what the report is. Next choose the data files which store the transaction details to be used in the report. Do this by clicking on the arrow at the end of the Report Type box (the default is Sales Ledger) and highlight your choice to select it.

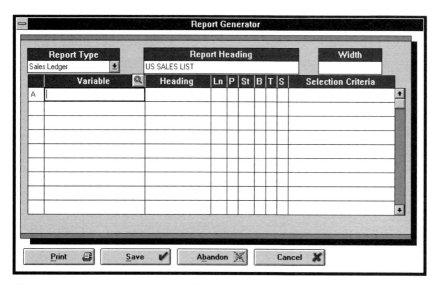

The Width box will show the width measured in characters as you design the report. Keep an eye on this figure, to make sure it will fit on your stationery. Start with the first line which begins with the letter A - each line will be a column on the finished report and you can identify the columns by this letter. The system of lettering is useful later when you need to make calculations using data from separate columns. This is done by setting mathematical formulae where columns are identified by their allocated letters.

Fill in the specifications for column A by pressing F4 while your cursor is in this line. Sterling +2 then lets you select the variables for the report layout by displaying the following screen:

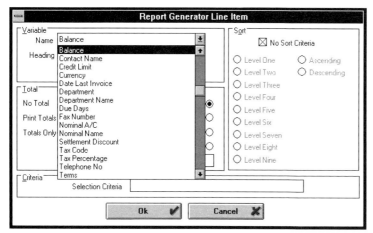

This window, headed Report Generator Line Item, lets you to set all the specifications for each column. It includes a list of variables which are automatically displayed. These variables can also be accessed by pressing the arrow at the end of the Name field in the Variable box. The variables will differ according to the data files you have specified in the Report Type field - the example screens show the Sales Ledger choices. Highlight the variable you want to include in column A - this could be the transaction number or the nominal account code, for example - and it will be entered in the Name field of the Variable box. If you click on OK, it will be entered as line A on the main report generator screen. Should you change your mind now or later about any of the column settings just click on the line and press F6 to remove it completely.

So far you have just set the variable for the column (line A) and Sterling +2 has set all the other specifications by default. To fill in the specifications yourself, don't click on OK but complete the rest of the Report Generator Line Item screen. Alternatively, do so later by clicking on the required line on the main Report Generator display and pressing F4. Start with the box labelled Variables. Change the Heading, if you want a different one to appear at the top of this column on the finished report. If you are setting a mathematical formula in this line, click on the Invisible check box as the formula shouldn't be printed out. Press Calculated Field if the figure in this column will be derived from calculations performed on data in other columns. Press OK when you want to return to the main Report Generator display and let the software use remaining default settings.

Tip

When you remove variables, the software automatically removes the space left in the design.

As these are financial analysis reports, you will also have to set criteria and mathematical formulae so that the software can make the necessary calculations. The software will take and manipulate data from some of the columns then display the result in a separate column. For example, you may want to give sales commission of 12% on all of your invoices and to do so you would use data in separate columns to perform the calculation. You would need to put the variable Net Amount in one column (for example column C) then get the software to calculate 12% of this to appear in a separate column. To do this you would press F4 on the third line, column C, and choose Net Amount as the variable. On the row for the column where you want the amount of commission to appear, you would specify that you want to multiply the amount of the invoice by 12%.

How do I specify instructions in the mathematical calculations?

Place the cursor on the line for the column where you want the result to appear. Press F4 to see the Report Generator Line Item window then click on the Calculated Field check box and enter a meaningful heading for the column in the Heading field - in the example above this could be commission. When you activate the Calculated Field check box the

Name field will be cleared automatically and the software will recognise that this line contains a mathematical command. Type the mathematical formula into the Name field using the standard computer symbols for each basic mathematical function. To find the correct commission for the example given above, you would type C*0.12. The asterisk is the computer command to multiply and this formula would take the figure from column C (Net Amount) and calculate 12% to appear in the commission column.

Warning

A Calculated Field can only perform a calculation using data from previous lines/ columns. For example, if the Calculated Field specifying the mathematical formula is line D it can only use data from lines A, B and C.

The mathematical symbols recognised by the software are:

+ addition   - subtraction

/ division   * multiplication

( ) brackets are used to prioritise calculations within a formula, i.e. the figures in the brackets are calculated before the rest in the total formula.

If you want to multiply row C by row D and then subtract row A the formula would be (C*D)-A or just C*D-A. However, if you want to subtract row A from row D and then multiply by row C it would be (D-A)*C.

Warning

Make sure you use capital letters to identify rows with upper case letters - there might be a row 'A' and also a row 'a' so incorrect typing can lead to confusion.

Tip

You can perform calculations on fields which include figures, such as the date field, as well as those with amounts taken from transactions or fixed values such as 0.12.

As you specify each column Sterling +2 automatically fills in the name of the variable plus a heading for the column in the field labelled Heading on the main Report Generator display. You can change the heading (press F4 to edit it) so long as you fit in with the maximum number of characters shown in the field called Ln. The Ln field is filled in by the software with the width of the column, as it will appear on the finished report. This is different for each variable you select. This figure does not include spaces as these will be added by the software, so you can use this number as your maximum allowance of characters.

Look at the rest of the fields on the main report generator window to see how they reflect your column specification. Under the letter P (for print) the letters Y or N will be automatically filled in to show whether or not the column will be printed on reports. On lines which just set the formula for calculations this will be N for no, whereas any that give textual and statistical information (including results of calculations) will be marked with a Y. This specification is set by activating or deactivating the Invisible check box on the Report Generator Line Item window.

If you have been specificying some of the fields for columns but letting Sterling +2 fill in the fields headed St, B, T, S and Selection Criteria with default settings, try amending these extra details. You can do this line by line as you work on columns, or later by pointing and clicking on the required column, pressing F4 and amending the boxes on the Report Generator Line Item window.

Tip
Instead of using F4 you can click on the magnifying-glass icon by the Variable heading.

The fields headed St on the main Report Generator window are used to specify which columns you want to have sorted automatically on the report. You can have the data in up to nine columns sorted and this includes alphabetic as well as numeric information. To do so, decide the order in which the columns should be sorted, specifying numbers 1 to 9 to show the sequence. You also need to decide if they should be sorted in ascending or descending order. Press F4 and make the specification in the box headed Sort. Start by clicking on the No Sort Criteria check box to activate sort by removing the X. Next click on the option button for the right level (from Level One to Level Nine) to show where this column falls in the order of priority, for sorting. Finish by pressing the Ascending or Descending option button. For example, if you choose Level One and Ascending, the software will do the calculation for this column first and the data will be sorted starting with the lowest and ending with the highest number, or starting at the beginning of the alphabet and continuing the list towards the end of the alphabet. If the column you are specifying should be sorted fourth and in descending order choose the Level Four and Descending option buttons - the software will do this calculation fourth and start with the highest numbers or from the end of the alphabet. On the main Report Generator window the figures 4D will appear in the St field.

Note

You need to set an order for the columns to be calculated, allocating the priority numbers 1 to 9.

The fields headed B are to specify a line or page break. If you specify a break here the software will automatically put a break in the report after this column is printed. Press F4 and click on the option buttons in the Break box to indicate if you want a Line or Page break. This works on the final report by moving to a new line or a new page each time the value of this field changes. It's also possible to put in a break if there is a change in the first 1 to 9 characters in the field. To do this put in the numbers 1 to 9 in the No field and press the On Chars option button.

Tip

Try out the page and line breaks in short sample reports to see how they work in practice.

The field headed T is to specify how you want total figures to be calculated and displayed. A T in this field will result in summary totals being printed in the places where you have inserted line breaks. Alternatively a Y in this field will result in totals being displayed in a variety of ways, depending on the number of breaks you have specified. If you put a Y and there are no breaks in the report there will be just one overall total for this column. If there is more than one break and a Y there will be subtotals at the breaks and an overall total at the end of the column. If you have specified multiple breaks and sorting instructions there will be a variety of subtotals at each primary and secondary break, plus an overall total at the end of the column.

These specifications can only be set when you press F4. Start by activating the Calculated Field check box under the heading Variable (make sure it has an X). In the box labelled Total you can then press the option buttons for No Totals, Print Totals (multiple totals at breaks plus a grand total), or Totals Only (summary totals at line breaks).

The field headed S is to specify that you want an indicator in the column showing

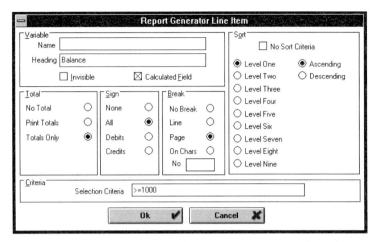

whether the amount is a debit or credit. This field displays the letters C, D or S for credit, debit or signed value. The signed value is taken from the transaction type as specified by the control account so the software will select the correct sign for both debits and credits. Press F4 and click on the Calculated Field check box to activate it and insert an X. Remember that some transactions are viewed as debits and some as credits depending on how they are treated by the control accounts in the nominal ledger - the way this is done is not always obvious to non-accountants. For example, sales invoices are posted to the debtors control account in the nominal ledger and have a positive sign as they are a credit to your company. Purchase invoices, on the other hand, are posted to the creditors control account in the nominal ledger and have a negative sign as they are debits to your company.

With some of the other control accounts it's not quite so obvious which types of transactions are debits and which are credits, and which have been given a negative or positive sign accordingly. Here is a list to help when you prepare reports:

Transactions with a positive sign (credits)

Sales invoices	Purchase credit notes
Purchase discounts	Purchase payments
Journal credits	Bank receipts
Cash receipts	

Transactions with a negative sign (debits)

Purchase invoices	Sales credit notes
Sales receipts	Journal debits
Bank payments	Cash payments

For some reports you may want to reverse the way debits and credits are viewed, so that the transactions listed as credits in the above example would be displayed as debits and the debit transactions would be shown as credits. To do this you specify that the report should multiply the figure by -1. For example, if the Net Amount is specified as column A and you want this to be reversed from credit to debit status, fill in line B with the formula 0-1*A in the variable field. Then press the Debits option button in the Sign box. You can also use this method with the same mathematical formula to reverse debits to credits by pressing the Credits option button, or press the All option button to reverse both debits and credits and fill in the signed value.

There are advanced ways of setting selection criteria so that Sterling +2 will know exactly which information you want to include in the report. You can set extremely precise criteria so that the software checks to see if figures and text fit all the requirements. These conditions are specified by pressing F4 and filling in the final box on the Report Generator Line Item window.

The criteria specifications work by making the software choose all records with a value greater than, less than or equal to the one you have stated. You can get more precise by having a combination of these, such as greater than one value and less than another. This works equally well for alphabetic information as letters can be equal to others if they are the same, and greater than if they are further ahead in the alphabet. The software can also be made to choose all the data which does not fit the specifications you have stated - this is useful if you particularly want to miss out information rather than to include it.

The software recognises these standard mathematical symbols in your formulae:

= equal to	!= not equal to
< less than	<= less than or equal to
> greater than	>= greater than or equal to

Tip

Remember to use the signs for greater/less than or equal to if you want to include the number you put in your formula or it will be missed out.

Test out a few formulae using these symbols: for example, if you have a column showing the Amount - Gross in the Variable field specify the data you want included in the Selection Criteria field of the same line. This could be >2000 to show that the software should take the data from all records where the figure is greater than 2000.

You can use the words AND and OR to set extra conditions to be met. For example, if you want the figure to be taken from all records where the amount is greater than 2000 but less than 3000, the formula would be >2000 AND <3000. In this formula both conditions must be met. If you want one or other of the two conditions to be met you would use OR, for example >2000 OR =1,500. You can also use brackets to include a combination of formulae, as in (>2000 AND <3000) OR =1,500. This last example would include all records which have values between 2,001 and 2,999 plus all the records which are exactly equal to 1,500.

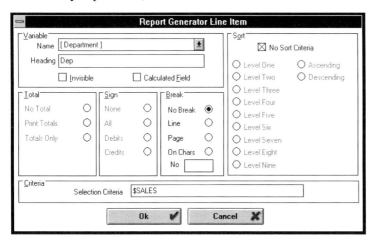

When setting specifications you can use wild cards - these are symbols which mean you don't want to set an exact character or set of characters. If you do this the software will accept all records with the characters you have specified regardless of the characters in the positions where you put the wild cards. If you just want to leave one character unspecified the sign is ?, but if you want a string of unspecified characters in a row you must put * (DOS users will already be familiar with these). For example, if you have a number of sales departments and want them all included you may set Department Name in the variable field, and under Selection Criteria put =SAL*. This would include all departments beginning with these three letters and finishing with any sequence of letters and numbers.

Tip

The wild cards don't have to be at the end of a set of characters or letters, they can be put anywhere within a number or group of letters.

For columns with textual information it is often necessary to search for a word or number of words to have the record included or excluded. This is done using the $ sign to find and include records with the specified word somewhere in the field, or with !$ to exclude these records. For example, you could specify sales departments by setting the criteria

$SALES to include records with this text, or exclude these departments by putting !$SALES. If you need to search for more than one word put the group of words in quotation marks, such as $"SALES TYPE".

Tip

Use double quotation marks, not the single ones, or the software won't recognise this command.

Searching for text need not mean looking for proper English words, it could also be used to find an account code including letters and numbers. You could search for customer and supplier codes using this technique - for example finding all accounts which have codes starting with the letters ABC by putting $ABC as the selection criteria. Alternatively this could be done by putting =ABC* as the selection criteria, but in this case the start letters would have to be ABC - the $ sign looks for the text in any position within the field. If you use the ? sign you can specify exactly where the characters should be found, so that ??ABC* would mean that ABC should be the third, fourth and fifth letters with any sequence of subsequent characters. Remember that you can also use negative signs to indicate you want records excluded if they contain certain characters, then set more conditions using AND and OR.

Once you are happy with all your specifications for the report, click on Save and you will be prompted to enter a report name. Now it's time to try out your tailor-made report by choosing Reports from the Toolbar, highlighting the one you have just created in the list, selecting the method of output and pressing Run. It's possible to set ranges on the Reports screen as with other Fixed Transaction reports. Your report will choose records which meet the criteria specified here and also defined on your report layout.

Using Preview

The Preview menu lets you view and change the whole appearance of your report by using a variety of typefaces and colours. Remember that you will also need a printer capable of handling your choice of settings! Press Preview on any of the report screens and try out the different menu options. Choose Print to print out the report as it is. This menu button displays the standard Windows printer control dialog box. Click on the option buttons to print out the whole report (All) or press Pages and fill in the first and last pages you want in the From and To boxes. Finish by pressing OK and the report will be printed.

The Setup button on the Preview window switches you to the standard Windows printer setup dialog box. Here you can click on the option buttons to choose the default printer or click on the arrow at the end of the Specific Printer box to choose a different one. In the Orientation box you can select Portrait or Landscape layout - Landscape is needed for wide reports as the lines are printed lengthways on each sheet of paper instead of from left to right.

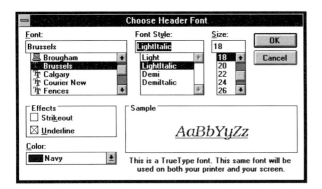

The remaining menu buttons are for specifying the font and colours for each part of the report, or you can press the Total button to have one font/colour setting for the whole report. If you want to have different settings for various sections press Header, Title, Text, and Message to specify fonts and colours for each. In the dialog box, you can choose the font by scrolling down through the list and highlighting it. Next choose the Font Style which may be just Regular or perhaps Bold for a Title. You may want the Title to be larger than the rest of the report, in which case scroll through the list of numbers in the Size box and click on a higher one to select it. To help you choose the font, font style and size there is a box called Sample which displays the text in the typeface and size you have specified. Try out the options in the Effects box: Underline will put a line under your text while Strikeout will put a solid line through your text. Finish by selecting the colour (if you have a colour printer) by pressing the arrow at the end of the Color field and highlighting the required shade. Finish by pressing OK. You can also use Options on the menu bar to access the font setting dialog box for each part of the report.

To the right of the Preview menu buttons there is a box showing the current page being displayed. Further right there are a set of buttons to help you move quickly through the pages of your report. From left to right these buttons perform the following functions: move to the first page, move back one page, move right one page, move to the end of the report, zoom in (enlarge the display), zoom out (miniaturise the display). Alternatively you can choose Page on the menu bar to move backwards and forwards through the pages of your report, while Options offers Zoom In and Zoom Out. Page on the menu bar also has a Page Layout option which lets you change the margin specification.

Adding graphs

Graphs are available from two areas of Sterling +2. Press Nominal, highlight any of the accounts and then Record and there will be a Graphs button at the bottom of the screen. There is also a Graphs button on the product sales display (press Product, highlight the required product, press Record, then press the Sales button). If there is information on record, the Graphs button will be active, not 'greyed out'. When you press it a line graph appears which uses the actual data, by default. You can press the Column button to change over to a bar graph, then click on the check boxes to have data from Actuals, Budgets or Prev (for previous) year. Switch back to the line graph by pressing the Line button. Choose a selection, such as Actuals and Budgets, to compare the figures against each other. A key to the graphs appears to show which figures are actuals and which are budgets. For product graphs you can switch between displaying a graph for the quantity sold or for the sales value.

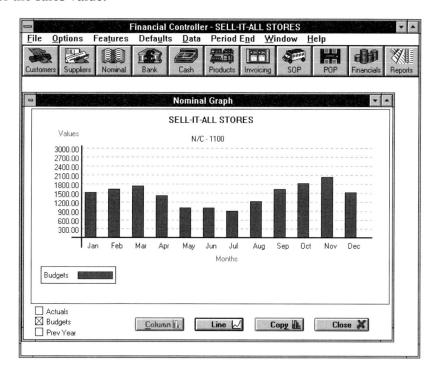

An extra button labelled Copy has been added to the graph display after the Sterling +2 manual was written. If you press Copy, the graph will be copied onto the Windows Clipboard so that you can transfer it to other documents and applications. To do this you need to use the Windows Program Manager, press Main then Clipboard (or ClipBook

Viewer). The graph will appear on the Clipboard display.

Tip

Don't worry if the Clipboard doesn't show the whole image of your graph. When you paste it into a document it will be complete.

Pasting the graph into another file or document is quite simple. For example, if you want to include it in a document produced on a Windows-based word processing package take the following steps. Copy the graph onto the Clipboard using the Copy button as described. Next load your word processing software and place the cursor at the position in the document where you want the graph to appear. Choose Edit on the menu bar and select Paste from the pull-down menu. The graph will be copied here. You can now use it to illustrate the point you are making in your text. Use the ClipBook Viewer to perform other tasks such as deleting or saving the graph image. Do this by pressing Edit on the menu bar then Delete on the pull-down menu to remove graphs you no longer need. To save an image, press File on the menu bar followed by Save As on the pull-down menu to store the graph to be used later. The Save As dialog box has the suffix CLP as default, so fill in the name of your graph - perhaps BOOKS.CLP for a product sales graph. When you need to use it, load the ClipBook Viewer then press File on the menu bar and then Open on the pull-down menu. Type in your file name BOOKS.CLP or click on it to select it from the list, then press OK.

Q&A

Can I add my company logo to reports?

You can do this by using a scanner to copy your company logo into a Windows bitmap file. Alternatively use Windows Paintbrush (available from Accessories on the Program Manager) or other graphic applications to design a logo and save it as a bitmap file. Next choose Defaults on the menu bar then Report Defaults on the pull-down menu. On the Report Defaults display, press the Browse button to see a list of bitmap files. The subdirectory C:\PLUS2\REPORTS will be automatically selected together with all files that have the suffix BMP (for bitmap). If you have stored the file in a different place double-click on c:\ in the right-hand box, scroll through the list of subdirectories and double-click on the correct one. If you have also specified a second level subdirectory such as PLUS2 then REPORTS, scroll down and double-click on the next subdirectory.

The complete path should appear under Directories at the top of the screen, for example C:\PLUS2\REPORTS.

The bitmap file will be listed in the box on the left, so click on it to select it and press OK. The Report Defaults display now shows your bitmap file. Click on the option buttons to have it positioned to the left, centre or right on your reports. Finish by clicking on the Print Graphics on Reports check box and the logo will appear on your reports. If you want to miss the logo out at any time return to this screen and click on the check box to deactivate it. Finish by pressing OK to save the setting.

What is the Wallpaper Defaults option on the pull-down menu under Report Defaults?

This lets you change the blank white Desktop area on the main Sterling +2 display. You can create a design using Windows Paintbrush, then use Wallpaper Defaults to incorporate your design on the Desktop. Choose Accessories from the Program Manager then Paintbrush and create your design. When you have finished, press File on the Paintbrush menu bar, then Save As on the pull-down menu. Choose the subdirectory C:\PLUS2\REPORTS as described above and give the file a name with the suffix BMP. Press File on the menu bar and Exit from the pull-down menu then return to Sterling +2. Choose Defaults from the menu bar, then Wallpaper Defaults. Press the Browse button and click on your bitmap file in the list to select it then press OK. The Bitmap Position box has option buttons which let you select the area on the screen where your design will appear - or press the Full Screen option button to cover the whole Desktop area. Click on the Display Wallpaper check box then OK and your Desktop will appear newly decorated with your design.

How can I store reports on file when I don't want to print them out immediately?

Select a report, such as Audit Trail which is available from the Reports option on the Toolbar. You will be given four output options. Display and Preview let you see the report on screen, while Printer should only be used to print out a report immediately to the default printer. To store the report use the File option button and Run (or File on the Display/Preview menu bars followed by Save As from the pull-down menu). The Save As display gives the suffix RPT as a default in the File Name box and you only need to replace the asterisk with a name for the report. This could, for example, be AUDIT.RPT. The file will be automatically saved in the subdirectory C:\PLUS2\LETTER (not in the REPORTS subdirectory as printed in the manual). To delete the file you will need to use

Windows techniques: choose Main from the Program Manager then File Manager. Click on PLUS2 in the left-hand box and LETTER in the list of subdirectories under PLUS2. AUDIT.RPT (or any other file you have stored) will then appear in the list on the right. Click on it to select it, press File on the menu bar and Delete on the pull-down menu. Finish by confirming the deletion then press File on the menu bar and Exit to leave this screen.

I have stored the report on file but can't use it with other applications as suggested in the manual. Why is this?

The report is not in the correct format to be read by other software applications such as spreadsheets. You will need to convert it into a different format and export it, in order to use it successfully (find out how in Chapter 12).

When I save the report I notice that there are different types of files apart from report files. What are they used for?

On the Save As display, you can click on the arrow at the end of the Save As File Type box to see the different formats available. When you save a report, the Report File format is automatically selected and the suffix RPT appears in the File Name box. The other formats are: Windows Write files (*.WRI), ASCII text only files (*.TXT), and comma separated value files (*.CSV). The software automatically selects the type of file according to the software you are working on.

CHAPTER 11

Multicompany Processing and Periodic Functions

Sage Sterling +2 Financial Controller can be used to handle a number of companies or one company with subsidiaries or subdivisions. Any of the companies you install can be treated as the parent company if required, otherwise you can keep independent accounts for each. Should you want to consolidate the accounts from a number of companies under a parent company, you can do this when you run the period end routines - described later in the chapter.

It's important to make sure each company you add has its own subdirectory on the hard disk, so that the data is kept completely separate for each one. The information for your first company is stored with Sterling +2 program files in the subdirectory C:\PLUS2. All of your accounting information, for example, is stored in C:\PLUS2\ACCDATA. Earlier you learnt how to change document designs using the subdirectory C:\PLUS2\LETTER. The other files for your first company are stored in C:\PLUS2 under \REPORTS, \CRITERIA and \MEMO. The names make it quite clear the type of information that is stored in each one.

You may only need to do accounts for one company. Even so you could set up at least one other company, which you could use to test out your expertise on the software, before risking any real damage to your actual accounting data! You will be asked to specify the directory where each company's information should be stored. Give this directory a meaningful name because it will appear on the Sage group window under its own icon. You will want to be sure you are choosing the right company each time. Sage suggests the directory C:\COMPANY2 as an example, but this is just a general name - you will probably want to put the names of your actual companies. For the demonstration data company to be used in training, you could put the directory C:\DEMO and the icon will be labelled with the word demo. You will have the option to set a different name for the icon but it makes sense to use the same tag for easy identification of files. The program files for Sterling +2 will be kept in the same directory as your first company. Each additional company will have its own set of subdirectories for accounting data, reports, document designs and criteria.

Tip

When you start the consolidation procedure the software treats the company you are working on as the parent. Choose the consolidation routine from the parent company and select which other companies you want to consolidate. You don't have to set up the parent company first.

Adding companies

It should be quite straightforward to add extra companies. You don't have to do anything new - the steps are similar to when you first installed Sterling +2. This time choose File from the main menu bar then select New Company from the pull-down menu. Start by adding a company which you can use to train staff or to try out complicated functions. Fill in the name and address, making it clear that this is not a real company. For example, call it Demonstration Company plc. The screen is just the same as the one you filled in when setting the configurations for your first company.

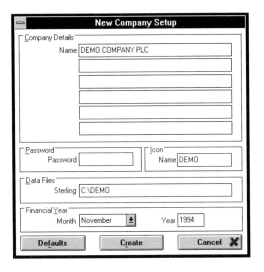

Each company can have a different password which you specify on this screen. You will not be able to click on the Create button to initialise the new data files until you specify the directory. Make sure you specify the path by using characters the computer can recognise. For the demonstration company you could type C:\DEMO in the Data Files box, by the label Sterling. You can also set a name to appear with the icon by Name in the Icon box. Here again Demo would be a good choice as you will easily be able to link the icon to the directory holding the data.

Use the Defaults button to change any of the standard Sage settings as you did when installing Sterling +2 (see Chapter 3 as a reminder). This will let you choose your method of VAT accounting and whether or not you want to use the default Windows colours set on your control panel or stay with the Sage colours - click on the check boxes to activate any choices. By now, some of the other defaults should make more sense. In the Editor box you will see NOTEPAD.EXE and it is this setting which makes Sterling +2 automatically switch to the Windows notepad when you need word processing facilities. The Function Keys box has CONTROL.EXE by F11, as this key loads the Windows Control Panel. F12 has been allocated to FINCVAR.EXE and automatically loads variables when you use Windows Write to redesign documents.

Once you have set all the defaults and typed the directory name for the new company, the Create button will become active and you can press it to complete the set up. You are now working on the files for the new company. You will see that the screen looks exactly the same as for the first company - there are just no records yet. Now it's time to create your database and carry on setting up the system just as you did the first time round.

Warning

The screens are identical for each company so check the company name at the top of the screen to make sure you're entering information in the correct company files.

How can I move from one company's data to another as I often have to work on several companies at a time?

It's quick and easy to move between companies. Choose File from the main menu bar, then Open Company from the pull-down menu, highlight the desired company in the list and click on OK. The company which you are currently working on will not be included in the list, so don't be surprised that your demonstration company doesn't appear the first time. By creating it you have automatically loaded it so be careful not to start inputting actual working data by mistake.

When you first switch on the computer and choose the Sage icon from the Program Manager window, you will see a choice of icons each labelled with a different company name. Make sure you choose the correct company and check from time to time to make sure you're not working on the wrong company or on demonstration files. If you use Open Company from the File menu, Sage will prompt you to finish all active transactions and close all windows before switching to a different company.

Consolidation

You may need to merge accounting data from several companies which work together as a group, perhaps a parent with subsidiaries or simply a company with subdivisions. This is called consolidation. However, you don't always have to consolidate the data from your separate companies. Even if you do, you might only want to select some of the companies for consolidation while others can be treated independently. You will need to decide which is the parent company and then run consolidation when this company's files are loaded. Don't worry if there are nominal accounts you have created in the subsidiaries which are not in the parent company - the software will automatically create them in the parent company's chart of accounts. However, you might want to change the chart of accounts by consultation with your accountant, before you consolidate the information.

Tip

Decide carefully how you want to organise your business into parent and subsidiaries before running consolidation. Once consolidation has been completed, the information in your parent company's nominal ledger will be overwritten by data from the subsidiaries.

Warning

Take a copy of your data from all the companies before running the consolidation procedure in case of error.

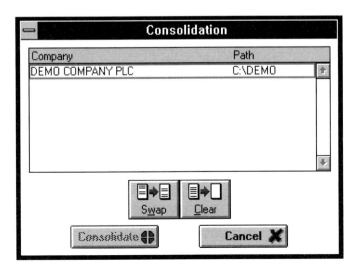

Consolidation should be run at month end for all subsidiary companies. Run Month End (described later) for the subsidiaries, then load the parent company and select Period End from the Menu bar. Next choose Consolidation and a window appears listing all the available companies. Highlight the companies you want to include in the consolidation. Only when you have selected them in this way, does the Consolidate button become active - press it and confirm that you want to continue. The data will then be merged with data stored in the parent company's nominal accounts. Accounts with the same codes will be added together and any new codes will be added to the parent company's chart of accounts. The trial balance for the parent company will now include data from all the merged company records and you should print out and check the balance sheet and profit and loss reports (available from Financials on the Toolbar).

Tip

Use the Swap button to choose all un-highlighted companies. Press the Clear button if you want to cancel your selections.

Any new codes which have been added to the parent company's nominal ledger must fit in with the existing structure so that they will appear in the correct reports. This will automatically happen if you set a standard range of codes for the profit and loss and balance sheet items and use this for all companies. You might have to make journal entries to adjust the figures before producing the final consolidated month end reports. After this you can run the complete month end procedure for the parent company.

Periodic functions

From the Period End option on the main menu bar, you can choose Month End and Year End as well as Consolidation. The other periodic functions you will need to run from time to time are Backup and Restore (on the pull-down menu under Data), remembering to back up your data as often as possible. Remember that in case of computer failure a recent set of printed out reports can help the company to keep working until the system is up and running again.

Month End

It's important to run the month end procedures on time because many of the transactions you have recorded will be waiting for this routine in order to be posted. In Chapter 9 under nominal ledger processing, you learnt how to enter details on prepayments and accruals. The month end routine will post these transactions to the correct accounts. The nominal accounts will be debited while the prepayment and accruals accounts will be credited and the transactions will be marked as posted in your records.

If you have set up depreciation for your company assets, the monthly amounts will be

calculated and posted to the fixed asset depreciation nominal accounts. The total figure for all assets will be updated in the depreciation control account. Only when this is done can you check for the accurate current value of your assets.

Tip

If you haven't set figures for depreciation of assets or for prepayments and accruals do so using Deprec, Prepay or Accruals on the nominal ledger menu (see Chapter 9).

The month end procedure can only be run if you have processed all of your recurring entries - these are the amounts you have set to be paid every month for items such as loans and insurance. The software carries out checks at month end, to see if these figures have been posted. If you haven't completed this procedure, then process the recurring entries now. Select Bank from the Toolbar, then Recurring and click on the Process button (see Chapter 6 for more details).

Warning

Take a copy of your data files before running the month end procedure.

When you press Month End on the Period End menu, the next window prompts you to click on the check boxes to indicate which routines should be run. The first are posting of accruals and prepayments, then depreciation. You should put an X in each of these boxes. You can also clear the audit trail and clear the stock, but these two choices are optional - do you want to run them or not? If you don't want to run these make sure there is no X in the box. Take heed of the warning at the top of the window which reminds you to take a copy of all your data in case you make a mistake and want to recover information. If you decide to clear the audit trail the software will clear all allocated, paid and reconciled transactions. Should you only want to clear audit trail transactions up to a certain date, replace the default date which appears at the bottom of the box. Finish by clicking on OK and the month end routines will all be run according to your specifications.

Warning

The Clear Stock option will remove all stock history files to the present date regardless of the date you set in the final box.

Year End

Warning

See Chapter 12 to find out how to prepare your final accounts and submit them to the Inland Revenue. Don't run Year End before you have a complete set of final accounts.

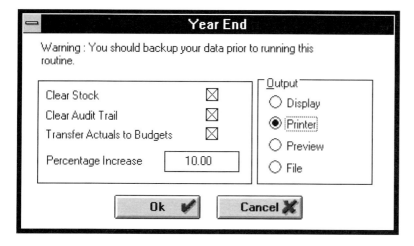

To run the year end procedures, select Period End from the main menu bar followed by Year End. The next display gives you the opportunity to clear the audit trail, clear the stock and transfer actual figures to create budgets. Click on the check boxes and make sure there is an X by the options you want to activate. Clear Audit Trail will clear out the transactions on the audit trail ready for a new start as another financial year begins. Clear Stock will clear all the stock history files - remember that the date you specify doesn't help limit this total clearance. If you choose to transfer actuals to budgets the software takes the nominal account balances for the year and uses them to create budget figures for the new year. These will then be used for comparison purposes.

Warning

Take a copy of all your data before running Year End as all the year's sales and purchase figures will be set to zero. Journal entries will be automatically posted so that the balances on all profit and loss accounts will be moved from the trial balance to the retained profit and loss control account.

If you choose to transfer actuals to budgets fill in the Percentage Increase box if you want to set a target for improved performance in the coming year. Finish by choosing how you want your year end report output - to disk file, printer or on-screen display. You will need a printout of this report as it lists all the postings carried out by the year-end procedure. Once you have carried out all of these steps press OK to run the year end function.

Backup and Restore

It's vital to back up your data before running periodic functions such as month and year end, which will change your files completely. However, it's also extremely important to keep regular backups, just in case you make a mistake and lose valuable data; or in case of computer failure, natural disaster or a computer fraudster in the office. Disgruntled staff can easily mess up the computer records, while events such as terrorist campaigns and plagues of computer viruses damaging and destroying data in the City of London show just how necessary backups are. The more recent your backup is, the more useful it will be and the sooner you will be able to get the business running again. Keep backups in fireproof safes and store extra copies away from the premises together with copies of the Sterling +2 master disks. In the event of computer failure or damage you can survive for a while with printouts of data, or even rent a PC to load your copies and recommence work immediately.

Tip

Remember that your hard disk will fail sooner or later making all the data files inaccessible - be prepared with up-to-date backups.

How often should I make a backup?

Run the backup routine at least once a day. This is not at all difficult as Sterling +2 not only automates all the steps and makes them easy to operate, it also reminds you to do so every time you exit and gives you the option to back up your data. When you are entering a large amount of information or doing major processing tasks, you should run the backup routines even more often. This will ensure that you don't waste hours of inputting time or find that you have processed transactions by mistake and want to return to an earlier version of your records.

When setting up the system you might want to run the Backup routine more than once a day. When you're up and running you'll probably only need to do so at the end of each day and before periodic functions such as month and year end. However, there may be days when you have to enter a large number of transactions - in that case run the Backup routine several times.

Sage recommends a standard method of keeping three sets of backup disks. There is the chance that by having just one copy all your data could be lost if the disks become damaged. Call your sets of disks A, B and C. On the first day make the backup onto the A set of disks, on the second day use set B and continue to use alternate sets of disks until the end of the week. On the last day of the week use set C for a weekly backup. At the start of the next week make the first backup onto set B and alternate daily between sets A and B. Make the weekly backup onto a *different* set C of disks each week. Keep each new set of C disks away from the office in case of natural disaster or fire. Make the final backups onto the latest set C before running month or year end routines.

Warning

Don't keep using the same floppy disks for your backup sets A and B. They will eventually become faulty so remember to replace them every few months and hopefully if you ever need to restore data it will only be out of date by one day.

Backup

Before running Backup, format a set of disks so that there are always some readily available to encourage staff to make copies of data. If this is the first time you're using a Windows application you may still be formatting disks using DOS commands, but the Windows method is easier. Choose Main from the Windows Program Manager window then select File Manager from the Main group window. Next choose Disk from the File Manager menu bar, put the floppy disk in drive A and select Format Disk from the pull-down menu. The next screen displays the formatting information about the disk in drive A and you just need to click on OK to have the disk formatted. At the end you will be given the option to format another disk and it's a good idea to format a whole set so that you're ready to take your backups.

With the first formatted disk in drive A select Data from the Sterling +2 Toolbar and select Backup from the pull-down menu. The next screen shows a selection of drives and subdirectories for you to select, but in fact the backup routine will back up all the

subdirectories and you can't just select a few. It's possible to choose a floppy disk drive (usually just A) or the hard disk drive C for your backup data. However, it makes sense to make the backup onto floppy disks, otherwise computer failure could lose your actual data and backup data.

Press the arrow in the Drives box to see a choice of disk drives and select a: by clicking on it. This will mark it out as the destination for backups - remember to insert a formatted disk ready to receive the data before pressing OK. When you back up your data onto floppy disk, Sterling +2 creates one file called SAGE.BCK. Make sure that you have at least one other disk containing the last backup, in case there is currently an error in the accounting data and you overwrite your only good set of backup data. If there is too much data for one disk you will be prompted to insert extra disks. In this case you should number them so that you know the correct order to insert them next time. Make sure you also date the disks accurately so that you will always know how old the data is should you need to use it to restore information - if you don't, you won't know how much and what work you need to re-enter to get the system up-to-date.

Warning

If there is a problem and you need to abort the backup in mid flow, delete all the data on the floppy disks. If you need some of it, keep the disks clearly labelled and away from the other backup sets. If you're not careful a disk used in an aborted backup may be used to restore data to the actual records and will only have part of the necessary information.

Restore

Should your computer fail or disaster strike you will be pleased with yourself for keeping regular backups because these can be used to restore the most recent copy of your accounting data. In less extreme circumstances, you may find that for some reason your

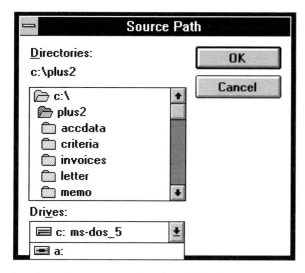

data has become corrupted and the software gives error messages when you try to access information. If you are using Sage support it's a good idea to ask for technical advice before running the Restore procedure, which will overwrite all your files with the last set of data copied onto backup disks.

Choose Data from the main menu bar, then the Restore option from the pull-down menu. Click on the arrow in the Drives box to see a list of disk drives. Click on a: to choose it, as the source of backup data. Insert the first disk from your most recent set of backup disks in Drive A. Finish by pressing OK to run the Restore routine.

Warning

This routine will replace all of your data files with the data from your last backup so don't use it to replace data in just some of your records. You must restore all the data at the same time - don't try to restore part of it. This may result in data corruption as the records will be incompatible until the full procedure has been run.

If the backup was onto a number of disks you must respond to the prompts to insert the disks in the correct order. Be careful to restore data from all of the disks used for the backup or your data files will be left incomplete. This should be straightforward if your disks are labelled well. If you do make a mistake and put the wrong disk in the drive the software will let you know so that you can try a different one. Sterling +2 finishes by displaying a message to tell you the restore has been successful. Don't forget that you will need to re-enter all the work done since the date of the backup.

Q&A

I have noticed that Sterling +2 doesn't automatically update opening and closing stock figures in the nominal ledger chart of accounts. What do I need to do to make sure stock transactions are reflected in the profit and loss account and on the balance sheet?

Make sure that you entered an opening balance in the opening stock account (5200 on the default chart of accounts) giving the value of your stock at the start of the financial year. Before you run month end procedures you should adjust the stock accounts in the nominal ledger - get in the habit of doing this regularly.

Imagine that you start with an opening balance for opening stock of £1,000 and at the end of the first month this has gone down to £500. You should post the following double entry:

N/C	Details	Debit	Credit
5201	Closing stock		500
1001	Stock	500	

At the end of the second month you should check your stock valuation again (print out the stock valuation report available by pressing Products on the Toolbar then Report). Imagine that the stock value has gone up to £750. You have to write back (reverse) the previous month's closing figure, then enter the current closing stock. To do this you need to make two double entries:

N/C	Details	Debit	Credit
5201	Closing stock	500	
1001	Stock		500
5201	Closing stock		750
1001	Stock	750	

Run the month end routine after the double entry has been made. If you keep your stock accounts updated every month your balance sheet report will have accurate figures throughout the year. If you don't do this task every month you must at least do it once a year. Remember to print out your stock valuation report before running the year end routine. Then either enter the closing stock figures yourself using the techniques above, or give the report to your accountant to make the necessary adjustments.

CHAPTER 12

Special Features

Sterling +2 has many useful facilities for error correction, reversing transactions and even clearing up data corruption. Although this part of the software, which has aptly been called Disk Doctor, has been designed for ease of use, many users don't take advantage of all the features it offers. Disk Doctor has already been mentioned in earlier chapters as the functions available here include the important method of compressing the data files, clearing the space which is still taken up by deleted and unnecessary records. Other Disk Doctor facilities are for checking the data to find any inconsistencies and to correct some types of errors. It's necessary to run the data checking function before you take the extreme step of restoring records from your backup disks as you may be able to cure some minor problems. Major corruption of files, on the other hand, means the only option is to revert to backup accounting data.

Tip

Use Disk Doctor to check for problems with your accounting data before taking backups.

The useful financial information put together in Sterling +2 reports can also be transferred to other applications and most businesses will want to do this in order to analyse the figures on a spreadsheet package. This can be done by transferring the files in the standard comma separated values (CSV) format, which is recognised by popular spreadsheets, databases and other financial applications. This format is called CSV as the files are transferred with each field separated from the next field by a comma. There is also an import facility which lets you transfer CSV files from an external source into Sterling +2.

Disk Doctor

Press Data on the main menu bar then Disk Doctor on the pull-down menu. This loads the data checking and correcting functions as well as the important data file compression routine. The three choices are Check, Correct and Compress; and heed the warning to take a backup before running Correct or Compress as these will change your data files. As soon as you press one of these buttons the procedure will be run.

Check data files

Before backing up your data it's a good idea to check for any errors or corruption. These can often be rectified before you copy them onto your floppy disks and ruin the backup. Select this option by running Disk Doctor with the required company loaded and press the Check button. The software will automatically check the files and point out three types of problem: errors, warnings and comments. If no problems are found these will all be marked with a zero, otherwise the number of inconsistencies will be displayed in the three boxes.

Tip

Double-click on the control-menu box in the top left corner to move quickly back through the Disk Doctor screens and to exit from this option.

If there are any problems the number will appear and the seriousness of these depends on the type of condition. The most serious are the errors which will need to be put right before you continue. A warning or a comment is less important and does not need to be fixed by the automatic routines - you will still want to find out what it is and correct it manually.

Disk Doctor checks for a variety of inconsistencies. The first type are input errors which can be recognised by the software if the amount is incorrect judging by the limits set within the program. Internal inconsistencies will also be found - these occur when transactions don't match up or values are incompatible. Missing data can be detected if files or pieces of vital data have been lost. Corrupt data is found when the software can't read damaged files or disks.

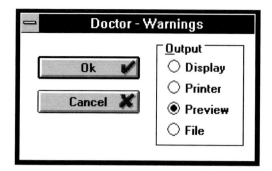

If errors, warnings or comments have been found by the data checking routine, the number will be indicated and the buttons at the top of the screen become active. For example, if there are just a few comments found, the Comments button will no longer be 'greyed out' - you can press it to see a full explanation of each problem. The software generates a report with errors, warnings and comments. It prompts you to choose a method of output for this report. Although you can just choose Display to see it on the screen it's a good idea to print it out.

Tip

Always print out the explanations for Errors, Comments and Warnings as you will need this for reference when you make manual adjustments to rectify the situation.

If any errors have been detected, press the Errors button to see exactly what is wrong. The explanations are quite clear and start with the words *Error on* then give the file name where the mistake has occurred. Next there is a colon and a description of the problem, perhaps a file name has been entered which does not exist (the spelling may be wrong), account codes may be duplicated so new ones will have to be set, and so on. These errors will have to be corrected, but it is not difficult to do so.

For warnings you need to press the Warnings button and here the list of explanations starts with the words *Warning on* plus the name of the file. Here the problems are less serious, but you may still want to take advantage of the warnings to put any minor mistakes right. Typical warnings would be if a field has been left blank in a record or if a file is too long. The message will also point out the correct size for this type of problem. Use all this information to set your records straight.

Should any comments be indicated, press the Comments button - again these are not serious problems. The explanations start with *Comment on* plus the file location to help you locate and correct the mistake. Typical comments would be if a field is the wrong length or if a cost price has been entered which is greater than the sales price. Again these are situations you will want to look into.

Compress files

To clear disk space which is being needlessly taken up by deleted records you will have to compress the data files from time to time. To do so, run Disk Doctor - making sure you have loaded the data files for the correct company if you have a multicompany version of the software. This routine is important to clear out all the deleted records which are still taking up disk space. Unless you do this periodically you may find the software starting to slow down. From the Disk Doctor menu choose Compress and the data files will be compressed freeing valuable disk space.

Correcting problems

There are two ways to put the mistakes right using Disk Doctor commands. From the main Disk Doctor menu you can choose Correct to change specific fields for individual postings. The software automatically displays the audit trail transactions. Use the scroll bar to move down to the ones on your Errors, Warnings or Comments reports in order to put them right. This option can also be used to reverse transactions which you have posted by mistake.

The other method is for more serious problems and is run by pressing Fix Data on the screen where the Errors, Warnings and Comments buttons are displayed immediately after the data check. The Fix Data functions are complicated and you should not attempt to carry them out if at all unsure. The corrections are made to a temporary file and if the software can use this to correct your actual records it will then do so.

If you select Fix Data, the software will prompt you through the necessary steps - but make sure you have a recent backup in case anything goes wrong. As the software attempts repairs you will be prompted with Yes or No questions to let it proceed or to abort the process, if in any doubt. It will ask if you want it to try to rebuild the audit trail and ledger file links, and if you press Yes the screen will display the progress as it tries to correct inconsistencies. If the software can't correct the error, it will point this out and give a message suggesting what you could do manually. If one problem is caused by a number of errors the software will only cure the most serious one and you will have to run this process again to make sure all the amendments are made.

The software will point out if it can't correct mistakes by giving the message that you must restore backup data. This means using your most recent set of backup disks using the Restore routine described in Chapter 11. Once you have done this, check the data again to make sure the errors were not already in the files when you made the backup.

This shouldn't be the case if you run the data checking routine regularly before making copies. If the restored data is error free, check the date the backup was made then re-enter all transactions which had been done between that time and the present.

Warning

You must restore all the data from the backup and not just the files containing errors.

When the software has attempted repairs it may then give the following prompt: *Run the data check again, after the Audit Trail links have been rebuilt, and see if the Account Balances are in fact correct.* This indicates that there are problems in the links between the ledger files and the audit trail and that some account balances are suspect. As this may have been caused by corruption prior to the rebuilding of the audit trail, there may no longer be a problem. A second check will show if this is the case. If you choose Yes at this prompt, you will return to the Disk Doctor main menu and can select Check again. This second check will hopefully show all your files are in order, but if this is not the case you will have to find the faulty account balances and amend them.

Once the audit trail has been rebuilt, the software will indicate if the trial balance figures don't balance with one of the two following messages: *Run data check again, after the Audit Trail links have been rebuilt, and see if the Trial Balance has been put right too;* or *Run data check again, after the Account Balances have been corrected, and see if the Trial Balance has been put right too.* If you run these options and the Trial Balance definitely does not balance, there's nothing you can do to correct the situation. Then the problem is serious! An inability to make the figures balance means that transactions have been lost or were not posted properly - the records can't be left in this state. You must restore the last error-free data from a recent backup and then re-do all work which has been input since that date or consult your Accountant.

Inconsistencies in the order processing files may be indicated by the message *You must have NO Purchase Orders with stock on-order before you can proceed to correct the Quantity Allocated/On-Order error.* If the software gives this message it means that the figures for stock which is allocated or on-order don't tie up with the figures recorded in the sales and purchase order processing files. Disk Doctor can correct this problem by setting all the stock allocated and on-order figures to zero. This step won't be taken until you clear all allocated and on-order stock from the sales and purchase order processing files. To do this, you need to unallocate all the allocated stock in SOP and remove all on-order stock in POP. Next time you run Disk Doctor it will reset the stock figures. Once the amounts match up you will have to use SOP and POP to reallocate stock and place stock on order.

The software may be able to rebuild the main control file (ACCOUNT.DTA) using information in the ledger files. It will ask if you want to do this with the message *Attempt a reconstruction of the ACCOUNT.DTA file based on the existing data in the other Ledger files?* It is possible for Sterling +2 to fill in missing files by searching the other ledgers and checking the posting records - the lost files will be recreated. If the software doesn't succeed in rebuilding the files, you will be informed by a variety of error messages. The main difficulty will be if the NOMINAL.DTA file is missing. In this case the software can't always find the control accounts in the nominal ledger. It may be able to identify the control accounts by the types of transactions contained in the files, or by using part of the account names or simply trying the default codes. If, however, the control accounts can't be identified, a message starting *Can't find* is displayed, such as *Can't find Debtors Control Account*, or *Can't find Petty Cash Account*. The only action you can take is to restore data from the last backup. This method of rebuilding files also relies heavily on the POSTING.DTA file, which records all transaction posting information. If this file is missing the software will recreate it. However, it will also create ledger files but not set up accounts except nominal ledger control accounts. There will be no transactions on the audit trail. You will have to revert to a backup copy of the data.

Tip

After a major rebuilding of files, run Disk Doctor a second time to check all is in order. You will be prompted to run another check and should reply Yes. Expect errors as there will be more inconsistencies for the software to correct.

If the POSTING.DTA file has gone missing, your transactions have also been lost and are irretrievable. You will need to restore your most recent backup. The software will also display the message *Create a new POSTING.DTA file and reset all the pointers in the Ledger files?* This option just creates a new file and makes sure there are no incorrect links between the ledgers and lost transactions.

Sometimes data corruption affects the links between transaction histories and the audit trail so that transactions might appear on the audit trail but will be lost in the ledger records. For example, a sales invoice transaction might appear on the audit trail but not in the right sales ledger transaction history. The software may be able to recreate the links and make sure the appropriate data is in all the right places. The prompt for this is the message *Rebuild all the Audit Trail and Ledger file links?* Unfortunately this procedure uses a great deal of computer memory as it needs to duplicate all the files being checked and rebuilt. Often there will not be enough disk space to proceed. The attempted reconstruction uses temporary files, so at least if it has to abort, these will be deleted and your original files will be left. The reconstruction might also fail, if there are transactions on the audit trail with account numbers which can't be found in the ledgers. If you want you can try adding the account numbers in the ledgers and re-running the process, but this may be unwise. This problem shows that you have corruption in both the transaction links and in your data files. If you add the missing account numbers and run the reconstruction procedure again it will use temporary files. If it fails you will be returned to your original files.

Should the software find transactions with missing or invalid tax codes, it will give you the chance to fill in all these fields with the code T0. The message is *Set the missing or illegal tax codes to T0?* You can reply with a Y for yes to this, but you should check your tax codes to find out why the problem has occurred. The code T0 will be entered for all incorrect or missing codes. The software can't make any allowances for the amounts entered in the net and tax amount fields so these will have to be amended.

If files are longer than is permitted by the software a message beginning *Reduce* will be displayed, such as *Reduce CATEGORY.DTA file to correct size?* In this case the software can shorten the file to the accepted length.

When corruption is found in the product files, the software prompts *Rebuild the Product Index, Record and Transaction files?* This routine involves using the original product index file to check product records and transactions for each product code. If the original product index file is checked and correct then a new index can be built together with new product and stock transaction files. The new set of files will be free from corruption, but records and transactions which have invalid links to the index will be removed and can't be retrieved. This process takes up a large amount of computer memory as the rebuild is first done to temporary files which only replace existing files if completed successfully. You will be warned if the computer has run out of memory.

Once you have unallocated stock and taken stock off order in SOP and POP, the software will prompt you to see if you want to return all the amounts for stock allocated and on-order to zero. The message is *Reset all Stock quantity Allocated and Quantity On-Order Values?* If you haven't yet removed all allocations and on-order amounts this procedure can't be carried out.

The software can calculate the quantity of stock by comparing movements of products. If the amounts on record don't match up the software will suggest a recalculation to set the files straight. The prompt is *Correct Quantity Used values in STKTRANS.DTA file?* You will be warned if the process has been unsuccessful. This will either be because the software can't deal with stock histories where the number of incoming transactions is greater than 50, or if there is a problem which can't be solved for individual product codes. When there are problems, the software will correct records for as many products as possible. Where errors have been pointed out you will have to make the amendments manually. Delete the product codes then create new codes and new records wherever problems prove impossible to correct.

There are three more ways in which the system can rebuild files. Remember that these will only be reconstructed wherever all the data can be found and matched up. Files will be removed completely if they are irretrievably corrupted and the missing data can't be copied from elsewhere. For invoices there is the option *Rebuild the Invoice Index, Record and Item files?* This will reconstruct the invoice index, record and item files retaining any item records which can be matched to invoice records without any corruption. Any corruption in the invoice index or records will mean complete removal.

The message *Rebuild the Sales Order Index, Record and Item files?* works in a similar way. It will only preserve records of orders with valid links and no corruption in the records. Similarly you may choose to rebuild the purchase order files by responding to the prompt *Rebuild the Purchase Order Index, Record and Item files?* All of these methods of rebuilding files require a large amount of memory space and you may be informed that your system lacks the capacity.

Warning

These procedures only retain files which are not corrupted so you will lose data from any corrupted sectors. If you are unsure about whether or not this is the best method for your particular problem consult a Sage technician. It may be better to use a backup copy of the last set of valid data using Restore as described in Chapter 11 and then repeat any work done since that date.

If any of the ledger files have disappeared, the software will ask *Attempt a reconstruction of missing Ledger file(s) based on the existing data in the other Ledger files?* This routine uses all available data to try and recreate the missing file. If any of the control accounts are missing these will be set according to the Sage defaults. If the POSTING.DTA file has been lost, none of the transactions will show on the audit trail. If the NOMINAL.DTA file is missing the control accounts will be reset as in the default chart of accounts. At the end you should take advantage of the prompt *Do you want to run the data check again?* as there will be errors in the links between files and the audit trail, but Disk Doctor can put this right.

Tip

It's always a good idea to run the data check again until it shows that there are definitely no more problems.

Error correction

When Disk Doctor has given messages indicating that you only need to amend specific fields in your transactions, this can be done using the error correction technique. To run this option choose Disk Doctor from the Data pull-down menu then press the Correct button.

The screen displays all the transactions on the audit trail which have inconsistencies. If they don't all fit on the screen use the scroll arrows to move up and down through the list. Choose the transaction you need to correct by highlighting it and click on Edit to see the full transaction details. Select the field in the transaction which you want to amend by

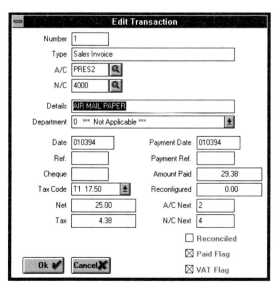

clicking on it or using the TAB key to move from field to field. If a field can't be altered the software will not let you select it, but if the field is available for correction you can type in the new data. Press OK to move on and do more correction. When you finish press Close to finish this task.

This option can also be used to reverse transactions such as invoices posted in error. To do this you must run the error correction routine, choose the transaction and change the amount to zero. The software will then keep a record of the original transaction but will post a reverse transaction for the same amount. As a result the two will cancel each other so you can delete them and then remove them from the records when you clear all reconciled transactions at period end. The reverse transaction will take the next available number on the audit trail so you will be able to check that it has been processed by looking at the audit trail report. This method can't be used for all types of transaction but it can be used for invoices, credit notes, bank receipts, bank payments, cash receipts and cash payments. Finish by printing out the transaction histories and audit trail and then check that you have made all the amendments, as suggested by Disk Doctor.

Warning

Remember to change the Payment Date field on the Edit Transaction display if you change the transaction date for payments or receipts. Otherwise the software can't use the information properly in reports.

Tip

If you need to change the VAT codes in any transactions, Sterling +2 won't automatically change the amount posted to the tax liability control accounts. It's better to post a reverse transaction to cancel the original one and then enter a new transaction with the correct figures.

Links to other applications

Sage offers a growing range of Windows packages which link into Sterling +2. Payroll completely automates personnel records, wages and salaries so that users can avoid the complex nominal ledger methods described in Chapter 9. TeleMagic for Windows is powerful contact management software which helps the credit controller and telesales staff (see Chapter 8). Microsoft and Sage have a joint software development agreement which means there are also seamless links between popular packages from both companies.

Whilst working on Sterling +2, you have already switched, fairly effortlessly, to Windows Write for word processing and document redesigning tasks. Sage has also set function key F11 to give quick access to the Windows Control Panel. Sterling +2 users will soon have a handy link to Word for word processing.

Microsoft also provides simple file transfer between Sterling +2 and its popular Office applications. Sterling +2 can work together with the Excel spreadsheet so that financial reports can be easily exported - one of the most complicated tasks to handle without easy links. Excel also has a menu option which provides a direct link to Sterling +2. Although users of the initial release of Sterling +2 Version 2 don't have this option on their menus. The technique works by transferring files to and from Excel via the Windows Write display. This means you work with the files using the importing and exporting techniques described below. The difference is that many of the steps are handled for you by the software making the connection appear seamless.

Even if you have other applications which do not have direct links to Sterling +2, you can export and import files. Data from Sterling +2 can be transferred to applications such as spreadsheets and databases for further processing and analysis. Information can also be imported from other sources using the standard CSV format. These options are particularly useful if you want to exploit your accounting data to the full. They also let you transfer files automatically rather than type all the figures into the spreadsheet or database. When you import files the data can be posted straight into your Sterling +2 files. The comma separated format divides fields using commas and quotation marks so that your applications can recognise exactly where the data needs to go.

Exporting files

To transfer data from Sterling +2 to a spreadsheet, database or other business application you need to create a CSV file containing the data. Do this by choosing File as the method of output on any of the report screens. For example, press Reports on the Toolbar, highlight one of the fixed transaction reports and click on the File option button as the method of output then click on Run. The software automatically displays the Windows display headed Save As. Click on the arrow at the end of the Save File as Type box and scroll down to highlight and select CSV file. The file name box automatically has *.CSV and you can replace the asterisk with the name of your file. To try it out just type EXPORT.CSV.

Tip

If you choose the Preview option button instead of File the method is slightly different. Press File on the Preview menu bar, then Save As from the pull-down menu. Continue as in the standard method.

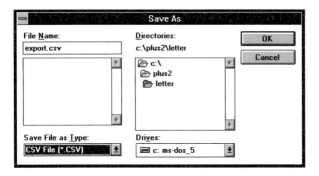

The file to be exported has been saved as C:\PLUS2\LETTER\EXPORT.CSV. Take a look at it by pressing F12 to switch over to Windows Write. Press File on the menu bar then choose Open from the pull-down menu. Click on the arrow at the end of the List of Files Type field, scroll down and choose All Files. A complete list of files will appear in the box on the left so scroll down until you find EXPORT.CSV. Click on it to select it, press OK, choose No Conversion at the prompt and the report will appear in CSV format.

What you need to do next with your file will depend on the software you want to transfer the data over to. However, there are other ways you can work on your CSV file. Should you want to delete it, you will have to use the Windows Program Manager: choose Main and then File Manager. Click on PLUS2 in the left-hand box and Letter in the right-hand box. Find EXPORT.CSV from the list which then appears on the right and click on it to select it. Press File on the menu bar and choose Delete from the pull-down menu. Confirm that you want to delete EXPORT.CSV when the prompt appears. Apart from deletion, File Manager offers other ways to work with your file, including opening, copying and renaming. When you want to leave the File Manager, press File and choose Exit from the pull-down menu.

Importing files

To import data from other sources you should select Data from the main menu bar then Import from the pull-down menu. The next screen gives you a choice of types of data files to import. Select the required one by clicking on the option button beside it. Choices are Customer Records, Supplier Records, Nominal Ledger Records, Transactions, Stock Records and Stock Transactions. Once the import has been completed, a report will be displayed to point out any errors that occured in the transfer. Inconsistencies are likely here and there due to missing commas and the like. Make sure that files in your spreadsheet or other applications have similar layouts to the files you are importing data to - the transfer will only be successful if the fields correspond, even if they are in a different order.

Tip

Familiarise yourself with CSV file layouts before attempting this routine. Take a look at export files to see how they are constructed - do this using Windows Write as described in the section on Exporting Files.

How do I create CSV files in my other applications ready to be imported by Sterling +2?

Before running the import facility you will have to produce compatible CSV files from data in your other applications. Sterling +2 will only accept data in files with the suffix CSV so you will have to give your files the following names: SALES.CSV (customer records), PURCHASE.CSV (supplier records), NOMINAL.CSV (nominal ledger records), TRANS.CSV (transactions), STOCK.CSV (stock records), STKTRANS.CSV (stock transactions). They will be copied into your actual accounting data files which have the same names but have the suffix DTA instead of CSV. Next you need to copy these files into the Sterling +2 subdirectory (C:\PLUS2). To copy the files, choose Main from the Windows Program Manager, then select File Manager. Click on the CSV files you have created one at a time, then choose File from the menu bar and Copy from the pull-down menu. A screen appears with the name and location of the CSV file and you just need to fill in the field labelled To with the correct directory - C:\PLUS2.

Warning

When you load Sterling +2 make sure you choose the right company to receive the data files if you're running Multico.

Next choose Data from the Sterling +2 main menu bar and then select Import from the pull-down menu. Once you click on the option button to choose which type of data is to be imported you can press Run. The next Window prompts you to fill in the source file which you have already prepared in CSV format. Sterling +2 automatically looks in the subdirectory C:\PLUS2 for any files with the suffix CSV and will expect standard names, such as SALES.CSV for customer records. If you have stored the file in a different subdirectory, type its name (including the path) into the file name box. For example, if you have called the file IMPORT.CSV and stored it in a subdirectory called EXCEL you will need to type C:\EXCEL\IMPORT.CSV. Finish by pressing OK.

The import routine starts by checking through the import data to see that there are no problems. Sterling +2 will then inform you of any errors so that you can correct them. If there are no difficulties the software will then go through the data a second time and transfer it to your accounts files. Then, it produces a report which shows exactly what has been imported successfully. Although errors should have been spotted in the first check, there is a chance the transfer will abort should mistakes be detected in the second check.

While the data is being checked and transferred, the software displays whether this is the first check or the second. It also shows the file line number to keep you informed on the progress being made. If you change your mind you can only abort during the first check by pressing escape - this can also be used to pause. Once the second check and actual data transfer begins you must let the whole process finish, because aborting at this stage would lead to a partial transfer and subsequent data corruption.

The report will point out any errors that stopped parts of the files being transferred. Typical errors would be failure to identify fields as the software looks for a comma at the beginning or end of a field; or quotation marks both at the beginning and end. Should one comma or a set of quotation marks be missing this will be pointed out. Fields with an opening quote and no final quote will give the message *Incomplete record*. Lines can only have 256 characters so you may get the message *Line too long for input buffer* if this limit is exceeded. You will also be warned if the field is too long as a maximum 32 characters will be permitted.

Tip

Don't be confused by two consecutive commas in a line - these enclose a field which contains no data. A single comma at the end of a line isn't an error - it means there is another field of zero length which has a meaning in this function.

Should there be too many fields, meaning more than necessary for data import, the screen displays *too many fields*, and if there aren't enough you will be told *invalid data*. If the number in a field is too high the message is *out of range*. You will also be warned if you don't have enough disk space, corruption in the files or problems making it impossible to read the data. The following warnings will be displayed: *Disk or File Error*, or *Disk or file access Error*. The message *Error while writing this data* means that you ran out of disk space during the second stage in checking and transferring files - a serious problem as this will have corrupted your records. If you get this last message you will have to restore data from your last backup.

If there is not enough disk space to display the final report, you won't know if the import has been successful. Use Disk Doctor (described earlier in this chapter) to check your data is free from errors. If the software returns to the main Import window after just one pass this means there were format and data errors in the import file and your original data has not been altered in any way. If all goes well, the software will progress from pass one to pass two and the IMPORT.RPT file will be displayed showing that the data has been successfully transferred. The second pass is much slower than the first because it is actually copying data from the source files to the target files in Sterling +2, whereas the first pass only has to read and check the source files.

BUSINESS*guide*

Preparing the final accounts

If your business is a limited company you are obliged to have your accounts audited by professional accountants. It makes sense to let them also prepare your final accounts for submission to the Inland Revenue. If, however, you have a different type of business you can prepare your own final accounts. Although this may sound a little daunting, many sole traders do all of their own accounting in a professional way. If you have followed the steps carefully and used Sterling +2 correctly, you will find that the software can actually do most of the work for you. If you are uncertain you could ask an accountant to prepare the accounts at the end of the first year and see if you feel confident enough to do it yourself in subsequent years. If your business is a partnership, however, the tax issues are complex - it's best to use a professional accountant.

Your final accounts may include a trading/manufacturing account and will definitely involve the profit and loss and the balance sheet reports. Trading and manufacturing accounts both serve the same purpose - one is for companies which manufacture goods while the other is for companies which offer services or buy and resell goods. The trading/manufacturing account subtracts the total cost of purchases from the income you have received from sales and the result is your gross profit.

The profit and loss account takes this gross profit and subtracts all the money you have paid out on overheads and direct expenses. The result is your net profit - the amount you have actually earned. With Sterling +2, all you need to do is print out your profit and loss report on the final day of your financial year because this gives both the gross and net profit figures. Choose Financials from the Toolbar, press P&L, click on the Printer option button and finish with OK. At the top of the report is the trading/manufacturing account. Beneath are the overheads and direct expenses with the total figure for net profit (or loss). The profit and loss report and the balance sheet figures give most of the information you need to fill in your tax return. The final accounts that you send should be typed out in the same way and will include the figures for the year (the Sterling +2 report also gives the amounts for the month). At the top of the page, you should show your business name and address. Next, state the period that the accounts cover - this should be the end date of your financial year. This information and the rest of the figures and layout can be copied exactly from the profit and loss report.

Warning
Run the month end routine before preparing your final accounts to make sure all the current transactions are posted (see Chapter 11). It's also important to print out the stock valuation report and update the stock accounts in the nominal ledger (see the Question and Answer section of Chapter 11 to find out how).

Tip
Contact Her Majesty's Stationery Office (HMSO) to ask for a guide to the layout of final accounts for submission to the Inland Revenue. Ask for the 1985 Companies Act which contains this information. Alternatively ask an accountant to show you how to do this in the first year and keep a copy to refer to in future years - the Sage layouts for the profit and loss and balance sheet reports conform to the regulations.

Next you should print out the balance sheet in the same way - press Financials on the Toolbar, then Balance, click on the Printer option button and finish with OK. Copy this report in the same way as the profit and loss report, remembering that you need the figures for the year to date and not the current month. The figures on the balance sheet will actually need to be adjusted in order to give a true picture of how your business is performing. The balance sheet includes the value of stock as an asset and this figure may need to be altered to account for lost and damaged goods. Refer back to Chapter 5 and see the Stocktaking section in the Business Guide for a full explanation of how this works and why it is so important.

Sterling +2 will have automatically made the other adjustments that an accountant would normally do for you if you had a manual set of records. This includes depreciation on capital items, such as computer equipment, so long as you have set the figures correctly using the methods described in Chapter 9. Sterling +2 uses the accruals method of bookkeeping to make adjustments to the figures at year end. This means it takes account of receipts and payments which have become due even if they haven't yet been settled. The accruals method also makes adjstments for payments which have been made, but which logically belong to a later period. For exampl, if you pay rent in advance on the last day of your financial year most of the payment relates to the new financial year. Tell your accountant Sage makes these adjustments as they will save him work.

Note

Set accruals and prepayments using the nominal ledger methods described in Chapter 9.

Once you have printed out the profit and loss report, adjusted stock valuation figures where necessary and printed out the balance sheet report, you are ready to send off your final accounts to the Inland Revenue (if you're a sole trader). If you trade as a limited company or partnership you will be fully prepared for the auditor's visit. Now you can run the Year End routine available under Period End on the menu bar (see Chapter 11) - make sure you back up your data first. The profit and loss and balance sheet reports will then show figures of zero for each account - they have been cleared and are ready for the new year's postings.

Q&A

What happens if I prepare the final accounts but have to wait for the auditor to check them? I'm worried in case my calculations are not accepted but I need to move on into the new financial year and set the accounts to zero.

It's important to run the Backup routine to store all your accounting data as it stood on the last day of your financial year, when you prepared the final accounts. Keep this disk copy safe in case your calculations are queried - you will be able to restore it and work on the files again just as you have learnt to do with demonstration data. Some companies clearly label all their monthly backups so that they can go back into their past records whenever necessary. Remember to back up your current data before using the backup in this way. If you have Financial Controller, you can use Restore to save your backup data at year end in the files of a demonstration company. This method is safer because there's no risk of damage if you forget to back up your current data, or to restore it once you have checked the past data. See the Training Tip in Chapter 2 if you don't remember how to set up and use demonstration data.

Our business is a partnership. How does this change the way we prepare final accounts?

The final accounts are prepared in the same way but there are other differences in the way you work on Sterling +2. Each partner who has invested capital in the business will have a separate Directors Capital account specifying his or her contribution (find out how to do this by referring to the Business Guide in Chapter 4). When you started the business you should have decided how the net profits would be divided between the partners (this should be set out in writing by a solicitor). At the end of the year you can take the net profit and share it between the partners, based on the agreed sums. During the year each partner can take drawings (the correct term for partners' earnings). You should create a separate drawings account for each partner, giving codes in the same section as other wages and salaries accounts in the nominal ledger (i.e. code numbers starting with the figures 70). When the actual drawings are made, you will make double entry postings between the bank account and the drawings accounts - do this in the same way you would for staff salaries (see the Business Guide in Chapter 9).

Preparing the accounts on Sterling +2 looks easy. I am a sole trader, do I really need an accountant?

If you have a small business some of your expenses may be shared between personal and business use. It's best to consult an accountant to find out what percentage the Inland Revenue is likely to allow on each of these items. For example, you may use the same car for business and domestic purposes and your accountant may suggest 75% business use. This will mean you can claim a deduction of 75% on all expenses relating to the car. The accountant will also be able to advise you of allowable expenses you may not have thought of. When you start out in business it's worth paying a fee to a professional who can save you money in the long term.

Do I need to send the Inland Revenue anything apart from the figures from the profit and loss and balance sheet reports?

If you have divided certain expenses between business and personal use you should state the percentages you have allocated to business use so that the Inland Revenue can decide whether or not to accept them. In future years you need only explain if you have changed one of these percentages - always keep it brief. It's also a good idea to explain any dramatic changes to your performance - tell them why your profit has suddenly increased or decreased by a massive amount. Always remember to keep your communications short and to the point.

Tip

Keep copies of everything you send to the Inland Revenue.

What should I expect the Inland Revenue to send back to me once they receive my accounts?

Don't worry if it takes a few weeks to get a reply - they will be looking at many sets of accounts at the same time. When they do write, it may be to ask you to explain a few of your figures. You shouldn't worry about this because they are only seeking clarification. After this you should get a letter letting you know that your calculations have been accepted. This will also state the agreed figure for your net profit - you will be taxed on this amount. When you finally receive your tax assessment you have 30 days to appeal if you think there is a mistake. Businesses pay their tax in one instalment, self-employed people pay in two parts.

Tip

Put the amount you owe into an interest earning account ready to pay on the due date. This will be January 1st for most businesses, or January 1st and July 1st for self-employed people.

I'm starting my first year in business. Do I have to inform the Inland Revenue, and how do I do this?

Contact the Inland Revenue and ask for their guide to starting in business. This will give you all the information you need on your business. You will also be provided with the necessary documents to register with the local tax office. You should also contact the Department of Social Security to make arrangements for your National Insurance contributions. Again they will send a guide and all the necessary forms. Contact the local VAT office (under Customs and Excise in the phone book) if you need to register for VAT.

My accountant is a member of Sage's Accountants club. What does this mean?

Members get extra help and support from Sage so that they can help their clients to run their accounts on the software. Sage also provides software called Sterling Auditor which helps the auditor to work on the clients' books and prepare the final accounts. All of this speeds up and simplifies the auditing process and should mean less work at year end.

I want to run my business as a limited company. How do I start?

The simplest technique is called buying a limited company off-the-shelf. This is not expensive - all you need to do is contact a company registration agent. Look under Company Registration Agents in the phone book.

Is there anything else I need to know?

By now you should have worked on all the Sterling +2 functions and learnt how to do your own accounting from the most basic tasks right through to preparing your final accounts. As you move into the next year on the system you can refer to the index to remind yourself how to work on each part of the software. In the next section you will see how two quite different companies are using Sterling +2 in practice to run their businesses.

Case Studies

Theatre de Complicité Ltd, London
Financial Manager: Sarah-Jane Hughes

The Theatre de Complicité in London chose to use Sterling +2 Financial Controller two years ago. As a touring theatre company this business has quite complicated accounting requirements even though there are only four full-time administrative employees. New productions mean constant changes to the cast of about 15 actors so it's difficult to computerise the payroll and personnel records. This is a unique type of business with extraordinary needs.

The Theatre selected Financial Controller, although there is actually no need for stock control, order processing or multicompany functionality. Like many buyers they opted for the top-of-the-range product, even though they could have saved financially by choosing Accountant which would have been adequate for their particular business. So far they have been unable to computerise the payroll because they would continually need to open and close files on casual workers. Their solution is to keep manual payroll records and then make journal entries to record the figures in the Sterling +2 nominal ledger.

As an accountant Hughes already had experience working on Sterling for DOS before moving onto Sterling +2. Her initial reaction was negative towards the Windows approach. She felt that the DOS version stuck more closely to accounting principles and liked the way reports were linked to the ledgers, not divided off into the separate Toolbar option Reports. The latest release overcomes this problem by allowing multiple windows to be displayed, so the Reports option can be opened alongside the ledgers.

The actual names of functions confused her because she was looking for traditional accounting terms. For example, she expected the day book to be accessed via a Day Book option as it is on the DOS version. She thought that there was no similar report available on Sterling +2, but this is one example where the information is available from Reports on the Toolbar and not from Customers or Suppliers. A professional accountant at heart, she would have also preferred sales and purchase ledger options on the Toolbar instead of Customers and Suppliers.

To non-accountants the term 'day book' would be more ambiguous. The sales and purchase ledger day books give details on transactions relating to specific dates, customers and suppliers. On more traditionally designed systems this information is accessed by choosing the sales or purchase ledger on the main menu, then the appropriate day book from the ledger menu. It's important to be able to choose the required customers or suppliers and also set a range of dates, nominal accounts and transactions. Hughes was finding it time-consuming to highlight the Customers and Suppliers she required and felt she had to look at full transaction histories with no way of specifying limits. The best method is to choose Reports on the Toolbar which offers a complete set of fixed transaction reports. Set the ranges to specify which transactions, customers, suppliers, dates or nominal codes you want to include at the bottom. Then you can choose types of transaction (invoices and credit notes are just two among many options). This is the day book although it might not have the same name.

Before installing Sterling +2, the Theatre used Microsoft's Excel Spreadsheet on an Apple Macintosh. They set up a cash book on Excel and took the figures off on a monthly basis just to review the accounts and make sure the wages had been paid. This meant putting together reports in an awkward fashion and calling in an accountant at year end to put the figures together in a more professional way. The main drawback was that this was an incomplete records system and the preparation of final accounts at year end was time-consuming and expensive.

The cost of the previous system was also causing problems with the Arts Council which funds the Theatre. They decided that they needed software capable of maintaining informative up-to-date records which could be broken down into categories for analysis. Other essential criteria were that the system must be extremely easy to use and integrated so that it could cope with a large amount of data. Information extracted from the software has to be presented to senior personnel at the Arts Council and the London Arts Board so it has to be timely and impressive.

The Arts Council recommended Sterling +2 and gave the Theatre a grant, all of which simplified the selection procedure. A software consultant supplied and implemented the system and the previous financial manager, Craig Sheppard, went on a Sage training course. Although he was a bookkeeper he needed more accounting training on the system to make the most of all the facilities. Many transactions were left unreconciled at the time Hughes arrived so the accounts needed careful sorting and processing. This is not an unusual situation as many businesses rely on the computer to take over the accounting and make all of the tasks automatic and obvious. According to Hughes it is still vital to have basic accounting skills - to know about sales, purchase and nominal ledgers and how they all interact. This book should help you understand these areas.

Setting up the new system on Sterling +2 was straightforward because the previous methods had been basic and there were no formal structures to follow. The Theatre chose to install the software in April, at the end of their financial year, so they only had to enter opening balances. They had to create nominal ledger codes to fit in with the standard structure used by the Arts Council and type in details from invoices. The financial manager ignored the sales and purchase ledgers and used the nominal payments facility available from the Bank option to post details on payments and receipts. The drawback with this approach is that it doesn't create transaction histories for the debtors and creditors. In retrospect Hughes feels it would have been better to enter details on individual customers and suppliers by entering details on each invoice. This can be done using the opening balance setup method on each customer or supplier record.

Installing the software in April was of definite benefit because only a trained accountant would have had the expertise to switch to a new system in the middle of the financial year. Many Sterling +2 users are non-accountants and they can avoid major difficulties in computerising accounts by doing so at year end. At this time of the year it's only necessary to make changes to the nominal ledger codes to fit in with the previous system and start anew with a blank sheet. Hughes's predecessor then had the monotonous task of entering all outstanding transactions and customer and supplier records.

The main advantages to the system have been the attractiveness of the Windows environment, the touch control and the extreme ease of use. Hughes now finds that it's not just appealing to look at but it does actually do the job efficiently. Disadvantages in Version 1 of Sterling +2 have largely been overcome - she complained about the way previous ledgers, reports and utilities were organised. In Version 2 these problems were resolved because the multiple windows allow the ledgers, reports and banking facilities to be viewed simultaneously.

Hughes is a frequent user of Disk Doctor so the fact that these utilities are now available from the menu bar is a definite improvement (on the previous version the user had to exit from Sterling +2 and choose a separate icon from the Sage Group window). The report generator was also more difficult to use in the earlier version and caused problems at the Theatre - a major complaint as this facility is of particular importance to Hughes. The new pop-up window with variables to set column specifications is a definite bonus as the software is now providing automatic prompts. For all the variables and settings Version 1 really did require technical expertise and a manual by your side for reference.

The software often seems more limited than it actually is because she finds the manual unclear about how to use certain functions. Reports are crucial to her work, but she wasn't sure exactly how to use Criteria, the report generator or some of the more advanced methods of sorting data and concluded that the reporting facilities were inadequate. This is not uncommon among Sage software users - the Sterling range can often handle more than they realise. Refer to Chapter 10 if you think you're not making the most of the reporting features.

The function Hughes missed most from her Sterling for DOS days was the F6 key. This let her copy the description field on a transaction from one line to the next, which is particularly useful if there are few or no changes. When putting on a production many of the details in the description line have to be repeated, this is possible on Sterling +2 using the Windows 'copy and paste' technique. Put the cursor in the field you want to copy, press the Control key and C simultaneously, then put the cursor in the field where you want to repeat the information and press Control V. Many Sage users may not have typing skills, so this technique can save time and frustration.

The most complicated task on accounting software is generally transferring data to and from other applications, such as spreadsheets. At the Theatre they would like to transfer figures to a Lotus spreadsheet but felt this was not possible. Many Sage software users don't realise that they can transfer their accounting data to other applications, including spreadsheets, by saving files in the CSV (comma separated values) format. It's a pity this facility is underused because transferring the data automatically saves time and effort and minimises errors such as typos. Financial managers need to use spreadsheets to analyse their figures and re-typing the data is a waste of effort. The process is explained in detail in Chapter 12.

Some users neglect the facilities offered by Disk Doctor, but Hughes exploits these to the full. It proves especially useful for error correction, so this is the technique she uses when she has made a slight mistake in a transaction description and wants to amend it. Although there are other methods of error correction she finds Disk Doctor the quickest and simplest. From time to time she runs the data file compression routine, which in general is another underused function. She also uses the reconfiguration options at month end. The reconfiguration options appear when you run month and year end and include clearing out the stock history files and reconciled audit trail transactions.

The software slows down as more data is added to it which is why she runs reconfiguration at month end. Her predecessor had left data for three months on the system and it was running slowly - many businesses do the same but mistakenly blame the software. It's vital to tidy up the records from time to time! For data security Hughes runs a monthly backup, and will sometimes increase this to once a week or more if she is inputting a large number of transactions. Sage recommends more regular backups so that you can always revert to the latest copy of your data should the computer fail.

The feature which the Theatre particularly needs is a cash flow model. Again this is an accounting term for facilities which Sterling +2 can provide from different options. Businesses need to watch their cash flow to see how much money is actually coming in and going out of the bank account. The books might look good if you have plenty of orders and have sent out a stack of invoices, but you will be in trouble if the customers aren't paying. Apart from watching the credit control you need to view the cash flow figures for current performance, and also use these to predict cash flow trends for future months.

A typical cash flow analysis report starts with the money in the bank account then adds all receipts from sales (the only money you have coming into the business). Then it subtracts all the payments to suppliers and all other items of expenditure. The main body of a cash flow analysis is available by pressing Financials on the Toolbar then P&L to see the profit and loss report for the current month. This shows all of your sales and purchases. View the balances in all of your bank accounts displayed in the main Bank window - Sterling +2 updates your bank balances automatically. The extra facilities, such as printing your own bank statements, help you keep an eye on cash flow. It is, however, important to process any payments and receipts immediately through the Bank option to keep your bank balances up-to-date.

The monthly figures on the profit and loss report can also be used for cash flow forecasts (to predict future trends). It's important to run the month end routine regularly so that the figures will be meaningful (this will also remind you to process recurring payments and update your bank balance). Once you have profit and loss reports for a few months (a year is ideal) you can use them to predict future performance. Do this by pressing Nominal then choosing 1200 bank current account and entering your calculations for future performance month by month. Take into account seasonal changes to business performance - for example a restaurant may do well in the run up to Christmas but may do little trade in January. This set of figures can also be printed out as a line or column graph. In later months you will be able to compare actual results against your cash flow forecast by looking at this record again and printing out a line graph showing budget and actual figures. The Theatre could include this type of information in impressive presentations for the Arts Council by copying the graph to the Windows Clipboard and transferring it to word processed documents (refer to Chapter 10).

The Theatre relies on the Sage technical support team for advice and didn't use their system supplier for extra help and consultancy after the software was implemented. As an accountant Hughes feels that the Sage support is adequate for her needs but that non-professionals would need extra backup from their suppliers. In future she would like to be able to transfer data between applications and is looking forward to using the links between Sterling +2 and the Excel spreadsheet.

Acoustics Records, Reading, Berkshire

Director: Simon Mayor

Acoustics Records is a small record company specialising in classical, folk and children's music. There are three directors and no employees on board so the payroll is simple. The directors do all the work themselves and as none of them are accountants, they deliberately chose software which was easy to use. Goods are constantly on order from suppliers and are despatched to customers as soon as they are received, so Sterling +2's stock control features are also put to the test.

The company chose Accountant Plus rather than Financial Controller, even though stock control is important. The software has been runing on an IBM compatible PC with a 486 processor for one year. Mayor installed Accountant Plus half way through the company's financial year to update from a previously manual system. The old methods had become too time consuming and there was a need for automatic up-to-the-minute records.

One of the major improvements of computerising was the ability to press a button and produce quarterly VAT returns which was causing confusion when done manually. At the end of the year the figures now tally which wasn't the case in the past. The software actually forces this business to keep the records updated on a daily basis.

One drawback is that the company depends heavily on the software getting the figures right automatically. Mayor trusts the VAT return to be accurate without doing any manual adjustments, but this may not always be the case. Any debts or transactions which have been written off using the automatic features will still leave an amount in the VAT liability account. This has to be adjusted manually and a record has to be kept in order to claim refunds - a fact which many users don't realise (see Chapter 9 for full details). Efficient credit control means Acoustics Records hasn't written off many transactions and hasn't lost money through leaving the VAT calculations completely up to the Sterling +2.

As retailers, Acoustics Records have product prices which frequently have 99p added instead of a round number of pounds sterling. This has led to some confusion when entering details on invoices if they type in the net value, then put the tax code and let the software calculate the gross amount (net plus VAT). This is because the system of calculating VAT rounds up the figures to the nearest penny and doesn't work in 0.5 pence. In fact Customs and Excise requires that businesses submit amounts to the nearest penny. The problem for retailers is that it's impossible to put a net figure in the amount column which will let the software calculate certain gross amounts such as £12.99.

For retailers the most important amount is the one that the customer will pay, so the best technique is to enter the gross amount first. Then put the tax code and use the Calculate Net button to work out the net value. Starting with the net figure then adding VAT using the tax code field will result in a gross amount ending in 98p. Another strange looking result is that if you enter a net price for two items followed by the tax code the result is sometimes an odd number where users expect a pair to be sold for an even amount. For example, Acoustics Records sell one product where the unit price is £5.10. Once VAT is added and the figures for both are calculated the result is £11.99 which Mayor would normally record manually as £11.98. The reason is that the software is actually more accurate in calculating the VAT - it doubles the net price to get £10.20 and adds VAT to this instead of working on each product separately. Again it's important to work in gross amounts because the customer won't be impressed by amounts rounded to the nearest penny.

Standard errors meant that large amounts of data were lost in the early days. This taught the company to keep regular backups, usually every day. There are six sets of disks for backup which are rotated as an extra security measure. Even this approach is not always enough, especially on days when a large number of transactions have been entered. When hours of work have been spent on entering records, several backups are necessary in a single day. At Acoustics Records time and effort spent entering data were wasted when a corrupt floppy disk destroyed backup data used in the Restore routine. It's important to use good quality floppies, change them regularly as they can soon start to fail, and use Disk Doctor to check the files for corrupt data before running Backup and Restore. See Chapter 11 for a complete guide.

When selecting software, Mayor looked for a product capable of handling VAT and stock control. The other main requirement was that it should be able to cope with the brisk mail order trade this type of business generates. The Customers database has about 1,000 names and addresses. He uses the analysis fields on the customer records to keep quite detailed demographic details on each one. This lets him filter out target customers for potential sales - a particular advantage as the types of music sold are in three such different categories and appeal to quite separate groups of buyers. When he wants to send a mailshot to the target customers he uses the Criteria button to select the right ones, then uses this information on standard letters he has produced. The same set of criteria can be saved and used to print out address labels. Although he feels a database could do the same task he prefers to have all of the features he needs in a single package. Sterling +2 has more advanced facilities for generating reports, but the Criteria method is so simple that he finds he doesn't need anything else.

The software was supplied by a local dealer who advised Acoustics Records that Sterling +2 was the product best suited to their requirements. They weren't originally thinking of buying accounting software and asked for separate database and spreadsheet products instead. Mayor is especially pleased that the dealer talked him out of buying other applications. He has contacts running similar businesses using the database and spreadsheet approach and feels that Sterling +2's integrated approach offering all the facilities is much more straightforward. It may not have the sophisticated abilities of a dedicated database, but it has all that he needs and doesn't need any extra programming or tailoring.

Mayor taught himself how to run the system and also how to do basic accounting. The company only employs an accountant at year end - they hope that their accounting costs will be reduced at the end of the next financial year, thanks to the software. There was no cost benefit in the first year of running in terms of professional accounting fees. This was mainly because the accounts were computerised half way through the year and the policy was to present the accountant with six months of records from the old system, plus six months of records from Sterling +2.

The main difficulties were understanding the accountancy terms and jargon, rather than in learning how to use the software. Mayor learnt by working through the manual and was more baffled by terms like 'posting an invoice' which initially made him think of going to the corner letterbox! He would like to see a manual with easier to understand expressions explaining the software to the many non-accountants who buy it. After installing the software he made use of the free 90 days support from the Sage technical team. He deliberately made sure that during this three month period he became completely familiar with the software and had the answers to his questions. This support was adequate for his needs - unlike many users, he registered in time to take advantage of the Sage hotline and exploited their service to the full.

The accounts were computerised in stages but it took less than three weeks to have the system up and running. The most time-consuming task was typing in the enormous database of customers, so he started with the active customers and added the rest gradually. Opening balances were worked out meticulously from the half year accounts produced on the old manual system. Mayor didn't have the time to enter opening balances specifying each invoice from the past six months for customers and suppliers. This would have given more accurate account histories but the volume of work would have been too great. For a business doing such a high amount of trade it would be difficult to put in all the figures halfway through the financial year.

Acoustics Records has such a large database of customers that the first release of Sterling +2 couldn't display the full list on the main Customers display. This limitation was actually caused by the Windows list box structures and the Sage programming team had to find a way around the problem. To display the missing customers the only way initially was to use Criteria to display only those at the end of the list. Sage overcame this problem in Version 2 by the use of compression techniques so that the list would use less memory. Now the sales ledger would have to be enormous before customers would disappear off the main window.

The second major problem has been that the software slows as more transactions are processed. Mayor felt that this was a defect due to Windows and was thinking of changing over to the DOS version of Sterling. In fact the software generally slows down if users neglect the housekeeping routines to tidy up their records and this would be exactly the same under DOS. The month end routine reconciles transactions and can also be used to clear out the stock and audit trail - it's important to run it every month to speed up the system. At Acoustics Records the month end routine was not run from March until September which was the end of the financial year. A second technique which was being ignored was the Disk Doctor file compression routine which clears the disk space taken up by settled and deleted transactions. Refer to Chapter 12 on Disk Doctor and Chapter 11 on Period End routines.

Although Accountant Plus is usually able to cope with the stock control requirements there are occasional hitches. A recent delivery of 500 CDs arrived from the supplier without an invoice. Mayor didn't want to enter details in the Products database to increase the stock level until he had an invoice providing the unit price - this decreases whenever he reorders a large number of certain goods. When he tried to send out 50 of the newly-delivered CDs to a distributor, this holdup in updating the stock levels led to extra problems. The software didn't recognise that there was enough stock to despatch -

the CDs were physically on the premises, but not yet in the computer records. In future he plans to try out Financial Controller to see if the extra sales and purchase order processing facilities would help to make invoicing and stock control more efficient.

Index

Other books from Computer Step include:

TITLE	AUTHOR	ISBN	PRICE
The PC Novice's Handbook 2ed	Kotecha	1-874029-04-0	£9.95
The PC Novice's H/book for Upgd & Mainten	Bunce	1-874029-14-8	£9.95
DOS for Beginners	Kotecha	1-874029-13-X	£11.95
Computing for the Terrified!	Greenwood	1-874029-09-1	£6.95
The Complete Gde to Sage Sterling & Accting	Jay	1-874029-10-5	£19.95
WordPerfect: The Joy of Six	Ingram	1-874029-08-3	£11.95
Windows in Easy Steps (V3.1)	Kotecha	1-874029-02-4	£9.95
Windows for Workgroups 3.11 in Easy Steps	Kotecha	1-874029-12-1	£14.95
Excel 5 in Easy Steps	Roach	1-874029-15-6	£14.95
Word 6 for Windows in Easy Steps	Basham	1-874029-16-4	£14.95
PageMaker 5 in Easy Steps	Basham	1-874029-06-7	£14.95
WordPerfect 6 for Windows in Easy Steps	Stewart	1-874029-11-3	£14.95

This is what they say about Computer Step titles:

"I've been successfully using Sage for ten years and STILL find this book helpful...."

Finance Dir., Wyvern Business Library

"...is quite the best book on this subject I have read." *The IBM PC User Group*

"...an excellent little book for the novice user..." *PC Today*

Computer Step also provides on-site training/consultancy on all areas of personal computing including all major software. For further details call 0926 817999.